CONTENTS

INTRODUCTION

Education in the United Kingdom: Facts and Figures has been written in the first instance as a set book for the Open University course EU208, *Exploring Educational Issues*. But it has been designed to stand independently of the course, and we hope it will also be found useful by people studying other courses, in the Open University or elsewhere, and indeed by anyone interested in education, whether as a parent, teacher, student or citizen.

This book has grown out of a previous one by the same authors, *The Education Fact File*, but it has been extensively rewritten and revised throughout. As we have to emphasise again and again in the chapters that follow, we are living in a period of rapid and profound change in education, beginning but certainly not ending with the Education Reform Act of 1988. Like its predecessor, the present book will inevitably become outdated in its turn, and the authors and publishers hope to produce new, up-to-date editions as the need arises. Accordingly, we would welcome any comments, criticisms, suggestions for inclusion, and above all corrections of any mistakes or misunderstandings.

This is not a work of original research. Almost all our information comes from published sources, mainly official publications but also academic research and other reference books more specialised than this one. These sources are acknowledged at the end of each chapter. (If any source we have used has inadvertently been omitted, we apologise, and ask to be told so that proper acknowledgement can be made in subsequent editions.) Our contribution has been to try to select the most significant information from those sources, and to present it in as clear and informative a manner as we can, in words and diagrams. Numbers in this book are usually 'rounded'; occasionally this means that percentages add up to slightly more or less than 100. Dates are usually given as they appear in the sources. Where two years are mentioned (e.g. 1992–3), this refers to a single academic year (or, where appropriate, a single financial year). It does not mean the two calendar years (1992 and 1993). Where a single year is mentioned (e.g. 1993), this usually refers to the point in the calendar year when the information was collected.

In preparing the book and its predecessors, we have received a great deal of assistance from many people and institutions, and we cannot acknowledge them all individually. We are extremely grateful nonetheless. Particular thanks are due to Geoffrey Walford, Dominic Newbould, Lorna Unwin, Martin Watkinson, Mary James and the staff of the Open University Library. We have been able to follow most though not all of their suggestions, and of course the responsibility for omissions and any remaining mistakes is ours.

*E*ducation in the UK: Facts and Figures aims to provide basic factual information in words, diagrams and numbers, about education in the United Kingdom today.

In Section One, we present some information about the social and historical background to current events and issues. Chapter 2 gives an outline of some social structures and processes that are important for education. Chapter 3 summarises the principal official reports on education and related subjects that have been prepared since the Education Act of 1944. And Chapter 4 outlines the most important educational legislation from the Education Act of 1870 to that of 1994.

In Section Two, we describe the educational systems of the four countries that make up the United Kingdom. The principal educational institutions are outlined in Chapter 5; the ways in which they are organised and controlled are explained in Chapter 6. Chapter 7 looks at the educational professionals who work in various ways within the systems. Chapter 8 outlines the recently introduced procedures of educational finance and resources – where the money comes from, and where it goes. Finally, Chapter 9 summarises the main qualifications available at every level within (and outside) the education systems.

Section Three covers a variety of processes occurring within these education systems. Chapter 10 looks at the school curriculum and its assessment, after the 1988 Education Reform Act. Chapter 11 provides information about a set of issues that have long been at the centre of educational debate and controversy – educational attainment, and its relationship to equality and inequality between children from different groups and categories. And Chapter 12 summarises the position today of young people just over school-leaving age: the new problems they face, the new possibilities open to them.

Section Four has just two chapters, both in the form of alphabetical lists: Chapter 13 is a glossary of important educational terms, and Chapter 14 deciphers some of the most widespread educational acronyms and abbreviations that are treated more fully in other chapters, as well as many that are not covered elsewhere in the book.

FACTS AND FIGURES

All these chapters are intended to be *factual*, to tell the reader what the educational world is like, not to give the interpretation or judgements – and certainly not the prejudices – of the authors or anyone else. This is a worthwhile aim, we believe, but one impossible to fulfil. Although we have done our best to fulfil it, we must offer some words of caution about taking the contents of this book as facts, let alone *the* facts about education.

First, and most obviously, the book is bound to contain errors. Some of these may come from our sources; others, alas, will be all our own work. We hope that these are few and trivial, but it is inevitable that a book of this character will have some.

Second, we have inevitably made choices about which facts to include, and which to leave out. Sometimes these have been slightly forced choices, because of gaps and limitations in the available data. But much more often, we have had to decide what we considered most significant and telling from an embarrassment of information. This is where interpretation is unavoidable, and prejudice a very real danger. We cannot, of course, claim to be unprejudiced; people are not normally aware of their own prejudices. What we can and do say is that we have never knowingly excluded or modified any information in order to favour our own beliefs, values or political preferences.

Third, even the categories in which data are presented depend on controversial judgements, and are open to unintended distortion. There are different ways of defining 'social class', for example, or of identifying ethnic groups, and these can lead to very different pictures of the class structure or ethnic composition of the country, and of the relationship between class or ethnicity and, say, educational attainment. The particular cases of social class and ethnic group are discussed in Chapter 11; here we want to make the general point that choosing categories for presenting 'the facts' is fraught with uncertainty and controversy.

Finally, we would like to warn against leaping too quickly to what may seem obvious interpretations of facts and their relationships, such as conclusions about cause and effect. Above all, we should be cautious about accepting plausible interpretations of one fact or set of facts in isolation, without at least checking that our interpretation fits in with other relevant information.

READING AND REFERRING

One of the first things we had to decide in preparing this book was whether it was to be primarily a reference book, to be consulted as required for some particular piece of information, or a genuine text, to be read through from beginning to end. As you will see, it has ended up as something of both. Four of the chapters are really elaborated lists: Chapters 3 and 4 present their reports and Acts in chronological order; Chapters 13 and 14 list their terms and acronyms in alphabetical order. We do not expect many people to read their way through these chapters; on the other hand, if you want to look up the main provisions of, say, the 1987 Teachers' Pay and Conditions Act, or distinguish GIST from GEST, you will find the information easily accessible there.

The other chapters, though, *are* designed to be read through as well as referred to. They deal with subject matter that does not so readily lend itself to division into self-contained entries. We hope that each chapter provides a clear and straightforward introduction to the basic facts and figures in the area it covers. The inevitable disadvantage is that it is not quite so easy to look things up in these chapters as it would be in a list. Besides, many topics do not fit neatly into one, and only one, chapter or section, however carefully these are devised. But the book has a comprehensive index, and cross-references within and between chapters. With judicious use of these, we hope, you should not have great difficulty in finding out what you want to know.

SCOPE

The book covers the whole of the United Kingdom – England, Scotland, Wales (which together form Great Britain) and Northern Ireland. (It does not cover the Isle of Man or the Channel Islands; they are not part of the United Kingdom, but Crown dependencies, with their own governments.) However, its coverage of these countries is far from equal. England, or for some purposes England and Wales together, receives much the most attention. Whether this is justified is open to argument; we are far from certain that we have always got the balance right. England is, of course, by far the biggest country in the United Kingdom, with 83% of its population (England and Wales together have 88%) (see Chapter 2, Figure 2.1). By virtue of its size, developments in English education usually exert greater influence on the other countries than theirs do on England. And a practical point: published data on English education are usually more extensive and detailed. We have tried to use United Kingdom data whenever we could, but often we have had to illustrate particular points from English, or English and Welsh, figures. We hope this does not mislead; we always try to make clear what countries or regions our figures cover.

Of course there are differences between the countries in the structure of their education systems, and in the processes within them. Northern Ireland, for example, still has its grammar schools, whereas maintained schools in England, Scotland and Wales are now almost entirely comprehensive. Scotland has its own system of school examinations and vocational qualifications; England, Wales and Northern Ireland share a common system. And so on. Differences in structure are spelled out in the appropriate chapters, and where we judge there to be significant differences in educational processes from country to country, we have pointed them out.

CHANGE

Finally, we are only too well aware that we have produced this book during what promises to be a period of the most profound, widespread and rapid educational change for many years – beginning, but certainly not ending with the 1988 Education Reform Act. The processes of change are well under way, but still far from complete, as this book goes to press (mid-1994). In almost every chapter, we have had to point forward to what seem to be the likeliest important developments in the near future, as well as describing things as they are now.

NOTE TO THE READER

In the references and bibliographies, the following abbreviations are used:

CIPFA	Chartered Institute of Public Finance and Accountancy
COI	Central Office of Information
CRAC	Careers Research and Advisory Centre
CSO	Central Statistical Office
DENI	Department of Education Northern Ireland
DES	Department of Education and Science
DFE	Department for Education
EDG	Employment Department Group
GSS	Government Statistical Service
HMSO	Her Majesty's Stationery Office
ILEA	Inner London Education Authority
ISIS	Independent Schools Information Service
NCC	National Curriculum Council
OFSTED	Office for Standards in Education
OPCS	Office of Population Censuses and Surveys
SCAA	School Curriculum and Assessment Authority
SED	Scottish Education Department
SOED	Scottish Office Education Department

Social factors of fundamental importance for the education system include the size of the population, its structure by age and sex, its distribution across nations and regions, its composition by social class and ethnic group and – not least – the ways in which any of these change from year to year.

POPULATION

The United Kingdom has a total population of about 55.6 million, divided unevenly among its four constituent countries as shown in Figure 2.1.

England is divided, for many official statistics, into eight standard regions. As Figure 2.2 shows, three of these are greater in population than Scotland, seven greater than Wales, and all eight greater than Northern Ireland. By far the largest is the South East, with 16.7 million; of these, about 6.4 million live in Greater London alone, which is thus more populous than any of the other regions of England, or any of the other countries of the United Kingdom.

Figure 2.3 gives, for Great Britain, the numbers of males and females in each of five age groups below the age of 25. These are the people most likely to be, now or in the very near future, full-time pupils or students in educational institutions.

The size of the population of school or college age has important implications for educational policy and planning. It affects the number of schools (see Chapter 5) and the number of teachers (see Chapter 7) required, and

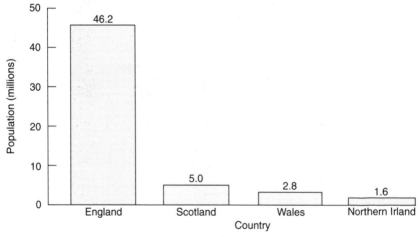

Figure 2.1   Populations of the four countries of the United Kingdom, 1991
(Adapted from OPCS, 1991, Table 2)

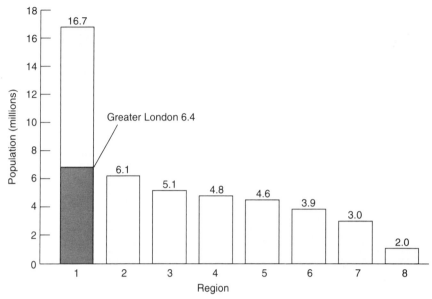

Figure 2.2   Populations of the eight regions of England, 1991
(Adapted from OPCS, 1991, Table A)
Key to regions: 1 South East; 2 North West; 3 West Midlands; 4 Yorkshire and
Humberside; 5 South West; 6 East Midlands; 7 North; 8 East Anglia

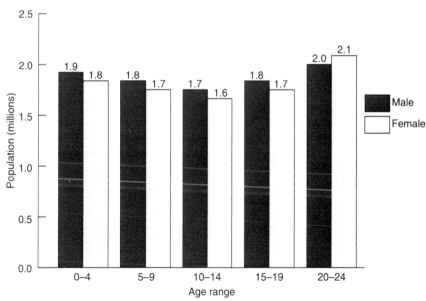

Figure 2.3   The under-25 population of Great Britain by age and sex, 1991
(Adapted from OPCS, 1993a, Table 1)

therefore affects the amount of expenditure needed by the education system (see Chapter 8). Changes from year to year in the number of people in each age group create difficulties for planning, especially as birth rates are notoriously difficult to predict; estimating what the school population will be in more than five years' time becomes increasingly speculative and uncertain. Figure 2.4 shows how the number of births in the United Kingdom has varied from year to year since 1964, when it reached its highest figure since the 1920s.

The population of Great Britain grew steadily from the end of World War II until the early 1970s (an increase of roughly 5% per decade), since when its total has remained stable. But the *age structure* within this total has changed, in the 1970s and 1980s, towards fewer younger and more older people. In 1991, 19% of the population were under 15 (compared with 24% in 1971), and 16% were 65 or over (compared with 13% in 1971) (OPCS, 1993b, Table 5).

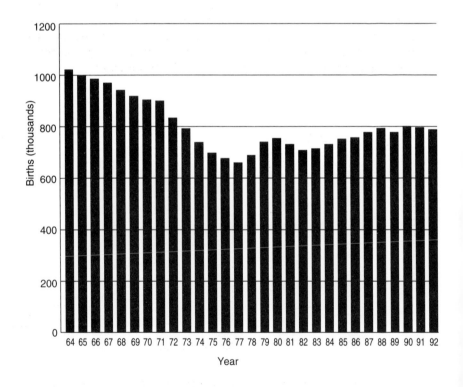

Figure 2.4   Births in the United Kingdom, 1964–92
(Adapted from CSO, 1982, Table 2.24; CSO, 1994a, Table 2.16)

HOUSEHOLD AND FAMILY

Half of all households in Great Britain had, in 1992, at least one dependent child. Of these children, 81% lived with an adult couple, and 19% with a lone parent (17% with a mother, 2% with a father) (CSO, 1994b, Table 2.6; OPCS, 1994, Table 2.24).

The majority of families are small. The average number of dependent children in all families with dependent children in 1992 was 1.8 (but see Figure 2.14 below). The distribution of family sizes among married couples in 1992 is shown in Figure 2.5.

Since World War II, births outside marriage have increased by over six times as a percentage of all births in the United Kingdom, from 5% (1951) to 32% (1992). During the same period, divorces have also increased: in England and Wales the increase was more than fourfold, from 0.3% to 1.4% of the married population per annum (CSO, 1994b, Tables 2.14 and 2.20).

Men are more likely than women to be 'economically active', that is, in effect, to be in or seeking paid employment (see Figure 2.8), but this difference is decreasing with time (see Figure 2.9). Women with dependent children are less likely to have full-time jobs but more likely to have part-time jobs, than women without. The younger her youngest child is, the less likely a mother is to have any employment, full- or part-time, as Figure 2.6 shows.

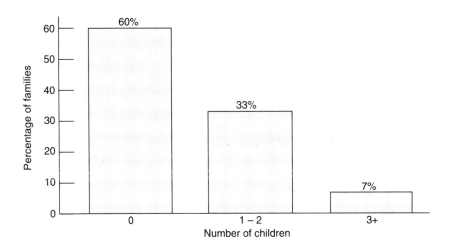

Figure 2.5   Percentages of one-family, married couple households with various numbers of dependent children aged under 18, England 1992
(Adapted from CSO, 1994b, Table 2.5)

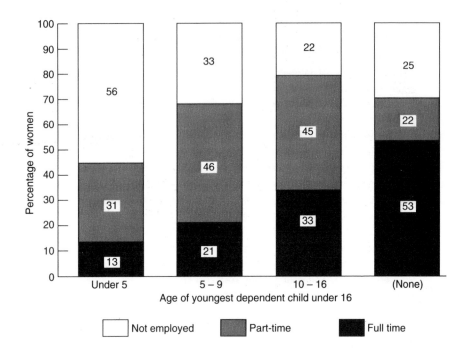

Figure 2.6   Percentages of women in employment, by age of youngest dependent child under 16, Great Britain, 1990–92 combined
(Adapted from OPCS, 1994, Table 7.12)

SOCIAL CLASS AND OCCUPATION

The terms 'working class' and 'middle class' are in almost universal use, but under many different definitions and interpretations, which can lead to different pictures of the class structure of the country. One way of obtaining figures for the classes is to ask people what class they think they belong to. When asked their social class, about 65% of people in Great Britain identify themselves as working (or 'upper working') class, and about 30% as middle (or 'upper middle') class. (Slightly more identify their parents as working class, and fewer identify their parents as middle class.) Figure 2.7 gives more detail about 'self-rated' social class.

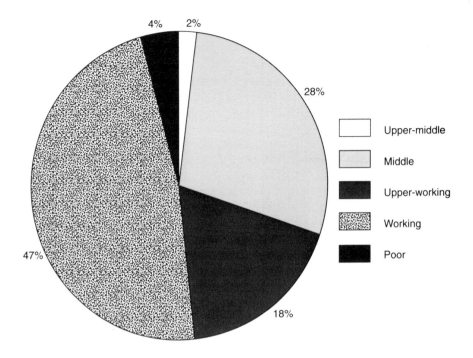

Figure 2.7   Self-rated social class, Great Britain 1991
(Adapted from Jowell et al. (eds) 1992, p. 177)

But demographers and social scientists also use more objective measures. The most common practice in educational research is to take *occupation* as the basis for identifying class, often adopting one of the official classifications of occupations used by the Office of Population Censuses and Surveys (OPCS) – socioeconomic classes, socioeconomic groups or, most usually, the one now called *social class based on occupation*, which is currently as follows (see OPCS, 1992a, paras 7.51–7).

I   Professional (this includes university teachers)
II   Managerial and technical (this includes school teachers)
III(N) Skilled non-manual
III(M) Skilled manual
IV   Partly skilled
V   Unskilled

Figure 2.8 shows the numbers of men and women in Great Britain in 1991 who were employed in the various OPCS social classes.

In practice, most educational researchers studying social class have used simplified or compressed versions of the OPCS classification. Frequently,

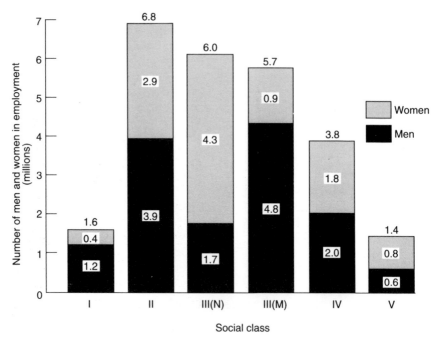

Figure 2.8   *Numbers of men and women in employment in each OPCS social class based on occupation, Great Britain 1991*
(Adapted from OPCS, 1992b, Table 6.13)

classes I, II and III(N) are taken to be middle class, and III(M), IV and V to be working class. Children are generally classified according to their fathers' occupations. For Great Britain as a whole this makes about 57% of the employed population middle class and 43% working class. But there are substantial variations from country to country and region to region. Scotland and Wales, and the North, North West, Yorkshire and Humberside, West Midlands, East Midlands and East Anglia regions of England have a lower percentage of their population in classes I, II and III(N) and a higher percentage in III(M), IV and V than Great Britain as a whole, whereas the South West and especially the South East have a higher percentage in I, II and III(N) and a lower percentage in III(M), IV and V than the British average. (The extremes are the West Midlands with 50% in classes I, II and III(N), and the South East with 64% (OPCS, 1992b, Table 6.14).)

Unemployment also shows geographical variation, being at present substantially above the United Kingdom average (of 9.8% of the workforce in 1992) in Northern Ireland (14.2%), the North of England (11.3%), the North West of England (10.8%) and the West Midlands (10.6%), and substantially below average in East Anglia (7.8%) (CSO, 1994a, Table 6.6).

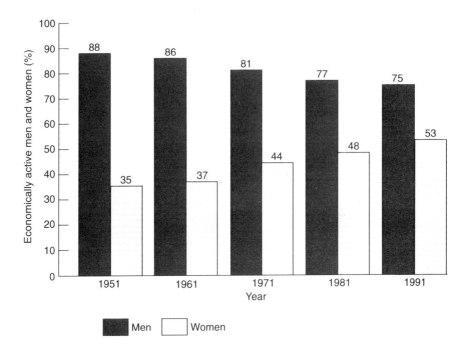

Figure 2.9   Percentages of men and women over school-leaving age who are economically active, United Kingdom 1951–91 (Adapted from CSO, 1989; CSO, 1994b, Table 4.7)

As Figure 2.8 shows, substantially more men than women are economically active. However, differences between the sexes in economic activity have diminished over the years. This is illustrated in Figure 2.9.

Women in employment are much more likely than men to be employed part time: 45% of female employees as compared with 6% of men (1993 figures self-assessed; CSO 1994b, Table 4.12).

In recent decades, the proportion of 'middle-class' people (that is, people in non-manual occupations) in the population has risen steadily, whilst that of 'working-class' people (in manual occupations) has fallen. This is illustrated in Figure 2.10.

ETHNIC GROUPS

The 1991 Census was the first to have a question on ethnic group membership. The ethnic categories used on the Census form, adopted after extensive

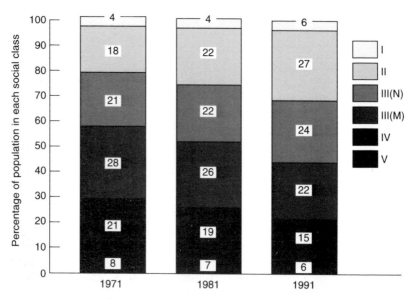

Figure 2.10   Social class composition of the population of Great Britain, 1971–91
(Adapted from OPCS, 1975, Table 29; OPCS, 1984, Table 16A; OPCS, 1992b, Table 6.13)

consultation and pilot-testing (see White, 1990), were: White, Black Caribbean, Black African, Black Other, Indian, Pakistani, Bangladeshi, Chinese and Other. According to the Census, the majority ethnic group (White) had 51.9 million members in Great Britain in 1991, of whom 49.7 million were born in the United Kingdom. The numbers for each minority ethnic group are shown in Figure 2.11.

A source of confusion in comparing different studies is that there is no single set of terms in use among researchers for the different ethnic groups. Sometimes differences in terminology are merely the use of different words for the same or similar groups (such as 'West Indian', 'Afro-Caribbean', 'African Caribbean' and 'Black Caribbean'); at other times, different sets of terms refer to different classifications and different ways of classifying. For example, a classification may be based on skin-colour, as in the OPCS Labour Force Survey's *White* and *Non-white*; or on country of origin or descent, as in the Rampton and Swann Reports' *West Indian, Asian* and *Other* (DES, 1981; DES, 1985); or on a mixture of both, as in Eggleston et al.'s (1986) *Afro-Caribbean, Asian* and *White*; or on country of birth of the head of household (as in the 1981 Census), with such categories of country as *the New Commonwealth and Pakistan*. Many terminological usages are controversial, and probably none is without its drawbacks. Here we adopt the categories used by our sources of data in each case. (The only exception is that instead of 'the New

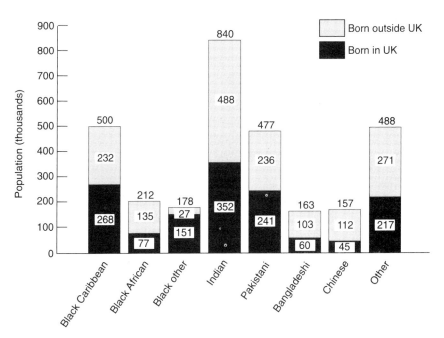

Figure 2.11   Minority ethnic groups in Great Britain, 1991
(Adapted from Teague, 1993)

Commonwealth and Pakistan', we say simply 'the New Commonwealth'. Pakistan rejoined the Commonwealth in 1989).

According to the 1991 Census, 94.5% of the population of Great Britain are White, while 5.5% belong to minority ethnic groups. The latter are concentrated in particular areas of the country. Two-thirds of all members of minority ethnic groups live in the former metropolitan counties of Greater London, West Midlands, West Yorkshire and Greater Manchester (compared with a quarter of the population as a whole). 45% of the ethnic minority population of Great Britain live in Greater London alone (compared with 12% of the population as a whole). By contrast, the regions of the North, East Anglia and the South West, plus the whole of Scotland and Wales, added together, contain 8% of the ethnic minority population of Great Britain (compared with 32% of the population as a whole) (OPCS, 1993c, Table 6).

This distribution leads to a very different ethnic composition of the population in different areas of the country. For example, 45% of the population of the London Borough of Brent belong to ethnic minority groups, as do 42% of the London Borough of Ealing, 29% of Leicester and 28% of Slough. By contrast, fewer than 0.2% of the population of the Isles of Scilly or the counties of Berwickshire or Sutherland belong to a minority ethnic group (Teague, 1993, Table 2).

Only a minority of immigrants to the United Kingdom have come from the New Commonwealth, and this minority has decreased in absolute terms, and even more in proportional terms, since the mid-1960s.

In 1965, there were about 206,000 immigrants to the United Kingdom, of whom 78,000 (38%) were from the New Commonwealth. In 1975, the total was 197,000, and the New Commonwealth figure was 66,000 (34%). By 1991, the total immigration figure had risen to 266,000, and the figure for the New Commonwealth was again 66,000 (24%).

Until the 1980s, there was more emigration from the United Kingdom than immigration to it. Thus in 1965, there were about 284,000 emigrants (compared with 206,000 immigrants), and in 1975 there were 238,000 emigrants (compared with 197,000 immigrants). However, in 1983, this pattern was reversed, and the number of people leaving the United Kingdom fell below the number entering – a pattern which has persisted in every subsequent year except 1988. In 1991, there were 239,000 emigrants (compared with 267,000 immigrants) (Bulusu, 1986, Table 1; Rosenbaum and Hornsey, 1992, Tables 1 and 2).

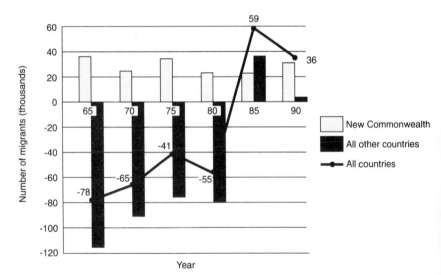

Figure 2.12   Net migration to and from the United Kingdom, 1965–90
(Adapted from Bulusu, 1986, Table 1; Rosenbaum and Hornsey, 1992, Tables 1 and 2)
Note: This diagram does not show the 1988 blip, when immigration briefly fell below emigration

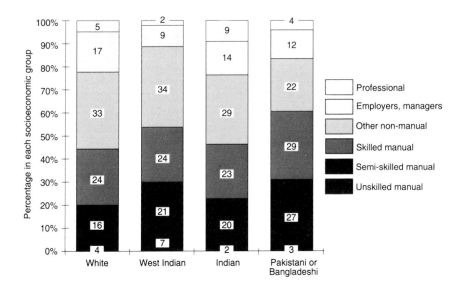

Figure 2.13   Percentages of White, West Indian, Indian and Pakistani/Bangladeshi people in each socioeconomic group, Great Britain 1989–91 (Adapted from OPCS, 1992b, Table 6.35)

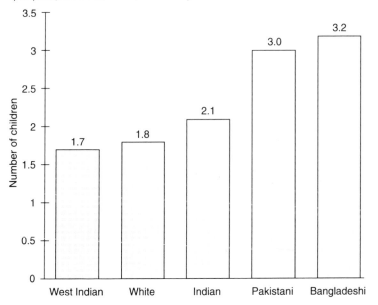

Figure 2.14   Average number of children per family in each ethnic group, Great Britain, 1987–9 (Adapted from Haskey, 1991)

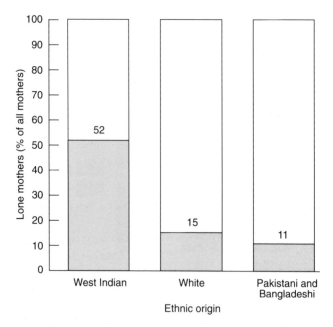

Figure 2.15   Lone mothers as percentages of all mothers, by ethnic group, Great Britain 1989–91
(Adapted from CSO, 1994b, Table 2.9)

The overall picture of migration to and from the United Kingdom from 1965 to 1990 is summarised in Figure 2.12: net immigration is shown as 'positive' migration (above the horizontal axis), and net emigration as 'negative' migration (below the axis).

With the passage of time, an increasing proportion of the ethnic minority population consists of people born in Great Britain. For example, the proportion of people of Indian, Pakistani or Bangladeshi descent living in Britain who were born in Britain rose from 38% in 1985–7 to 44% in 1991. For people of Afro-Caribbean descent, the proportion also rose, though more slowly: from 52% to 53% in the same period (Haskey, 1988; Teague, 1993).

The ethnic minority population is young; according to the 1991 Census, 33% were aged under 16 and 6% aged 60 or over (compared with 20% under 16 and 21% 60 or over in the population as a whole) (OPCS, 1993c, Table 6).

As well as age differences, ethnic groups show differences in their occupational structure (see Figure 2.13) and family patterns (see Figures 2.14 and 2.15).

SOURCES AND FURTHER READING

Bulusu, L. (1986) Recent patterns of migration from and to the United Kingdom, *Population Trends*, No. 46.

CSO (1982) *Annual Abstract of Statistics*, No. 118, London: HMSO.

CSO (1989) *Annual Abstract of Statistics*, No. 125, London: HMSO.

CSO (1994a) *Annual Abstract of Statistics*, No. 130, London: HMSO.

CSO (1994b) *Social Trends*, No. 24, London: HMSO.

DES (1981) *West Indian Children in our Schools: Interim Report of the Committee of Inquiry into the Education of Children from Ethnic Minority Groups*, Cmnd 8273, London: HMSO ('The Rampton Report').

DES (1985) *Education for All: Report of the Committee of Inquiry into the Education of Children from Ethnic Minority Groups*, Cmnd 9453, London: HMSO ('The Swann Report').

Eggleston, J., Dunn, D., Anjali, M. and Wright, C. (1986) *Education for Some: the Educational and Vocational Experiences of 15–18-year-old Members of Minority Ethnic Groups*, Stoke-on-Trent: Trentham Books.

Haskey, J. (1988) The ethnic minority populations of Great Britain: their size and characteristics, *Population Trends*, No. 54.

Haskey, J. (1991) Estimated numbers and demographic characteristics of one-parent families in Great Britain, *Population Trends*, No. 65.

Jowell, R. et. al. (eds) (1992) *British Social Attitudes: 9th Report*, Aldershot: Dartmouth.

OPCS (1975) *Census 1971: Great Britain: Economic Activity Part IV*, London: HMSO.

OPCS (1984) *Census 1981: Economic Activity: Great Britain*, London: HMSO.

OPCS (1991) *1991 Census: Preliminary Report for England and Wales*, London: HMSO.

OPCS (1992a) *1991 Census: Definitions: Great Britain*, London: HMSO.

OPCS (1992b) *Labour Force Survey 1990 and 1991*, London: HMSO.

OPCS (1993a) *1991 Census: Sex, Age and Marital Status: Great Britain*, London: HMSO.

OPCS (1993b) *1991 Census: Historical Tables: Great Britain*, London: HMSO.

OPCS (1993c) *1991 Census: Report for Great Britain (Part 1) Volume 1*, London: HMSO.

OPCS (1994) *General Household Survey 1992*, London: HMSO.

Rosenbaum, M. and Hornsey, D. (1992) International migration 1991, *Population Trends*, No. 70.

Teague, A. (1993) Ethnic group: first results from the 1991 Census, *Population Trends*, No. 72.

White, P. (1990) A question on ethnic group for the census: findings from the 1989 test, *Population Trends*, No. 59.

This chapter contains summaries of the principal findings and recommendations of some of the major official reports on education and related topics from 1944 until the present day. Inevitably, not all reports can be covered, and the summaries of those included are brief and highly selective. (See the 'Sources and further reading' section at the end of this chapter.)

Almost all of these reports were prepared by committees of inquiry appointed directly by government ministers (though we have also included a small number of particularly important reports produced by working parties or study groups attached to government ministries). All recent committees of inquiry, and some in the past, have been set up specifically for the task in hand, but between 1944 and 1967 many of the inquiries were undertaken by the Central Advisory Councils for Education (CACE) for England and for Wales, bodies set up under the 1944 Education Act to advise ministers on important educational issues. The reports are usually best known by the name of the committee's chairperson – 'The Plowden Report', 'The Warnock Report' and so on.

Where reports have led to legislation (see also Chapter 4), or were otherwise very influential, we have tried to indicate this, with brief comments in square brackets. In some cases, though, reports seem to have had little impact, and in many others their effects are difficult to assess.

Unless otherwise indicated, the reports apply to England and Wales.

1944 FLEMING – PUBLIC SCHOOLS AND THE GENERAL EDUCATION SYSTEM

The Fleming committee was set up to consider how public schools (defined as those belonging to the Headmasters' Conference or the Governing Bodies Association, together with 'comparable schools for girls') could develop and extend their association with the general education system. The report recommended that public schools should progressively be integrated into the state system by taking pupils who would be given state grants. To begin with, it was suggested, they should allocate a quarter of their places to this scheme, but eventually all their places should be open to pupils with state grants. [Though well received by the public schools, the scheme never came into effect, mainly because of the unwillingness of either central government or LEAs to take responsibility for payment of the grants.]

1944   MCNAIR – TEACHERS AND YOUTH LEADERS

This report was concerned with the supply, recruitment and training of teachers (and youth leaders). It recommended (for both) increases in salary, and the extension of training courses to three years' full-time study.

1945   PERCY – HIGHER TECHNOLOGICAL EDUCATION

This report investigated the needs of higher technological education in England and Wales, and the role of universities and technical colleges in meeting them. It recommended expansion of universities' science teaching and the creation of colleges of advanced technology. In addition, it recommended the establishment of organisations to coordinate the work of universities, colleges of technology and technical colleges at both local and national levels.

1946   BARLOW – SCIENTIFIC MANPOWER (Cmd. 6824)

This report argued that more university places were needed, especially for science students. [More places were provided.]

1947   CLARKE – SCHOOL AND LIFE (CACE England)

This was the first CACE report. It examined 'the transition from school to independent life'. The committee interpreted its brief very widely, embracing all levels of education. Greatly increased expenditure was called for, particularly to reduce pupil/teacher ratios and improve unhealthy and unsuitable school buildings. Recommendations were made about a wide range of topics: relationships between school, home and neighbourhood; youth clubs and voluntary organisations; the health of children at school and young people at work; and 'compensatory' further education for workers in routine jobs. The main conclusion about education and employment was that purely educational aims came first: schools should not prepare pupils for particular types of employment; industry itself benefited from the teaching and learning of basic educational skills.

1948   CLARKE – OUT OF SCHOOL (CACE England)

Following up some of the conclusions of the first CACE report (see 1947 Clarke) this inquiry considered 'the natural interests and pursuits of school children out of school hours'. It urged that LEAs increase and improve facilities for children's play and recreation outside school hours, and that the government give financial support to voluntary bodies serving the out-of-school interests of school children. It further recommended that LEAs provide training courses for parents and all those who work with children.

1949   EVANS/AARON – THE FUTURE OF SECONDARY EDUCATION IN WALES
(CACE Wales)

The report from this investigation made detailed recommendations for the organisation and curriculum of secondary education in Wales under the 1944 Education Act, and its relationship with primary and further education. It argued that education should be child-centred; it could take the form of either 'multilateral' schools or a dual system of grammar/technical schools and modern/technical schools (rather than a tripartite system), but must take into account variation in ability and aptitude between children. It recommended that the curriculum should emphasise free creation and cooperative inventiveness rather than passive assimilation, and that the study of history, geography and literature should give a central place to Wales. Particular attention was given to two issues: the rural and sparsely populated character of much of Wales, and the problems caused by the prevalence in Wales of two languages. As regards the latter, the committee recommended concentration on the pupil's first language, be it Welsh or English, with emphasis on conversation and oral work, but with a due subordinate place for written work. It argued that English must be taught well in predominantly Welsh-speaking areas, and that Welsh should be available as an option for all children in predominantly English-speaking areas.

1954   GURNEY-DIXON – EARLY LEAVING
(CACE England)

This committee considered the factors influencing the age at which pupils left 'secondary schools which provide courses beyond the minimum school leaving age' – in practice, grammar schools. Research was commissioned, with data being gathered principally from a 10% sample of all grammar schools, whose headmasters supplied details of the 'background, school record and potentialities' of the 1946 intake. The report concluded that a pupil's performance was closely related to his or her father's occupational status: the higher that status, the better a pupil's performance, not only in leaving school less early but in having a better academic record and, in the headmaster's judgement, more 'promise'. These differences increased during secondary education; children from lower-status occupational groups declined from their 11-plus position relative to higher groups. The report offered some speculative explanations of these differences, most involving aspects of home background, including shortage of money, 'bad living conditions', and lack of educational experience and unfavourable attitudes to education among parents in the lower-status occupational groups. This was the first major investigation of the working of the 1944 Education Act (see Chapter 4), and it cast doubt on the effectiveness of the Act in reducing social-class-based inequalities in education. It recommended that more grammar school places be provided, and that financial provision be improved for pupils who remained at school after the minimum leaving age.

1955   UNDERWOOD – MALADJUSTED CHILDREN

The term 'maladjusted children' entered common usage after the 1944 Education Act, and it was the aim of this committee to investigate the education of such children. Recommendations included the use of day, rather than boarding, schools wherever possible; the setting up of a comprehensive Child Guidance Service in every LEA, with a strengthened role for educational psychologists; and the introduction of preventive measures such as increased nursery provision.

1959   CROWTHER – 15 TO 18 (CACE England)

The Crowther committee was set up to consider the education of boys and girls between the ages of 15 and 18, and it was specifically asked to make recommendations about the place therein of exams below GCE level. The extensive research that was commissioned confirmed earlier findings (see 1954 Gurney-Dixon) about the relationship between fathers' occupational status and pupils' educational attainment. The higher the father's status, the greater the child's chance of attending a grammar rather than a secondary modern school, though the occupational group 'skilled manual workers' was so large that their children were by far the largest single group in all types of school. It was argued that there was considerable 'wastage' of talent, and much attention was paid to the 'neglected educational territory' of pupils who left school at 15 to follow a craft or technical, rather than an academic, career. The report recommended that there should be more further education. Of 16–18-year-olds, half should be in full-time further education by 1979, compared with 12% at the time of the report. [In the event, major expansion in further education came slightly later, in the 1980s, with high unemployment of school leavers and such schemes as YTS.] It accepted that some comprehensive schools could be set up, but on the whole endorsed the existing tripartite system, and indeed suggested further divisions within it (and within further education). The report argued that, in secondary modern schools, the top third of pupils were capable of taking and benefiting from external exams below GCE level [the future CSE, first examined in 1965], but that the majority of pupils there should be spared them. It was also recommended that early subject specialisation should be discouraged (although study in depth was still desirable in the sixth form); and that two clauses from the 1944 Act which affected older pupils should be implemented, namely the raising of the school leaving age to 16 and compulsory part-time further education in county colleges. [The school leaving age was eventually raised, in 1972, but compulsory part-time further education has not been introduced.]

1960 ALBEMARLE – THE YOUTH SERVICE IN ENGLAND AND WALES

This committee was set up to review the Youth Service, which was thought to be demoralised and unprepared to deal with the increasing demand from the 'baby boom' children who were reaching adolescence. It recommended better training and status for youth leaders, a building programme of new premises and facilities, and the setting up of a Youth Service Development Council. It supported the continuation of a mixture of statutory and voluntary provision. [Most of the recommendations were implemented: the Development Council was set up to advise on a 10-year development programme; a large amount of building work was authorised and a special college opened in Leicester to train youth leaders, whose numbers doubled by 1966.]

1963 NEWSOM – HALF OUR FUTURE (CACE England)

This investigation considered the education of pupils between 13 and 16 of average and less than average ability. The terms of reference show some overlap with those of the Crowther Committee; there was considerable overlap in the pool of CACE research on which the two committees drew, and some similarity in the recommendations offered (see 1959 Crowther). Like Crowther, Newsom accepted the tripartite system, believing there to be different levels of natural ability in children which could best be catered for by different kinds of school. But it did not accept that schools for the less able should be poorer in buildings, quality of teaching, or any other respect. It recommended maintenance of existing structures, but with a redistribution of spending to the benefit of the less able (for example, the rebuilding of inadequate secondary modern schools in slum areas). Again like Crowther, it strongly recommended the raising of the school leaving age to 16 [this eventually happened in 1972] and the provision of a more stimulating and demanding curriculum so that pupils had a wider choice of courses, including some 'broadly related to occupational interests', and others concerned with personal and social development, and 'imaginative experience through the arts'. It advised that all 16-year-old school leavers should be provided with some form of 'internal leaving certificate' containing a 'general school record'. [In practice, the curriculum for many less-able and average pupils became geared towards the new external CSE exam, contrary to Newsom's explicit recommendation. Only in the late 1970s did many schools begin to use pupil profiles and records of achievement similar to what Newsom had recommended.] Other miscellaneous recommendations were offered, including the provision of adequate religious instruction and positive guidance on sexual behaviour, the extension of the school day for older pupils, and the establishment of an experimental building programme 'to try out different forms of school organisation and teaching methods in buildings designed for the purpose'.

1963–4 ROBBINS – HIGHER EDUCATION
(Cmnd. 2154)

Appointed to review the pattern of full-time higher education in Great Britain, and advise on its long-term development, this committee commissioned extensive new research and examination of existing research. Looking particularly at entry into higher education, it found, like previous reports (see 1954 Gurney-Dixon, 1959 Crowther, 1963 Newsom), a high correlation between social class and educational achievement. (At the extremes, a child of professional parents was about 20 times more likely than a child of semi-skilled and unskilled workers to enter full-time higher education.) Even with controls for measured intelligence, the correlation remained high. The *proportions* of children from each class entering higher education remained much as in the 1920s, although the *absolute numbers* had increased steadily with the expansion of educational provision. However, social-class influence on attainment seemed to cease with university entry: once admitted, working-class students performed as well as middle-class students. Robbins concluded that there was a huge, untapped, and indeed often unsuspected, 'pool of ability' in the population, especially in lower socioeconomic groups. It recommended a massive expansion in higher education (from 216,000 places in 1962–3 to 390,000 in 1972–3 and 560,000 by 1980). Also recommended were: the establishment of the Council for National Academic Awards (CNAA) to grant degrees to students in non-university establishments [this happened the following year]; the raising of the status of teacher training colleges to colleges of education offering BEd degrees, and their integration into universities [the former has happened, but the latter only in part]; the granting of university status to the 10 colleges of advanced technology [this was accepted], and in due course to other colleges [this did happen eventually, in the 1990s]; and the establishment of special institutions for scientific and technological education and research (SISTERS) [this has not been implemented].

1967   PLOWDEN – CHILDREN AND THEIR PRIMARY SCHOOLS (CACE England)

The Plowden Report examined primary education in England 'in all its aspects'. Based on extensive research, it concluded that parents' attitudes to education were of supreme importance in influencing children's educational success – more so than the parents' educational or occupational status, than material circumstances at home, and than schools themselves. It approved of 'progressive', child-centred teaching methods, a broader curriculum and increased parental involvement; it recommended that schools should become more involved in their communities – suggesting that there should be positive discrimination to help schools in deprived or 'educational priority areas' (EPAs). It also recommended expansion of nursery provision, the ending of corporal punishment in primary schools, and greater attention to the needs of slow learners, handicapped children and the children of immigrants. It argued that more teachers should be encouraged into primary schools (especially men, graduates and those who had specialised in maths or science), and a new group of staff called 'teachers' aides' should be recruited with a similar status to nursery assistants [never widely implemented]. It suggested that primary education could be reorganised into first and middle schools. [The Plowden Report had a profound effect on the way both professionals and parents viewed primary education, but few of its practical recommendations were immediately acted upon. Teachers in 'difficult' schools received an extra £75 annually (as against £120 recommended by Plowden). An expansion of nursery provision did not begin until 1973 (and was cut back not long afterwards). Money was found for school building projects, especially in EPAs, but 10 years later 20% of all primary pupils were still being educated in pre-1903 buildings, many with outside lavatories. A programme of action research was set up to establish and monitor EPAs. The concept of greater parental involvement was favourably received, and this involvement has increased in the years since Plowden. Corporal punishment was forbidden in *all* state schools from 1987.]

1967   GITTINS – PRIMARY EDUCATION IN WALES (CACE Wales)

Set up at the same time as Plowden, with the same terms of reference and some overlap of membership, this report shared Plowden's philosophy of education, and reached similar general conclusions. (See 1967 Plowden.) In addition, it considered some specifically Welsh issues, mainly the prevalence of two languages in school and community, but also the existence of large rural areas with sparse population, and the high respect widely felt for education and for teachers. It recommended a considerable increase in the advisory staff employed by LEAs, and in in-service training for teachers; improved coordination of primary education in Wales; and the fostering of both Welsh and English, especially Welsh as a second language in predominantly English-speaking areas.

1968 NEWSOM – PUBLIC SCHOOLS COMMISSION, FIRST REPORT

This commission was set up by a Labour government to advise on the future of boarding public schools in the light of comprehensivisation. Public schools were defined as those belonging to the Headmasters' Conference, Governing Bodies Association or Governing Bodies of Girls' Schools Association. It concluded that they could be abolished, integrated into the maintained system, or allowed to remain but without their traditional tax privileges – though the commission's terms of reference favoured integration. It recommended, as a step towards integration, that a number of public schools should accept some of their pupils (eventually at least half) from maintained schools, using criteria of comprehensive selection and social needs (rather than selection according to ability); these pupils would receive financial assistance. These arrangements should be voluntary if possible, but statutory if necessary. [The recommendations met considerable opposition and were never implemented.]

1968 SUMMERFIELD – PSYCHOLOGISTS IN THE EDUCATION SERVICE

This report recommended that the educational psychologist's brief should be extended beyond the traditional testing and assessing of children plus some remedial teaching to include 'an extended range of treatment'. (Treatment had previously been the responsibility of the psychiatrist within the Child Guidance Service.) It also recommended an increase in the numbers of educational psychologists, aiming at a proportion of one per 10,000 children.

1968 DAINTON – THE FLOW OF CANDIDATES IN SCIENCE AND TECHNOLOGY INTO HIGHER EDUCATION

The swing away from science in the sixth forms of secondary schools, which ran counter to the expansion of science and technology in the universities, was the subject of this investigation. The report called for changes in the sixth form, with less specialisation and some mathematics for all pupils. [The recommendations were not well received, and came up against a shortage of appropriately qualified teachers and the determination on the part of the grammar and public schools to defend the notion of sixth form study in depth.]

1969   HASLEGRAVE – TECHNICIAN COURSES AND EXAMINATIONS

The committee reviewed the training of technicians and recommended the establishment of a Technician Education Council and a Business Education Council, to oversee courses and examinations. [These were set up, and later amalgamated to form the Business and Technician Education Council (BTEC).]

1970   DONNISON – PUBLIC SCHOOLS COMMISSION, SECOND REPORT

The terms of reference for this commission were similar to Newsom's in 1968, but concerned with independent day schools and direct grant schools. The report recommended that they should either admit pupils without charging fees and without selecting by ability, or forgo state aid. [Direct grant schools were required to choose either comprehensivisation or withdrawal of state aid in 1975.]

1972   JAMES – TEACHER EDUCATION AND TRAINING

The James Report examined the arrangements for the education, training and probation of teachers in England and Wales, looking at course content, the role of different types of institution, and the relationship between intending teachers and other students. It proposed a radical reorganisation of teacher training to involve three stages (referred to as 'cycles'): general higher education, professional training and in-service training. The first cycle could take the form of a degree or a new qualification, a two-year Diploma in Higher Education. The second cycle would consist of a year's professional studies followed by a year as a 'licensed' teacher (replacing the existing probationary year), after which students would be awarded a BA (Ed). The third cycle, of in-service training, should amount to at least a term's worth every seven years for all teachers in post. [There was strong opposition to the 'licensed teacher' proposal from the teachers' unions, and little action was taken to try to implement this. The principle of integrating teacher training into higher education was accepted by the government, and throughout the 1970s colleges of education merged with other FE establishments, such as technical and art colleges, to form colleges and institutes of higher education.]

1973   RUSSELL – ADULT EDUCATION: A PLAN FOR DEVELOPMENT

After examining non-vocational adult education in England and Wales, this report suggested little change in the existing division of responsibility for adult education between LEAs, the university extra-mural departments and voluntary bodies such as the WEA. However, it did recommend the establishment of a national development council, regional advisory councils, and local organisations in every LEA, with a strengthening of the role of central government in both financial support and guidance to LEAs. It advised that employees should have a right to paid educational leave, and also that adult education courses should charge fees, but that these should be small. [No action on the report was taken until 1977, when the Advisory Council for Adult and Continuing Education was set up: a central body like the proposed national development council but lacking the strong government support called for by the report. The local organisations have not been established.]

1974   FINER – ONE-PARENT FAMILIES

This report examined the particular needs and problems of one-parent families (one in 10 of families with children by 1971), and many of its recommendations had educational implications: expansion of day care and nursery provision, encouragement of pregnant schoolgirls to continue their education, radical changes in the secondary school curriculum and in the careers guidance offered to girls to enable them to compete equally for better paid, traditionally male jobs, greater home–school contact with more support from guidance staff for children known to be in one-parent families. [The Finer Report was not debated in parliament until over a year after it was published, and few of its recommendations on housing, law and benefits were implemented. The Sex Discrimination Act of 1975 provided the legal basis for equal opportunities for girls, but the 'radical changes' in girls' curriculum choices have not yet been introduced. Nursery and day care provision have expanded but still do not meet the demand. Care for school-age children outside school hours and in the holidays has received little attention. Little information is available on the extent to which schools are aware of, and providing for, the special needs of children from one-parent families, which now form a fifth of all families with children.]

1974   SWANN – THE FLOW INTO EMPLOYMENT OF SCIENTISTS, ENGINEERS AND TECHNOLOGISTS

A parallel report to Dainton (see 1968 Dainton), Swann investigated the flow of science and engineering graduates out of, rather than into, higher education.

It concluded that the best graduates in these subjects tended to stay on at university rather than go into industry or teaching. It recommended that, in postgraduate training, there should be more emphasis on the links between the academic world and industry, and that scientists should be encouraged, in various ways, to contribute to the work of schools.

1975   BULLOCK – A LANGUAGE FOR LIFE

'All aspects of teaching the use of English, including reading, writing and speech' was the subject of this report. It was concerned mainly with England, though it took some evidence from other English-speaking countries (including Scotland). It emphasised that it was not concerned with reading alone, arguing that reading is not a discrete skill that can be considered in isolation from general language development. The evidence on standards of reading was examined: while the committee judged these inadequate for present-day society, they found no strong evidence of actual *decline*. The report provided a lengthy and thorough account of the acquisition and use of the entire range of language skills, stage by stage, from infancy to adulthood, and the problems and difficulties that can occur. Language teaching in 2,000 schools was surveyed: there was widespread commitment to basic skills, and much emphasis on formal practice. Insisting that there was no simple way in which reading and the use of English could be improved, and that improvement required 'a thorough understanding of the many complexities, and . . . action on a broad front', the committee offered 333 conclusions and recommendations; only with reluctance was it prepared to select 17 of these as its principal findings. These included exhortations addressed to teachers, schools, LEAs and public attitudes, as well as direct recommendations to the government for specific action. The committee called for greater emphasis on language at all educational levels, with increased spending on staffing, accommodation and other resources. Detailed recommendations included: that every school should have a policy for 'language across the curriculum' and a suitably qualified teacher to support it, and that LEAs should appoint special advisers to support the schools; that there should be screening procedures to identify language difficulties at an early stage, and specialist assistance available at both school and LEA level for those in need; that language in education should form part of initial training for every teacher; that in-service education in reading and language should be expanded; and that a system of monitoring be set up, using new instruments to assess a wider range of attainments than in the past and establishing new criteria for literacy.

1975   ALEXANDER – ADULT EDUCATION: THE CHALLENGE OF CHANGE

After investigating voluntary, non-vocational adult education in Scotland, the committee recommended that adult education should be combined with the youth and community service into a community education service. [Most Scottish education authorities adopted this arrangement.]

1976   COWAN – REORGANISATION OF SECONDARY EDUCATION IN NORTHERN IRELAND

Ways of changing the Northern Ireland bipartite selective system (of grammar and secondary intermediate schools) to a non-selective system were investigated. The adoption of a dual system of 11–16 and 11–18 comprehensive schools was recommended; the former could have a two-form entry, but the latter required a six-form entry. Pupils could transfer from 11–16 to 11–18 schools for sixth-form courses. [These proposals were widely opposed, and they were abandoned by the new Conservative government in 1979, although much groundwork had been done in the meantime on the legal and administrative aspects of implementing them (see 1979 Benn, 1979 Dickson).]

1977   TAYLOR – A NEW PARTNERSHIP FOR OUR SCHOOLS

The arrangements for the 'management and government' of maintained schools in England and Wales were examined. It was recommended that every school have its own governing body, consisting of equal numbers of representatives of the LEA, school staff (including the headteacher ex officio), parents ('with, where appropriate, pupils') and the local community. The report suggested that all the powers relevant to school government should be formally vested in the LEA, but that it should delegate these as far as possible to the governing body of each school, who should in turn allow as much discretion as possible to the head. Specifically, governors should be given responsibility for defining the broad aims of the school; they in turn should invite the head and staff to devise means of pursuing them, and should themselves monitor the school's progress towards them. LEAs should provide initial and in-service training courses for governors, and all governors should attend them. [The main recommendations were implemented in the 1980 Education Act, and further extended in the 1986 Education Act; but the 1988 Education Reform Act introduced radical changes in the relationships between parents, governors, teachers, LEAs and central government (see Chapter 4).]

1977   MUNN – THE STRUCTURE OF THE CURRICULUM

Munn and Dunning are usually, and reasonably, considered together (see also 1977 Dunning). They were set up in close succession by the Secretary of State for Scotland to study the curriculum (Munn) and assessment (Dunning) in the third and fourth years of Scottish secondary schools; they kept in close touch with each other throughout their deliberations; and they presented their reports with complementary recommendations at the same time. The Munn Committee identified a number of problems with, and criticisms of, the traditional Scottish secondary curriculum, notably those arising from two major recent developments, the rapid expansion of comprehensive schools, and the raising of the school leaving age to 16. These had left too many pupils of average ability or below either struggling with work beyond their abilities or following 'improvised' courses. For pupils of high ability, too much of the curriculum was often taken up with preparation for exams, and too little done to stretch them in the earlier years. At the same time, new subjects were being urged for inclusion in the school curriculum. The committee recommended that the curriculum in these two years should consist of a *core* and an *elective* area. The core would consist of seven subjects, four (English, maths, PE and RE) to be taken by all pupils, the other three (a social studies subject, a science, and a creative arts subject) to be chosen from a short list. The elective area would be wide-ranging, and a further two or three options would be chosen from it. Each course should have three syllabuses of different (but overlapping) levels of difficulty to cater for pupils of different ability, with some limited opportunities for transfer between them. The first year of secondary schooling, at 12 plus in Scotland, ought not to differentiate pupils, the committee thought, but differentiation should begin in the second year, and be well established by the third. [Unlike that of England and Wales, Scotland's 'national curriculum' has not been established by law, and how much influence Munn has actually had on schools is uncertain.] (See also Chapter 10, Figure 10.3.)

1977   DUNNING – ASSESSMENT FOR ALL

The Dunning Report on assessment should be taken together with the Munn Report on curriculum (see 1977 Munn). Dunning considered the assessment of third- and fourth-year pupils of all levels of academic ability in Scottish secondary schools. The committee recommended that O grades, taken only by the abler pupils, be replaced by an examination that matched comprehensive education, and that all pupils should be assessed for a single national certificate in each subject. To cater for pupils of different ability, however, and to ensure that everyone could gain a certificate, Dunning endorsed Munn's proposal for three syllabuses of different levels of difficulty, and recommended that certificates should be awarded at three corresponding levels, covering the entire ability range. These were termed Credit (the highest), General and Foundation, the last of these to be divided into Pass and CC (Course Completed). Awards should be based on continuous assessment of course work as well as on a final external examination. [The major recommendations of the Dunning Committee were accepted, and embodied in the Standard grade examination system, which has replaced O grades in Scotland (see Chapter 9).]

1978   OAKES – THE MANAGEMENT OF HIGHER EDUCATION IN THE MAINTAINED SECTOR

This report identified the principal tasks for management as gathering information on supply and demand, planning for change, allocating resources and general supervision. It proposed a new division of responsibility for finance between central and local government, and a structure of regional and national bodies to advise both the Secretary of State and LEAs on management tasks, while leaving considerable freedom of decision with both the LEAs and individual institutions.

1978   WADDELL – SCHOOL EXAMINATIONS

This report stemmed from the recommendation of the Schools Council in the early 1970s that the dual examination system of GCE and CSE should be replaced by a single system at 16 plus. The committee agreed that a single system was desirable, and suggested ways in which it could be implemented without excessive financial or administrative difficulty. They recommended using three modes, as in CSE, and a single grading system, though with special papers in some subjects for pupils of low or high ability. There should be regional grouping of GCE and CSE exam boards (four in England, one in Wales). They suggested that the unified courses could be offered from 1983, with the first exams in 1985. [In the event, the first GCSE courses were introduced in 1986, and the first exams took place in 1988. (See Chapter 9.)]

1978   WARNOCK – SPECIAL EDUCATIONAL NEEDS

The Warnock Report reviewed educational provision in Great Britain for children and young people 'handicapped by disabilities of body or mind'. It introduced the concept of 'special educational needs', recommending that it replace categorisation of children by the 10 existing statutory categories of handicap. It suggested that up to 20% of the school population might have such needs at some time in their school career (previously around 2% of children had been legally classed as 'handicapped'). It also recommended that children whose needs could not be met within the resources of the ordinary school should have a record (which came to be called a 'statement') of their special educational needs drawn up by a multiprofessional team. A detailed procedure was proposed for assessing and 'statementing' children with special educational needs, with parents having rights to be involved and make known their views. Wherever possible, children with special needs should be educated in ordinary schools alongside their peers (the principle of integration). [The Warnock Report strongly influenced the 1981 Education Act; see Chapter 4. See also Chapters 5 and 11 for further information about the education of children with special needs.]

1979   KEOHANE – PROPOSALS FOR A CERTIFICATE OF EXTENDED EDUCATION (Cmnd. 7755)

The purpose of this study was: to examine proposals (from the Schools Council) for a certificate of extended education (CEE) – a single-subject qualification at 17 plus, for pupils staying on after the compulsory leaving age but not taking A levels; to study pilot schemes already in operation; and to advise the Secretary of State as to whether the CEE should be given official recognition. The report recommended approval and development on a national basis, but with modifications so as to ensure that those taking the courses were prepared for employment. The committee felt that basic communication and numeracy skills were most important for this purpose, and so it was suggested that all CEE certificates should record proficiency scores in English and mathematics. In addition, it suggested that more courses should be developed that related directly to the world of work, and had titles informative to employers. The committee did not endorse the Schools Council's wish to see CEE courses closely linked to CSE courses and grades; it would prefer to see CEE courses more closely linked to FE courses (themselves in need of a simpler structure) and more vocational in emphasis.

1979   MANSELL – A BASIS FOR CHOICE

This was a report of a DES study group set up to consider full-time courses (mainly one-year courses) for young people of average ability and attainment, who had left school and needed neither GCE studies nor preparation for specific jobs. The group found that many such courses existed, but that they lacked coordination. It therefore recommended a unifying and rationalising curriculum structure, in the form of a set of criteria that existing and future courses might satisfy, with national validation but allowing scope for flexibility and local initiative. It was suggested that courses should consist of three main elements. First, there should be a common core of general education, occupying 50–60% of the course. The remainder should be tailored more to the vocational interests of the students, and be divided equally between vocational studies related to a general idea of employment and studies specific to a particular job. Students' final assessment should take the form of a profile, recording course work and subjective evaluations of abilities as well as the results of objective tests. A nationally recognised qualification should be awarded on successful completion of a validated course. The study group emphasised three principles underlying their recommendations: though not requiring an initial vocational commitment from students, courses must encourage the development of 'a realistic vocational focus' as they progress; attainment in vocational studies should receive equal recognition with academic attainment, and should not restrict future prospects; and the experience of learning is important in itself, as well as the attainment of certain levels of performance.

1979   ASTIN – REPORT OF THE WORKING PARTY ON THE MANAGEMENT OF SCHOOLS IN NORTHERN IRELAND

Set up after publication of the Taylor Report for England and Wales (see 1977 Taylor), this working party recommended that each school in Northern Ireland too (with the possible exception of small primary schools) should have a board of governors.

1979   BENN – REPORT OF THE WORKING PARTY ON VOLUNTARY SCHOOLS

This report investigated ways of allowing voluntary schools in Northern Ireland to continue (as direct grant schools) in the new non-selective system of secondary education recommended in the Cowan Report (see 1976 Cowan). [It became inapplicable when, after a change of government in 1979, the Cowan recommendations were abandoned.]

1979   DICKSON – REPORT ON PREPARATORY AND BOARDING DEPARTMENTS; REPORT ON THE STAFFING OF SECONDARY SCHOOLS; REPORT ON IN-SERVICE TRAINING

These were reports of investigations of various legal and administrative aspects of the new non-selective system of secondary education recommended in the

Cowan Report (see 1976 Cowan). [They became inapplicable when, after a change of government in 1979, the Cowan recommendations were abandoned.]

1980   CHILVER – THE FUTURE STRUCTURE OF TEACHER EDUCATION IN NORTHERN IRELAND

An interim report of the Higher Education Review Group for Northern Ireland (see also 1982 Chilver), Chilver investigated implications for the teacher education system of falling school rolls. It recommended that the three Belfast teacher training colleges come together on a single site. [The proposal aroused strong opposition from both Catholic and Protestant churches, and was not adopted.]

1981   RAMPTON – WEST INDIAN CHILDREN IN OUR SCHOOLS (Cmnd. 8273)

The 'Rampton Committee' was set up in 1979, late in the life of the Labour government (its membership was finalised by the new Conservative government) to investigate the education of children from all ethnic minority groups. First, though, it was required to produce an interim report on West Indian children. Research commissioned by the committee appeared to show considerable underachievement by West Indian children, on average, compared with White and Asian children. Various possible explanations were considered, with particular attention paid to racism, a factor frequently mentioned in evidence to the committee. While believing that few teachers were intentionally racist, and while not accepting that racism was the sole cause of West Indian underachievement, the committee concluded that unintentional racism (in the sense of stereotyped, negative or patronising views of West Indian children) was widespread and did influence children's performance. Other contributory causes that were suggested included the inadequacy of preschool provision and its particular unsuitability for West Indian families; prejudice on the part of some teachers against West Indian children's use of English; inappropriate curricula and teaching materials; and the discouraging effect of the relatively poor employment prospects of West Indian school leavers resulting from discrimination in the labour market. At the same time, the committee believed, some West Indian parents did not do enough to support schools and teachers. In a long list of detailed recommendations, the committee urged institutions and organisations at all levels to recognise these problems and work to solve them. The main requirement, as they saw it, was for a change in attitude in the community at large towards acceptance of ethnic minorities. In specifically educational matters, stress was laid on both initial and in-service training of teachers to attune them to the needs of ethnic minority groups and to improve their understanding of a multicultural approach to education. (See also 1985 Swann.)

1982   CHILVER – THE FUTURE OF HIGHER EDUCATION IN NORTHERN IRELAND

This was the final report of the Higher Education Review Group for Northern Ireland (see also 1980 Chilver). It set out to predict likely demand for higher education until the end of the century, and to provide guidelines for meeting it. Recommendations were that the New University of Ulster move towards more emphasis on mature students, distance learning and non-degree work; that Ulster Polytechnic increase emphasis on vocational studies; and that Queen's University Belfast continue largely as before, though with more emphasis on broadly based and part-time courses, and, where possible, three-year degree courses (instead of four-year). [In the event, the New University of Ulster and Ulster Polytechnic amalgamated in 1985 to form the University of Ulster.]

1982   COCKCROFT – MATHEMATICS COUNTS

The subject of this investigation was mathematics teaching in primary and secondary schools in England and Wales, in the light of the mathematical needs of pupils when they proceed to further or higher education, employment and adult life generally. It attempted to identify these needs, and addressed detailed recommendations for meeting them to central government, LEAs, examination boards, teachers, training institutions and funding bodies for research and curriculum development. More general recommendations were addressed to the public at large. These included: that the diversity of pupils' abilities should be recognised, and a 'differentiated curriculum' and range of examination papers provided; that the quality of the maths teaching force be improved – by the recruitment and retention of more well-qualified mathematicians through financial incentives, flexible salary structures and guarantees of employment, and through increases in in-service training and support; that the subject should be approached by teachers in a variety of different ways, including exposition, discussion, practical work and problem-solving, as well as mental and oral work; and that curriculum materials be developed reflecting a 'foundation list' of mathematical topics identified by the committee.

1982   SWINNERTON-DYER – THE SUPPORT OF UNIVERSITY SCIENTIFIC RESEARCH

This report investigated postgraduate education, especially as supported by such bodies as the Science and Engineering Research Council and the Social Science Research Council, and its success in meeting national manpower requirements. It recommended that the councils monitor the rates of submission of theses by research students in every university, so as to be able to impose sanctions on universities whose rates were unsatisfactory. It was also recommended that the DES should encourage postgraduate conversion courses, by means of maintenance grants, and that a single national body should be set up to identify manpower requirements and commission courses to meet them.

1982   THOMPSON – EXPERIENCE AND PARTICIPATION

This was a review of the Youth Service, set up by the recently elected Conservative government. It recommended that a government minister be appointed to coordinate the work of all departments concerned with youth affairs, and that there should be more funding and clearer national objectives. It suggested that the Youth Service should be attempting to meet the 'crucial social needs' of the 11–20 age group, especially the unemployed, the handicapped, girls and young women, and ethnic minorities. [Most of the report's recommendations were rejected in the government's formal response two years later.]

1985   SWANN – EDUCATION FOR ALL (Cmnd. 9453)

Just before what had been the Rampton Committee published its interim report (see 1981 Rampton), Mr Antony Rampton was replaced as chairman by Lord Swann. The final report – almost eight times as long as the interim – was able to cover the same ground in more detail and also to extend the coverage to a wide range of ethnic minority groups. Further research studies confirmed the earlier picture of West Indian pupils' underachievement, on average, compared with Asian and White pupils, but showed that the gap appeared to be diminishing significantly as time passed. The committee remained convinced that largely unintentional racism was an important factor behind West Indian underachievement, a claim not undermined by the high achievement of Asians, since stereotyped views of them were generally much less negative, and racism might have different effects on different groups. Of other possible causes of these disparities in achievement, IQ differences were considered at length, but not found to be a significant factor. Differences in socioeconomic conditions, however, were found to provide a partial explanation for the relatively low attainment not only of West Indian but probably also of Bangladeshi children. Socioeconomic differences themselves often resulted from racial discrimination, especially in employment and housing. The committee also considered, rather more briefly, the educational needs of Chinese, Cypriot, Italian, Ukrainian and Vietnamese children, and the particular needs of Travellers' children and 'Liverpool Blacks'. The committee's general conclusion was that the response to these issues must lie in the education of *all* children, not just of ethnic minority children. All LEAs and schools must lead pupils to understand what is involved in Britain's being a multiracial and multicultural society; this must permeate all the work of schools. Racism must be fought, and inherited myths and stereotypes attacked. More detailed recommendations included giving first priority in language teaching to English. Although linguistic diversity was considered a positive asset, bilingualism in maintained schools was not supported. Separate schools for ethnic groups, though permissible in law, were not supported either. The committee believed that if its proposals were adopted, the demand for such schools would be greatly reduced. In this connection, central government and LEAs were urged to be sensitive to the wishes of some groups to have their daughters educated in single-sex schools. It suggested that more attention should be given to multicultural matters in both initial training and in-service training of teachers, and that the effectiveness of racism awareness training should be investigated. It further recommended that greater effort should be made to employ and promote teachers from ethnic minority groups, though without positive discrimination or lowering of standards.

1985   LINDOP – ACADEMIC VALIDATION IN PUBLIC SECTOR HIGHER EDUCATION

This report recommended a variety of methods of validation. It suggested that some polytechnics and colleges should be given complete autonomy by the Secretary of State to validate their own courses; others should be allowed more limited autonomy, in specific areas; while in yet others external validation should remain. It also proposed that there should be a national organisation to coordinate the activities of universities in validating public sector colleges' degree courses. [Since 1992, all polytechnics – now universities – and several colleges have autonomy to validate their courses.]

1987   BLACK – NATIONAL CURRICULUM TASK GROUP ON ASSESSMENT AND TESTING: A REPORT

As part of the preparations for what became the 1988 Education Reform Act (see Chapter 4), the Government set up a Task Group on Assessment and Testing (TGAT), under the chairmanship of Professor Paul Black, to devise assessment arrangements for the national curriculum. It recommended that pupils be assessed at the end of each of four *key stages*, at the ages of seven, 11, 14 and 16 respectively. At the first key stage, assessment should only be in the core subjects of the national curriculum (English, mathematics and science plus Welsh in Welsh-speaking schools in Wales). At subsequent key stages it should be in all the foundation subjects (the core subjects plus art, geography, history, music, physical education, technology, a modern foreign language at the last two stages, and Welsh in non-Welsh speaking schools in Wales). At the first three key stages, assessment should be formative for individual pupils; at the final stage it should also be summative. At each stage, the pupils should be assessed against appropriate *attainment targets*, grouped into a small number (the Task Group recommended no more than four) of *profile components*, reflecting the range of knowledge, skills and understanding the subject encompasses. For each profile component, there should be a progression through criterion-referenced *levels* of achievement – 10 levels for subjects taught throughout the full age range of five to 16. The same scale of levels should be used to assess children at every stage. This would allow direct comparison of the attainments of all children, regardless of age, and, it was argued, make children themselves more aware of their progress over the years. Assessment should combine two different methods: first, the teachers' judgments of their pupils' attainments, based on their work in class; and secondly, the pupils' performance on *standard assessment tasks* (SAT) set nationally. A wide range of SATs should be available, from which teachers could select so as to be able to incorporate them into the work they and their pupils were doing, and use them for formative and diagnostic as well as summative purposes. Procedures should be established for monitoring teachers' assessments, especially where they disagreed with the SAT results. At the final key stage (age 16), assessment should, for the present, be through the existing GCSE examinations (see Chapter 9), though this would eventually need to be modified. The results for individual children should be kept confidential, and made available only to their parents and teachers. But aggregated test results – by class and by school – should be published for Key Stages 2, 3 and 4, to enable parents to judge how well teachers and schools were performing. However, such results should be published only as part of a broader report – by a school about its work as a whole, and by the local authority about the socioeconomic characteristics of the area that are known to affect schools' and children's performance. [Most of the recommendations of the TGAT Report were initially accepted by the Secretary of State – though aggregated results for schools were published in the form of 'league tables', and not only in the context of reports by schools and LEAs. The TGAT model was used as a framework by the national curriculum subject working groups in drawing up programmes of study and attainment targets. But the assessment arrangements were widely criticised as too complicated, time consuming and costly – criticisms ministers came to share. In addition, ministers became uneasy about the TGAT's concern with formative and diagnostic as against summative testing, and its emphasis on the judgements of teachers. Over the next few years, teachers' assessments were reduced in importance, as compared with external national tests. The wide range of SATs originally proposed was replaced by a narrower range of more limited tests, simpler and quicker to administer. Some changes were made to the TGAT framework: for example, attainment targets were no longer grouped into profile components, but were themselves divided into *strands*. Finally, still more simplification of the system of national assessment was proposed in the Dearing Report and accepted by the Secretary of State. See 1994 Dearing, and Chapter 10 below.]

1988   KINGMAN – REPORT OF THE COMMITTEE OF INQUIRY INTO THE TEACHING OF ENGLISH LANGUAGE

The committee was established to recommend a model of how the English language (whether spoken or written) works, which would form a basis for teacher training and professional discussion of English teaching; to recommend how and how far this model should be made explicit to pupils; and to recommend what pupils should be taught and be expected to understand by the ages of seven, 11 and 16. The model recommended is in four parts. The first describes the *forms* of English, spoken and written, at various levels from individual letters or sounds to connected discourse. These include vowel and consonant sounds, intonation and stress; the alphabet, spelling and punctuation; the formation of plurals and comparatives, and the use of metaphors and idiomatic expressions; the structure of phrases and sentences, the characteristics of verbs (such as tense, aspect, mood and number agreement), nouns, adjectives, adverbs, adjuncts, disjuncts and conjuncts; and the structure of units of discourse larger than the sentence. The second part describes *communication* by speakers or writers and *comprehension* by listeners or readers. This includes consideration of the context and type of discourse, of the intentions and attitudes of both speaker and listener, and of various processes of inference used in deriving meaning from sounds, forms and contexts. The third part describes the ways in which children *acquire* the forms of language, and *develop* their ability to use and understand them, with consideration of what might be found easy or difficult at different stages of development. The fourth part describes *variation* in English, over time and from place to place. Other dialects and creole languages differ systematically from Standard English; their forms and phrases are not 'bad grammar'. The report recommends that children should learn to write clearly and accurately in Standard English, and argues that they can be helped in this by learning to use descriptive technical terms to talk about language. But it does not favour a return to 'old-fashioned formal teaching of grammar' or learning by rote. How explicit the report's own model of language should be made to *pupils*, and when, is a matter for the professional judgement of teachers. The report favours the setting of attainment targets for children at seven, 11 and 16 (though with some publicly expressed reservations by Sir John Kingman himself about whether English can be 'mastered rung by rung' as in climbing a ladder (Nash, 1988)), and spells out in some detail what these should be. At all three stages, these targets include both skills in *using* English, and explicit knowledge *about* the language – its rules and conventions, its historical and geographical variation, and so on. Considerable attention is paid to the linguistic knowledge and skills required of teachers, and the ways in which these can best be learnt. Detailed recommendations are made about the amount and kind of training in English language teaching appropriate for primary teachers, and for English teachers and teachers of other subjects in secondary schools; the report's own model is recommended as a basis for these. As well as occupying a more important place in initial teacher training, English language should become one of the 'national priority areas' for in-service training of teachers.

1988   HIGGINSON – ADVANCING A LEVELS

The committee was set up to examine the principles that should govern GCE A level syllabuses and their assessment. It recommended a thorough revision of present arrangements. There should be more coordination of the work of the GCE examining boards, with more uniform standards of marking, a reduction in the number of separate syllabuses in each subject and a compulsory core common to the remaining syllabuses. A fifth of A level assessment should be based on course work rather than the final examination. The recommendation most widely noticed was that full-time students should normally study a wider range of subjects – five A levels plus one AS level, rather than three A levels as at present. [The recommendations of the report were rejected by the Secretary of State immediately on its publication.]

1989 ELTON – DISCIPLINE IN SCHOOLS

The committee was established to recommend action to secure the orderly atmosphere necessary in schools for teaching and learning. It judged the main discipline problem facing teachers to be not the rare serious incidents of physical aggression, but the cumulative disruptive effects of relatively trivial but persistent misbehaviour. It offered no simple diagnosis of causes, or simple remedies, but instead made a wide range of recommendations to teachers, headteachers, governing bodies, LEAs and parents. Central to these were ways of helping teachers become more effective classroom managers – in both initial and in-service training. Others include the following. Schools should attempt to create a positive atmosphere based on a sense of community and shared values. Heads' management styles should encourage a sense of collective responsibility among teachers, and of commitment to school among pupils and parents; their management training should be directed towards this. School buildings should be kept in a good state of repair and appearance. Parents need to provide their children with firm guidance and positive models of behaviour; schools should do more to prepare pupils for the responsibilities of being parents. Pupils themselves should be given more responsibility, and their non-academic achievements should be given more recognition.

1992 HOWIE – UPPER SECONDARY EDUCATION IN SCOTLAND

The Howie Committee was set up in 1990 to review the curriculum and examinations in the fifth and sixth years of secondary education in Scotland. The Committee was highly critical of present arrangements. It concluded that the curricular breadth on which Scotland prides itself is not reflected in actual attainment. Many pupils obtain only one or two Highers, and many others none at all. Even the ablest pupils compare badly in breadth of attainment with those in European countries. At the same time, Higher courses give little opportunity for study in depth, as pupils have to learn too much, too quickly after Standard grade (see Chapter 9 below), whose own pace is too slow. Many pupils are therefore insufficiently prepared for higher education. Vocational education is too sharply divided from academic, and held in low esteem. There is too much flexibility, leading to arbitrary course choices and making coherent course planning difficult. To meet these criticisms, the Committee suggested that Standard grade courses should be started earlier and completed by the end of the third year; and that in the fourth, fifth and sixth years, pupils should follow one of two routes: either a one- or two-year programme leading to a Scottish Certificate (SCOTCERT); or a three-year programme leading to a Scottish Baccalaureate (SCOTBAC). The SCOTCERT programme would be aimed at the majority (60–70%) of fourth-year pupils, but would also be available to adults and in further education colleges. It would cover a combination of 'core skills', general education and vocational education, in a modular structure (with 16 modules per year). The modules would be based, in part, on existing National Certificate modules, and amalgamated with the new GSVQs (see Chapter 9 below). It would prepare pupils for employment, further training or more advanced education. The SCOTBAC programme would offer two 'lines of study', one in arts, the other in science, but with some academic and vocational variants. There would be a 'core' common to both lines (English, modern languages, mathematics, science, social subjects, music, art, history and information technology), but the weighting of subjects within the core would vary between the lines. In addition, there would be optional subjects, but these would be restricted in number and required to form a coherent programme of study (which could be vocational as well as academic in emphasis). Courses would be based, in part, on existing Higher and CSYS courses, but major core subjects would be taken to a level well beyond Higher and in some cases beyond CSYS level; optional subjects would be taken to at least Higher level. SCOTBAC would be the normal route to higher education. Assessment in both SCOTCERT and SCOTBAC would be criterion referenced, and partly internal, partly external. The SCOTBAC would be awarded with an overall grade, on a scale A–D; pupils need not pass every subject, and good performance in some could to some extent outweigh poor performance in others. Arrangements should be made for pupils to be able to transfer between the two programmes. [Just over two years after the publication of the Report, the government published its response. By and large, it rejected the Howie recommendations, though they have had some influence on the government's own plans. Standard grade courses are to remain in the third and fourth years. For the fifth and sixth years, Highers will remain, but with modifications (see Chapter 9 below). The proposed 'twin-track' structure of SCOTCERT and SCOTBAC had met much opposition, on the grounds that SCOTBAC would inevitably be held in much higher esteem than SCOTCERT. As few schools would be able to offer both tracks, a system of 'SCOTBAC schools' and 'SCOTCERT schools' might develop. There would be strong parental pressure for pupils to attend the former, leading to high rates of drop-out or failure.]

1993 DEARING – THE NATIONAL CURRICULUM AND ITS ASSESSMENT

This is the final report, after consultations and an interim report, by an individual (Sir Ron Dearing, the Chairman of the School Curriculum and

Assessment Authority) not a committee. Dearing was asked by the Secretary of State for Education to review the national curriculum with a view to 'slimming down' the curriculum, simplifying its assessment arrangements, considering the future of the 10-level scale of attainment, and improving the central administration. Dearing recommended that for these purposes there should be an immediate, closely coordinated review of the curriculum orders in all the subjects of the national curriculum. For Key Stages 1–3 (i.e. pupils aged five–14), these reviews should aim to reduce the statutory curriculum enough to free about 20% of teaching time for use at the discretion of schools. This reduction should be achieved, not by removing any subjects from the compulsory curriculum, or by altering the basic content of programmes of study, but by identifying an essential core for each subject, and reducing the number of attainment targets so as to concentrate on that core. Statements of attainment should also be reduced in number and made less specific, or perhaps even replaced by a smaller number of more general 'level descriptors'. Schools should use the discretionary time thus made available primarily for basic literacy, oracy and numeracy, and then for deepening pupils' knowledge and understanding of the national curriculum subjects. They should be accountable to their governing bodies for their use of this time. For Key Stage 4 (i.e. pupils aged 14–16), the schools' discretion should be extended. Only English, mathematics, science, and PE should be compulsory, together with short courses in a modern foreign language and (from 1996) technology; the remaining national curriculum subjects (art, geography, history and music) should be optional. (Dearing notes that religious education and sex education will also be compulsory at this stage, but outside the national curriculum.) For the teaching time thus freed, vocational as well as academic options should be considered. The 10-level scale of attainment should be retained for the subjects that use it, but it should be used only until the end of Key Stage 3. (The subjects that do not use the scale – art, music and PE – should continue to use end-of-key-stage statements instead.) The national curriculum thus revised should not be altered for five years. National tests should be simplified as far as possible without sacrificing validity or reliability; calls on teachers' time for administering tests, conducting teacher assessment and keeping records should be reduced. (Except for the core subjects in primary schools, statutory teacher assessment should be postponed until the curriculum had been slimmed down in accordance with the recommendations above.) The national curriculum and its assessment arrangements should continue to be available for pupils with special educational needs, and the levels defined in curriculum orders should be broadened to take account of this. Teachers of pupils with special needs should be consulted over this, and parents of pupils with special needs should be involved by schools in the development of appropriate curricula for their children. [These recommendations were accepted by the Secretary of State, with minor modifications and additions, the proposed reviews were duly conducted, and new draft curriculum orders were issued in May 1994, for consultation and planned implementation from August 1995 (see Chapter 10 below).]

SOURCES AND FURTHER READING

Although official reports are usually best known by the names of the chairpersons of the committees of inquiry that produced them, they are rarely to be found under those names in the author indexes of libraries. The official authorship of reports is varied and sometimes confusing; usually the easiest way of finding official reports in libraries is to look under the titles in title indexes.

In addition to the reports themselves, the following are useful sources. Evans et al. (1994), contains summaries, mostly briefer than ours, of a wide, though still selective, range of reports, including a number not covered here. Corbett (1978) and Rogers (1980) have longer summaries and discussions than ours, but of a smaller number of reports, and of course do not cover the most recent reports.

Corbett, A. (1978) *Much To Do About Education*, 4th ed., London: Macmillan.

Evans, M. et. al. (eds) (1994) *Education Yearbook 1995*, Harlow: Longman.

Gathorne-Hardy, J. (1977) *The Public School Phenomenon*, London: Hodder & Stoughton.

Gordon, P. and Lawton, D. (1984) *A Guide to English Educational Terms*, London: Batsford.

Mackinnon, D. (1976) *Social Class and Educational Attainment*, Milton Keynes: Open University Press (a component of OU Course E201 *Personality and Learning*).

Nash, I. (1988) Kingman sets stage for new English working party, *Times Educational Supplement*, 6 May 1988.

NICER (1984) *Register of Research 1978–82*, Belfast: Northern Ireland Council for Educational Research.

Rogers, R. (1980) *Crowther to Warnock: How Fourteen Reports Tried to Change Children's Lives*, London: Heinemann.

This chapter summarises the main Acts of Parliament concerned with or directly relevant to education, together with a small number of particularly important ministerial circulars, regulations and orders. It is inevitably highly selective, both in the Acts it covers and in what it includes from each Act. No attempt is made to use legally precise terms or statements in the summaries. We begin with the 1870 Education Act – which in many ways represents the beginning of the modern education system – but concentrate on legislation since 1944. The 1988 Education Reform Act, seems likely to stand alongside that of 1944, if not that of 1870 itself, in the scale of its consequences for education.

Except where otherwise specified, these Acts apply to England and Wales.

1870 ELEMENTARY EDUCATION ACT ('The Forster Act')

The aim of this Act was to provide elementary schools throughout the country, filling the gaps in the existing provision established by the churches, private benefactors and guilds. It divided the country into school districts, and, in those districts with inadequate provision, required school boards to be elected which would raise money through the rates to provide public elementary schools (often called 'board schools'). These schools were to be non-denominational and open to inspection. School boards were allowed to prescribe weekly fees and to pass byelaws requiring attendance by all children between five and 13 years of age.

1880 EDUCATION ACT (The 'Mundella Act')

This Act required school boards to pass byelaws to secure attendance (although pupils older than 10 could be exempted if they had achieved a certain standard of attainment, or a satisfactory record of attendance). Fees in elementary schools were limited to 9d per week.

1888 LOCAL GOVERNMENT ACT

This Act created county councils and county borough councils, which were later used as the framework for educational administration (see 1902 Education Act).

1891 EDUCATION ACT

In effect, this Act made elementary education free.

1892 EDUCATION ACT (IRELAND)

This introduced compulsory school attendance in Ireland, and required local authorities to create School Attendance Committees to enforce it.

1899 BOARD OF EDUCATION ACT

This Act set up a Board of Education to supervise the education system.

1902 EDUCATION ACT ('The Balfour Act')

The 1902 Act established a system of secondary education as the 1870 Act had done for elementary education, by filling the gaps in the existing provision with non-denominational state schools (they were not free until 1944). The Act abolished the school boards and replaced them with a system of local education authorities based on the county and county borough councils of the 1880 Local Government Act. In the county areas, however, responsibility for elementary education was given to non-county boroughs with a population exceeding 10,000 and urban districts with a population in excess of 20,000. These were known as Part III Authorities (and were abolished by the 1944 Act).

The new LEAs took over the responsibility to provide adequate facilities for elementary education and in addition were authorised to provide 'education other than elementary', either by setting up new secondary schools or by aiding existing ones in their areas. They were allowed to raise and spend rates, within set limits, to fulfil these responsibilities. In some areas this resulted in generous secondary provision, whilst other areas did as little as possible. Section 6 of the Act stipulated that all elementary schools had to have managers and laid down how many of these should be LEA representatives. Governors for secondary schools were dealt with under regulations made under the Act between 1902 and 1908.

1906 EDUCATION (PROVISION OF MEALS) ACT

LEAs were authorised by this Act to spend public money on meals for undernourished elementary school children.

1907 EDUCATION (ADMINISTRATIVE PROVISIONS) ACT

With this Act LEAs were required, for the first time, to provide for the medical inspection of children in elementary schools.

1910 EDUCATION (CHOICE OF EMPLOYMENT) ACT

By enabling LEAs, if they wished, to set up Juvenile Employment Bureaux, this Act laid the foundation for a careers service.

1918 EDUCATION ACT ('The Fisher Act')

The 1918 Act required LEAs to submit schemes of development, when requested by the Board of Education, to ensure that a fully national system of public education was being set up. It abolished the limits set on secondary educational expenditure in 1902, and removed the exemptions to the requirement to attend school between the ages of five and 14. It also abolished the 'half-time' system by which children worked for part of the day and attended school for the remainder. It recommended that school leavers aged 14 to 16 should attend 'continuation' schools for the equivalent of a day a week (this was never implemented). If they wished, LEAs were allowed to set up nursery schools or classes for children below school age, and to provide physical and social educational facilities, such as school camps. All fees for elementary schools were abolished.

1923 EDUCATION ACT (NORTHERN IRELAND) ('The Londonderry Act')

This Act created County and County Borough Education Authorities, and Regional and County Borough Education Committees, in Northern Ireland. They were given powers to ensure adequate elementary and higher education within their areas; and provision was made for existing schools to transfer to these new authorities. These authorities were made responsible for the 'catechetical instruction' of children in elementary schools, according to their parents' denomination. Education was to be funded from both taxes and rates.

1930 EDUCATION ACT (NORTHERN IRELAND)

The 1930 Act gave the Education Minister power to nominate up to a quarter of the membership of Education Committees in Northern Ireland (it being understood that the nominees would be clergymen); regulated the membership of School Management Committees; and required local education authorities to provide Bible instruction in any school if the parents of 10 or more children demanded it.

1944 EDUCATION ACT ('The Butler Act')

The Butler Act replaced almost all previous educational legislation and laid the foundation for the modern education system. It replaced the Board of Education with a Ministry of Education, and gave the Minister at the head of this a creative rather than a merely controlling function, charging him or her with promoting education in England and Wales.

- It abolished the distinction between elementary and higher education, and set up a unified system of free, compulsory schooling from the age of five to 15 (to be raised when practicable to 16). Pupils could receive this education in the LEAs' own schools, in schools maintained by other organisations, or, in certain circumstances (under Section 56 of the Act), 'otherwise' – in effect, at home.
- It extended the concept of education to cover the needs of those above and below school age, and to include the community's needs for culture and recreation. LEAs could provide nursery schools and classes; they could provide or finance holiday classes, camps, play schemes, swimming baths, community centres and recreation facilities; and were given the responsibility (never implemented) to ensure that all young people up to age 18, and not otherwise in education, received part-time further education by attending a 'county college' for the equivalent of one day a week.
- It created a variety of services to support the basic structure of primary and secondary education, e.g. transport, free milk, medical and dental treatment. School meals were to be provided for all children who wanted them (an obligation on LEAs removed by the 1980 Education Act).
- It formulated a relationship between the county and voluntary sectors which has lasted with little change. Voluntary schools were given the choice of becoming 'aided' or 'controlled' schools and provision was made for a few 'special agreement' schools (see Chapter 6). Standards were set to which all school premises had to conform.
- It named the Minister of Education (who became the Secretary of State for Education and Science in 1964) as the arbiter in disputes between LEAs, LEAs and governors, and LEAs and the public. He or she was given considerable powers, and had to be consulted by LEAs over their general development plans and any specific proposals to establish, close or alter schools (this changed under the 1980 Act).
- It set up two Central Advisory Councils for Education (CACE), one for England and one for Wales, to advise the Minister of Education. A number of major reports were produced in this way (see Chapter 3), but no CACE has been constituted since 1967, and later government reports have been issued by committees set up to consider particular issues.
- It laid down guidelines for religious instruction. All schools (county and

voluntary) must start the day with a corporate act of worship, although parents have the right of withdrawal and LEAs may rule that it is impracticable to assemble all the pupils (e.g. in very large or split-site schools, or where pupils follow many different religions). All schools must also provide religious instruction (the only part of the curriculum prescribed by law, until the 1988 Education Reform Act), and this must be non-denominational except in voluntary schools.

- It required LEAs (in Section 34) to ascertain the needs of children in their areas for special educational treatment, and recommended that they be educated in ordinary schools wherever possible. Ten categories of handicap were established, including the new 'maladjusted'. (These were abolished by the 1981 Education Act.)
- It required every LEA to appoint a chief education officer.
- It removed restrictions on married women teachers.

1946 EDUCATION ACT

This Act specified the responsibilities of LEAs and governors for the maintenance of voluntary schools, and of LEAs in some circumstances for the enlargement of controlled schools.

1947 EDUCATION ACT (NORTHERN IRELAND)

Public elementary education in Northern Ireland was abolished by this Act. In its place a unified system of primary, secondary and further education was set up. Education was to be compulsory from five to 15 years of age. Collective worship and religious education were to be compulsory in all county schools. Each local authority was required to estimate the needs of primary, secondary and further education in its area, and to submit plans for meeting them to the ministry. Local authorities were also required to provide books and stationery; to provide facilities for recreation and physical training; and to ascertain which children in their areas required special education, and provide special schools as necessary. The authorities were enabled to grant scholarships, and to give vocational guidance. Medical inspection was made compulsory for all children. Provision was made for the setting up of voluntary schools. Rules were laid down for the management of schools, and the provision of finance by local authorities.

1948 EMPLOYMENT AND TRAINING ACT

The basis for a Youth Employment Service, which subsequently became the Careers Service, was established by this Act.

1948 EDUCATION (MISCELLANEOUS PROVISIONS) ACT

This Act enabled LEAs to recover the costs of providing primary and secondary education for pupils not belonging to their areas (repealed in the 1980 Education Act); and allowed LEAs to provide clothing grants.

1953 EDUCATION (MISCELLANEOUS PROVISIONS) ACT

This Act authorised LEAs to pay for pupils to attend independent schools, and enabled LEAs to recover the costs of providing further education for students not belonging to their areas (repealed in the 1980 Education Act).

1958 EDUCATION (AMENDMENT) ACT (NORTHERN IRELAND)

Local education authorities in Northern Ireland were required by this Act to set up management committees for further education institutions, with some degree of autonomy, instead of managing them directly.

1962 EDUCATION ACT

The 1962 Act required LEAs in England and Wales to provide grants for all first-degree courses in accordance with national rules and income scales ('mandatory awards'), and allowed them to provide grants for further and postgraduate education ('discretionary awards'). It authorised the Secretary of State to award grants for postgraduate courses and for older students. (These various powers and responsibilities were modified in the 1973 and 1975 Education Acts.) It also set school leaving dates.

1963 LONDON GOVERNMENT ACT

Implemented in 1965, this changed the administration of education in the Greater London area by creating the Inner London Education Authority (responsible for the 12 inner London boroughs and the City) and 20 outer London boroughs, each being a separate LEA. The ILEA was unique in that it dealt only with education, whereas all other local authorities had education alongside other local government responsibilities, such as housing, transport and social services. (The 1988 Education Reform Act abolished the ILEA from April 1990.)

1964 EDUCATION ACT

This Act amended the 1944 legislation which had divided schooling between primary and secondary at age 11, by allowing the break to come between the ages of 10 and 12, to cover the development of middle schools. Such schools have to be 'deemed' either primary (normally eight–12) or secondary (normally nine–13) schools for purposes of classification.

1965 REMUNERATION OF TEACHERS ACT

Committees for negotiations on teachers' pay were set up by this Act, which also laid down procedures for arbitration where agreement could not be reached. (It was repealed by the 1987 Teachers' Pay and Conditions Act.)

1965 TEACHING COUNCIL (SCOTLAND) ACT

This set up the General Teaching Council for Scotland to deal with the training, registration and professional conduct of Scottish teachers.

1965 CIRCULAR 10/65 ORGANISATION OF SECONDARY EDUCATION

This Circular declared the (Labour) government's objective of ending selection at 11 plus and eliminating separatism in secondary education. It requested LEAs to prepare and submit to the Secretary of State plans for reorganising secondary education on comprehensive lines, and offered guidance as to methods of achieving this. (This circular was withdrawn in 1970 by Circular 10/70, and effectively reinstated in 1974 by Circular 4/74 (DES)/Circular 112/74 (Welsh Office). See also the 1976 and 1979 Education Acts.)

1966 LOCAL GOVERNMENT ACT

This Act introduced the Rate Support Grant, made LEAs (rather than central government) responsible for paying for school meals and milk, and allocated funds (under Section 11) to local authorities for payment of staff employed specifically for the education and welfare of immigrants.

1967 RATE SUPPORT GRANT (POOLING ARRANGEMENTS) REGULATIONS

Under the 1966 Local Government Act, these Regulations provided for the pooling of expenses incurred by LEAs on teacher training, advanced further education, the education of pupils not belonging to the area of any authority, and the training of educational psychologists.

1967 EDUCATION ACT

Existing responsibilities of LEAs (under the direction of the Secretary of State) for controlled schools were extended to apply to middle schools.

1968 EDUCATION ACTS

Two Education Acts were passed in 1968. The first allowed LEAs to establish comprehensive schools, and to convert existing schools into middle schools. The second required the establishment of boards of governors for poly-technics and other LEA-maintained colleges, and the specification of the governors' functions *vis-à-vis* those of the LEAs and of the colleges' principals.

1968 EDUCATION AMENDMENT ACT (NORTHERN IRELAND)

The 'maintained' school in Northern Ireland was created by this Act. It is a special category of voluntary school on whose management committee the education authority is represented, and for whose buildings and equipment the education authority takes financial responsibility.

1969 CHILDREN AND YOUNG PERSONS ACT

Local authorities were given powers and responsibilities for children not receiving proper education, or in need of care and control.

1970 EDUCATION (HANDICAPPED CHILDREN) ACT

Responsibility for the education of severely subnormal children in England and Wales was transferred by this Act from the health authorities to the local education authorities; LEAs were thereafter responsible for all establishments caring for mentally handicapped children.

1970 EDUCATION (EXAMINATIONS) ACT (NORTHERN IRELAND)

This set up an Examinations Council, GCE Board and CSE Board in Northern Ireland.

1970 CIRCULAR 10/70 ORGANISATION OF SECONDARY EDUCATION

This Circular withdrew Circular 10/65, and affirmed the (Conservative) government's intention to allow individual LEAs to determine the shape of secondary education (selective or comprehensive) in their areas. (This was withdrawn, in its turn, in 1974 by Circular 4/74 (DES)/Circular 112/74 (Welsh Office). See also the 1976 and 1979 Education Acts.)

1970 CIRCULAR 18/70 (DES); 108/70 (WELSH OFFICE) PRIMARY AND SECONDARY EDUCATION IN WALES

The responsibility for primary and secondary education (and related school matters) in Wales was transferred from the Secretary of State for Education and Science to the Secretary of State for Wales. The Secretary of State for Education and Science retained responsibility for a number of educational services in Wales, but these have also been transferred subsequently, apart from those concerning the teaching profession.

1970 CHRONICALLY SICK AND DISABLED PERSONS ACT

This Act required new educational buildings to be made accessible to disabled people, unless this was incompatible with the efficient use of resources.

1971 EDUCATION (MILK) ACT

The 1944 Act was amended so that free milk was provided to pupils over the age of seven only if they attended special schools or qualified on medical grounds. (The 1980 Education Act and the 1986 Social Security Act each further restricted the supply of free milk.)

1971 EDUCATION (AMENDMENT) ACT (NORTHERN IRELAND)

This restricted the provision of free milk in Northern Ireland.

1972 LOCAL GOVERNMENT ACT

Implemented in 1974, this Act reduced the number of LEAs in England and Wales from 163 to 104, by creating some new and larger authorities. In the new system there were 39 counties, eight enlarged Welsh counties, 36 metropolitan districts and, as before, 20 outer London boroughs and the Inner London Education Authority (ILEA). It reaffirmed that LEAs must set up education committees and appoint a chief education officer, but the Secretary of State need no longer be consulted about the appointment of the latter.

1972 RAISING OF THE SCHOOL-LEAVING AGE ORDER

The school-leaving age was raised to 16 (nearly 30 years after this was recommended in the 1944 Education Act).

1973 EDUCATION ACT

Postgraduate education was excluded from eligibility for LEA discretionary grants (it had been eligible under the 1962 Education Act). The Secretary of State was authorised, in some circumstances, to award supplements to LEA mandatory grants.

1973 EDUCATION (WORK EXPERIENCE) ACT

This Act enabled LEAs to arrange for children under school-leaving age to have work experience as part of their education in the last year of compulsory schooling.

1973 EMPLOYMENT AND TRAINING ACT

This required LEAs to set up a careers service. It also set up the Manpower Services Commission (MSC) under the Department of Employment. (The MSC was disbanded as a separate organisation in 1988.)

1973 NATIONAL HEALTH SERVICE REORGANISATION ACT

The school health service was transferred from LEAs to area health authorities, but LEAs were required to provide facilities for dental and medical inspection of pupils.

1974 EDUCATION (MENTALLY HANDICAPPED CHILDREN) (SCOTLAND) ACT

Responsibility for the education of severely mentally handicapped children was transferred from the health authorities to the local education authorities under this Act. (It was similar to the 1970 Education (Handicapped Children) Act for England and Wales.)

1974 CIRCULAR 4/74 (DES)/CIRCULAR 112/74 (WELSH OFFICE) ORGANISATION OF SECONDARY EDUCATION

This Circular withdrew Circular 10/70, and reaffirmed the (Labour) government's objectives of ending selection at 11 plus and creating a unified system of secondary education. It required those LEAs who had not already done so to submit to the Secretaries of State, by the end of the year, information about their plans for making their schools comprehensive. (See also the 1976 and 1979 Education Acts.)

1975 EDUCATION ACT

The provisions of the 1962 Education Act were extended to require LEAs to award mandatory grants to students taking the DipHE, HND and initial teacher training courses, and to authorise the Secretary of State to award grants for adult education courses. (It was repealed by the 1993 Education Act.)

1975 SEX DISCRIMINATION ACT

This Act prohibited sex discrimination in admission to schools, appointment of teachers (with exceptions for single-sex schools) and careers advice, and stipulated that neither girls nor boys should be refused access to 'any courses, facilities or other benefits provided' solely on the grounds of their sex.

1975 DIRECT GRANT GRAMMAR SCHOOLS (CESSATION OF GRANT) REGULATIONS

These Regulations specified how and when direct grants were to be phased out.

1976 RACE RELATIONS ACT

This Act prohibited discrimination on the grounds of race in admission to schools, appointment of teachers, careers advice, access to facilities and the award of discretionary grants. 'Positive discrimination' in favour of disadvantaged racial groups is not normally allowed, e.g. in recruitment or promotion. In some closely defined circumstances, however, where it can be shown that a particular racial group has a special need with regard to education or training, access to facilities may be restricted or allocated first to its members.

1976 EDUCATION ACT

This attempted to abolish selection by ability for secondary schools. It laid down the general principle of comprehensive education which would have ended selection over a period (but this was repealed in the 1979 Act). Added to the main Bill were six miscellaneous sections. One limited the powers of LEAs to pay for places in independent schools, another (Section 10) encouraged the education of handicapped children in ordinary schools (but see the 1981 Education Act).

1976 EDUCATION (SCHOOL-LEAVING DATES) ACT

This Act set the date in the summer term after which children aged 16 are no longer required to attend school. (It was repealed by the 1993 Education Act.)

1979 EDUCATION ACT

This repealed the obligation placed on LEAs by the 1976 Education Act to provide plans for comprehensive reorganisation.

1980 EDUCATION ACT

The provisions of this Act were as follows:

- The obligation to provide free school milk and to provide school meals was removed, allowing LEAs to provide milk or meals or not as they wished, at whatever cost or standard they chose (including free milk or meals, if they wished, for families on low incomes), apart from a responsibility to provide free meals for children of families receiving Supplementary Benefit or Family Income Supplement, and to provide facilities free of charge for pupils to eat food brought from home. (These powers and responsibilities were altered in the 1986 Social Security Act.)
- The Assisted Places Scheme was created, whereby pupils can be transferred from maintained to particular independent schools, with the government paying part or all of the tuition fees; the Secretary of State was authorised to establish the details of the scheme by issuing regulations.

- It required all independent schools to be registered, and abolished the previous category of 'recognised as efficient'.
- Parents were given a right to choose the school they wanted their child to go to, although the LEA could refuse on the grounds of inefficient use of resources (and the parents could appeal).
- Parents were given rights to be represented on school governing bodies. LEAs and school governors were required to provide information to parents on such matters as criteria for admission, exam results, curriculum, discipline and organisation. (But see the 1986 Education Act and the 1988 Education Reform Act.)
- It affirmed that provision by LEAs, of education for under-fives was discretionary not compulsory.
- Section 13 of the 1944 Act, concerning the establishing, closing or altering of maintained schools by LEAs, was repealed. Now the Secretary of State's approval was required only if there were local objections to a proposal.
- It introduced greater control over the advanced further education pool (known as 'capping').
- The Secretary of State for Wales was authorised to give financial assistance to LEAs for the teaching of Welsh or the use of Welsh as a medium for teaching other subjects.
- It restricted the rights of LEAs to refuse to provide primary, secondary or further education for pupils or students not belonging to their areas, and their powers to recover the costs of providing it.

1980 EDUCATION (SCOTLAND) ACT

A largely consolidating Act, this incorporated measures enacted separately during the 1960s and 1970s, and reaffirmed the legal framework for education in Scotland. It covered all types of school – public (i.e. maintained), grant-aided and independent. It empowered the Secretary of State for Scotland to issue regulations governing the conduct and the responsibilities of local education authorities. In addition, it defined the responsibilities and rights of parents; established the Scottish Examination Board to conduct Scottish Certificate of Education (SCE) examinations; set up committees for negotiating teachers' pay settlements, laying down arbitration procedures where agreement could not be reached; and made provision for children with special educational needs.

1981 EDUCATION ACT

Following the recommendations of the Warnock Report (see Chapter 3, 1978 Warnock), this Act altered the law relating to the education of children with special educational needs. It replaced the previous categories of handicap with the concept of special educational needs, defined as existing where a child has significantly greater difficulty in learning than the majority of children of the same age, or has a disability that prevents or hinders him or her from using the educational facilities normally available. LEAs were given carefully defined responsibilities, to identify the needs of children with a learning difficulty which, in the view of an LEA, calls for it to determine the provision required for the child. The Act set up a detailed assessment procedure for ascertaining these needs, giving parents the right to be consulted, and to appeal against an LEA's decision about appropriate provision. It also reaffirmed, with greater emphasis than the 1944 Act, the principle that children with special educational needs should normally be educated in ordinary schools provided that their needs can be met there, that the education of the other children does not suffer, and that it is compatible with the 'efficient use of resources'. (It was almost entirely repealed by the 1993 Education Act.)

1981 EDUCATION (SCOTLAND) ACT

This gave parents in Scotland the right to choose which school their children should attend.

1984 EDUCATION (GRANTS AND AWARDS) ACT

This allowed the government to allocate sums of money to LEAs for particular educational purposes, thus reducing the local authorities' control over how the block grant was spent. This reserved money was offered in the form of education support grants (ESGs) of up to 75% of the cost of each project, in areas of education that the Secretary of State had deemed to be important.

1986 EDUCATION ACTS

Two Education Acts were passed in 1986.

The first introduced the Local Education Authorities Training Grants Scheme for in-service training of teachers (see Chapter 8).

The second Act required every maintained school to have a governing body, and set a formula for the numbers of parent, voluntary body and LEA representatives, which depended on the type and size of the school. Parent representation was strengthened. It required governors to present an annual report to parents at the school, and to arrange a meeting with them to discuss it. It gave governors the responsibility for determining sex education policy in the school, and preventing 'political indoctrination'. Governors were also to 'use their best endeavours' to ensure that children with special educational needs were identified and suitable provision made. Corporal punishment was prohibited in state schools from August 1987; independent schools may still use it, but not on pupils whose fees are paid by the state.

1986 SOCIAL SECURITY ACT

From 1988, the provisions of the 1980 Education Act concerning free school meals and milk were abolished. LEAs no longer have the power to supply free school meals or milk to any children other than those from families receiving Income Support; and they no longer have any obligation to supply free meals or milk to *any* children (even those from families receiving Income Support).

1987 TEACHERS' PAY AND CONDITIONS ACT

This Act abolished the negotiating procedures set up in the 1965 Remuneration of Teachers Act, replacing them until 1990 by authorising the Secretary of State to appoint an interim advisory committee and to impose teachers' pay and conditions. (It was repealed by the 1991 School Teachers' Pay and Conditions Act.)

1988 LOCAL GOVERNMENT ACT

This included an amendment (Section 28) forbidding local authorities to 'promote teaching in any maintained school of the acceptability of homosexuality as a pretended family relationship'. (There is still uncertainty as to whether this clause has any practical effect on schools, because of vagueness in the wording of the amendment. See Macnair, 1989.)

1988 EDUCATION REFORM ACT

The main provisions of the Act are as follows:

- It empowered the Secretary of State to prescribe a common curriculum (to be called the national curriculum) for pupils of compulsory school age in maintained schools (for details, see Chapter 10), to set attainment targets for each of its constituent subjects at the ages of seven, 11, 14, and 16, and to make arrangements for assessing how well these are met; established a National Curriculum Council (for England) and a Curriculum Council for Wales to oversee the implementation and assessment of the national curriculum; required LEAs, school governors and headteachers to ensure that the national curriculum is taught in all maintained schools. (These provisions apply to 'grant-maintained' schools (see below). They do not apply to independent schools.)

- It established mechanisms to ensure that the limits set by LEAs or governors on the number of pupils a maintained school admits are not lower than the school is physically capable of accommodating, normally the number admitted in 1979, when school rolls were at their highest. Parents may send their children to any school that has room for them, provided that it caters for their age and aptitude. (These provisions apply to 'grant-maintained' schools (see below).)
- It required LEAs to delegate certain responsibilities for financial management and the appointment and dismissal of staff to the governing bodies of schools; permitted the governing bodies to delegate many of these responsibilities to headteachers (see Chapter 8).
- It allowed a maintained secondary school, or a primary school with over 300 pupils (extended in 1990 to all primary schools), on the resolution of its governing body, with the consent of a majority of those parents who vote in a secret ballot, and with the approval of the Secretary of State, to opt out of LEA finance and control, and be given 'grant-maintained' status. (If fewer than half the parents vote, a second ballot must be held within 14 days. The results of the second ballot will be binding, regardless of how many parents vote in it.) The school will then own its own premises, employ its own staff, and receive an annual grant directly from central government. The character and size of a grant-maintained school cannot be altered, or the premises sold, without the consent of the Secretary of State.
- It empowered the Secretary of State to enter into long-term agreements to fund city technology colleges (see Chapter 5).
- It removed polytechnics and certain other colleges of higher education from LEA control, making them 'free-standing statutory corporations', under the direction of boards of governors whose members are initially appointed by the Secretary of State (see Chapter 5).
- It required LEAs to delegate certain responsibilities for financial management and the appointment and dismissal of staff to the governing bodies of the larger colleges remaining under LEA control.
- It placed the funding of higher education in the hands of two statutory bodies, a Universities Funding Council (UFC) (replacing the University Grants Committee), and a Polytechnics and Colleges Funding Council (PCFC) to administer funds for higher education provided directly by the Secretary of State. The councils had the power to attach terms and conditions to the provision of funds to any institution. Both bodies were independent of government. Their members were to be appointed by the Secretary of State, with between 40% and 60% of the membership to come from higher education.
- It forbade the granting of academic tenure (see Chapter 7) to new university academic staff; withdrew tenure from staff in posts who move to a different university or accept promotion within the same university. At

the same time it affirmed that academic staff may not be dismissed for holding particular beliefs or following particular lines of inquiry, and that senior staff may not be dismissed to be replaced by more junior, and cheaper, staff.

- It abolished the Inner London Education Authority (see Chapter 6) transferring its responsibilities from April 1990 to the inner London boroughs and the City of London.

1988 SCHOOLS BOARD (SCOTLAND) ACT

This established school boards for Scottish schools, with strong parental and community representation. The boards have extensive rights to be informed and consulted about their schools' educational, disciplinary and financial policies and achievements, and to participate in the appointment of senior staff.

1989 SELF-GOVERNING SCHOOLS ETC. (SCOTLAND) ACT

This established procedures whereby Scottish schools could 'opt out' of finance and control by education authorities, and receive funding directly from the Scottish Central Government. (By 1994, just one school had done so.)

1989 EDUCATION REFORM (NORTHERN IRELAND) ORDER

By this Order, Northern Ireland follows the main thrust of the English and Welsh reforms. There is a similar, though not identical, common curriculum and pattern of assessment, and a comparable scheme for delegation of financial management to the governing bodies of schools. 'Opting out' is also permitted, but only where a school seeks 'grant-maintained *integrated* status' and chooses to progress towards full integration of Protestant and Roman Catholic pupils.

1990 EDUCATION (STUDENT LOANS) ACT

This act empowered the respective Secretaries of State to issue regulations making arrangements for students in higher education in England, Wales and Scotland to receive, and repay, loans towards their maintenance. (For details of the arrangements currently in force, see Chapter 8 below, p. 136.)

1991 SCHOOL TEACHERS' PAY AND CONDITIONS ACT

A review body was established, its members appointed by the government, to make recommendations to the Secretary of State for Education about teachers' salaries and conditions of employment. Final decisions are then made by the Secretary of State, after consultation with LEAs, teachers' representatives and other interested parties, and set out in a School Teachers' Pay and Conditions Document. (The 1987 Teachers' Pay and Conditions Act was repealed.)

1992 TRANSFER OF FUNCTIONS (NATIONAL HERITAGE) ORDER AND TRANSFER OF FUNCTIONS (SCIENCE) ORDER

Responsibility for sport and recreation in England was transferred from the Department of Education and Science to the Department of National Heritage, and for science in England to the Cabinet Office. The Department of Education and Science was renamed the Department for Education.

1992 FURTHER AND HIGHER EDUCATION ACT

Further education colleges became corporations independent of local education authorities, funded by central government largely through two new Further Education Funding Councils (FEFC), one for England, the other for Wales. Sixth-form colleges were removed from LEAs' control, and joined the further education sector as free-standing colleges, funded through the FEFCs.

The funding of higher education (universities, polytechnics and other colleges of higher education) was unified. The Universities Funding Council and the Polytechnics and Colleges Funding Council were replaced by two unitary Higher Education Funding Councils (HEFC), one for England, the other for Wales. All institutions of higher education now have to compete for funding for both teaching and research.

(Although the funding of further education colleges is now largely through the FEFCs, and of universities through the HEFCs, it is the HEFCs that fund any higher education courses in further education colleges, and the FEFCs that fund any further education provision in universities.)

The Council for National Academic Awards, which had validated the degrees of institutions of higher education other than universities, was dissolved. Subject to the approval of the Privy Council in each case, polytechnics and other institutions of higher education may become degree-awarding bodies in their own right and, if they meet certain criteria, may take the title of university. Colleges of higher education that are not permitted to award degrees in their own right may have their degrees validated by a university. [All the polytechnics and several other institutions had adopted the title of university by the end of 1993.]

1992 FURTHER AND HIGHER EDUCATION (SCOTLAND) ACT

This act reformed further and higher education in Scotland along lines very similar to those of the 1992 Further and Higher Education Act (for England and Wales). Responsibility for providing further education was transferred from education authorities to the Secretary of State, who was required to make funds available for further education, and authorised to establish a Scottish Further Education Funding Council to assist him or her in allocating these funds. [No such Funding Council has as yet been established.] Colleges of further education are to be managed by new Boards of Management, corporate bodies independent of education authorities and subject to the direction of the Secretary of State. The funding of higher education was unified, with the establishment of a Higher Education Funding Council for Scotland, taking over the functions of the Universities Funding Council in Scotland (for universities) and the Scottish Office Education Department (for other institutions of higher education). Subject to their meeting certain criteria, all institutions of higher education could take the title of university. [Five had done so by the end of 1993, giving Scotland 12 universities in all.]

1992 EDUCATION (SCHOOLS) ACT

This Act and the Education (Schools Inspection) Regulations 1993 issued under it establish new arrangements for the inspection of schools. Inspection of schools is to be the responsibility in England of the Office for Standards in Education (OFSTED), a non-ministerial department, independent of the DFE, headed by Her Majesty's Chief Inspector of Schools; and in Wales of the Office of Her Majesty's Chief Inspector of Schools in Wales (OHMCI Wales), similarly independent of the Education Department of the Welsh Office. OFSTED and OHMCI are to identify, train and register a suitable body of *Registered Inspectors* and *Independent Inspectors*, not in the employ of OFSTED or OHMCI. Actual inspections of schools and colleges will now normally be conducted by teams of these Independent Inspectors, headed by a Registered Inspector, and including at least one *Lay Inspector* who has not been involved professionally in education. A team will be offered a contract by OFSTED or OHMCI for the inspection of a school or college, after it has invited tenders from at least two Registered Inspectors. Every maintained school (including grant-maintained schools and CTCs) and some independent schools (notably those catering for children with special educational needs) is to have a four-yearly inspection, lasting not more than two weeks, and normally not more than one. The inspectors must report on the quality of education provided, the educational standards achieved, the efficiency of financial management and the 'spiritual, moral, social and cultural development' of the pupils. Her Majesty's Inspectors of Schools (HMIs), who traditionally conducted school inspections, will now have a more organisational, administrative, training and supervisory role.

1993 EDUCATION ACT

This act contains a number of miscellaneous provisions.

New provisions are made for grant-maintained schools. They are to be financed through two new bodies, the Funding Agency for Schools (for England) and the Funding Council for Wales. Members of these bodies are to be chosen by the Secretaries of State for Education and for Wales, respectively, who are empowered to issue directives to them. In addition to being responsible for the funding of grant-maintained schools, these funding bodies may in time assume all or part of the responsibilities currently held by local education authorities for the provision of education in their areas. When the percentage of the primary or secondary pupils in an LEA's area who attend grand-maintained schools reaches 10%, the Secretary of State is empowered to transfer part of these responsibilities; when it reaches 75%, he or she is empowered to transfer all the responsibilities. The process for LEA-maintained schools to become grant-maintained by 'opting out' of LEA control is simplified. And other ways of establishing grant-maintained schools are introduced. Independent schools may 'opt in' to grant-maintained status, or entirely new schools may be set up within the grant-maintained sector, on the initiative of the Funding Agency or Council, or of local 'promoters'.

Methods are introduced of dealing with schools identified as unsatisfactory by school inspectors. In the first instance, the LEA may appoint new governors, and withdraw delegated management from such a school. If the school continues to be judged unsatisfactory, central government may put it under the management of an appointed Educational Association, centrally financed, until its performance is judged acceptable.

Pupils excluded from schools must now be excluded either permanently or for a fixed term not exceeding 15 school days in any one term; the category of indefinite exclusion is abolished. LEAs must provide education for excluded pupils in Pupil Referral Units, which must offer a broad and balanced curriculum, but need not offer the full national curriculum.

In addition, the National Curriculum Council and the School Examinations and Assessment Council are replaced by a unitary School Curriculum and Assessment Authority. Parents are permitted to remove their children from sex education lessons. The provision of religious education is extended. The Secretary of State is empowered to issue regulations and a code of practice concerning the education of children with special educational needs. Finally the allocation of school places is rationalised.

1994 EDUCATION ACT

This Act deals with two separate topics, teacher training in England and Wales, and students' unions in England, Wales and Scotland.

The Act establishes a Teacher Training Agency for England and Wales. Its membership is to be decided by the Secretary of State, who is to have regard to the desirability of including persons with successful experience of teaching, teacher training, the provision of education, and industrial, commercial or financial matters or the practice of any profession. The Agency is to provide information and advice on teaching as a career, and to act in England as the funding agency for teacher training courses and related activities which the governing bodies of eligible institutions consider necessary or desirable. (The funding agency for teacher training in Wales is to be the Higher Education Funding Council for Wales.) Institutions eligible for funding include all institutions of higher or further education, all schools, and any partnerships between eligible institutions. The objectives of the Agency include securing the involvement of schools in all courses for the initial training of teachers, and establishing 'an appropriate balance' between courses provided wholly or mainly by schools and other courses. The terms and conditions under which grants are made by the Agency must not refer to the content of particular courses of study or research programmes, or the way in which they are taught, supervised or assessed.

The Act also regulates the conduct of students' unions in England, Wales and Scotland, in establishments of higher or further education funded by the appropriate Higher or Further Education Funding Councils or the Scottish Office. The governing bodies of such establishments must ensure that students' unions operate in a fair and democratic manner, and are accountable for their finances. Any student must have the right not to be a member of a union or to be represented by it, without thereby being unfairly disadvantaged in any way, including the provision of services. Appointment to major union offices must be by election in a secret ballot in which all members are entitled to vote. No person should hold sabbatical office or paid elected office in any union for more than two years. Allocation of resources by the union to groups or clubs must be fair and open. Affiliation of the union to any external organisation must be open, and subject to at least annual review by the members.

SOURCES AND FURTHER READING

The standard, regularly updated, reference work on educational law in England and Wales is Liell and Saunders (1989); it has a special supplement on the 1988 Education Reform Act. It is detailed and rigorous, but consequently difficult for those untrained in law to tackle. Much more approachable for the lay reader is the journal *Education and the Law*, a useful source of information about new legislation, regulations, orders, DES circulars and court cases.

A number of books and booklets offer detailed summaries of the 1988 Education Reform Act as it finally passed into law. Maclure (1989) is especially valuable, though no longer up to date about developments after the Act itself.

Advisory Centre for Education (1988) Guide to education welfare benefits, *ACE Bulletin*, No. 22, March/April.

CIPFA (no single date) *Financial Information Services*, Vol. 20, *Education*, London: Chartered Institute of Public Finance and Accountancy.

Hyndman, M. (1978) *Schools and Schooling in England and Wales: A Documentary History*, London: Harper & Row.

Liell, P. and Saunders, J. B. (1989) *The Law of Education*, 9th ed., London: Butterworth.

Maclure, S. (ed.) (1986) *Educational Documents, England and Wales, 1816 to the Present Day*, 5th ed., London: Methuen.

Maclure, S. (1989) *Education Re-Formed: A Guide to the Education Reform Act*, 2nd ed., London: Hodder & Stoughton.

Macnair, M. R. T. (1989) Homosexuality in schools – Section 28, Local Government Act 1988, *Education and the Law*, Vol. 1, No. 1, pp. 35–9.

Sallis, J. (1981) *ACE Guide to Education Law*, London: Advisory Centre for Education.

This chapter describes, with some basic facts and figures, the range of institutions that make up the United Kingdom's education system.

> **F A C T** The United Kingdom has over 34,000 schools in total (30,000 in the maintained sector), with half a million teachers and over nine million pupils (1991–2 figures: GSS, 1994, page 2).

(A) PRESCHOOL

Preschool provision by an LEA may take the form of:

- *Nursery schools* – Separate schools for 2–5-year-olds, each with its own headteacher and a number of classes staffed by teachers and nursery assistants who have trained under the National Nursery Examination Board (NNEB). The recommended child/adult ratio is 13 to 1 (or 22 to 1 if qualified teachers only are counted).
- *Nursery classes within primary schools* – Separate classes for 3–5-year-olds which are an integral part of a primary school, with staffing as for nursery schools.
- *Reception classes* – Children who are just under compulsory school age can gain early admission to the first (reception) class in an infant or first school.

There is no obligation on LEAs to provide preschool education (except for children identified as having special educational needs) and provision varies greatly, both in amount and in type. In Wales, 69% of 3- and 4-year-old children go to maintained nursery or primary schools, full- or part-time, compared with 54% in Northern Ireland, 53% in England and 42% in Scotland. In Northern Ireland, 87% of the 3- and 4-year-olds in preschool education attend full-time, compared with 60% in Wales, 50% in England, and 25% in Scotland (GSS, 1994, Tables 1 and 16). Considerable variation in amount and type of provision is also found between regions, and between individual LEAs. (This is illustrated for England in Figures 5.3 and 5.4.)

Preschool children may also attend *day nurseries*, which are provided by local authority Social Services Departments, and regulated by the Department of Social Security. Private provision, including *playgroups* and *childminders*, has to be registered with local authority Social Services Departments. In 1991–2, in the United Kingdom, some 30,000 children attended local authority day nurseries, 105,000 attended other registered day nurseries, 297,000 went to registered childminders and another 496,000 went to registered playgroups

(CSO, 1994, Table 3.2). Figure 5.1 shows how these forms of provision have changed over time.

There are also *independent schools* that cater for preschool children. There are two main types: those that are basically preparatory schools – preparing very young children for entry to a highly academic independent school later on – and those that are a fee-paying alternative to maintained nursery schools, either because preschool places are in short supply or because the school adopts a particular educational philosophy, such as the Montessori method. Since 1979, they too have been required to register with local authority Social Services Departments, and are not counted in the official education statistics.

Some common patterns of early childhood experience are shown in Figure 5.5.

F A C T   In the United Kingdom in 1991–2, there were 1,380 publicly maintained nursery schools catering for some 85,000 children, 81% of them on a part-time basis. But the majority of under-fives received their education in primary schools, in either nursery or reception classes – 677,000 children, 47% of them part-time. Another 49,000 under-fives went to private school, 41% of them part-time. Altogether just over half (53%) of the 3- and 4-year-old population received some education at school, mostly on a part-time basis (GSS, 1994, Tables 1 and 16).

(B) PRIMARY

The legal definition of primary education covers children aged 5–11 years in England, Wales and Northern Ireland, and 5–12 years in Scotland. Primary schools consist mainly of:

- *Infant schools* – for children aged 5–7 years.
- *Junior schools* – for those aged 7–11 years.
- *Combined junior and infant schools* – these are the most common and cater for children of both age groups.

An alternative system, introduced in some areas in the late 1960s, is the three-tier system, of *lower* (or *first*), *middle* and *upper schools*, based on the idea that the age of 8, 9 or even 10 was a more appropriate time for children to make the transition between the informal teaching of the early years and the more formal subject teaching offered later.

Middle schools developed in a variety of patterns; some catered for 8–12-year-olds (deemed primary), others for 9–13-year-olds (deemed primary or

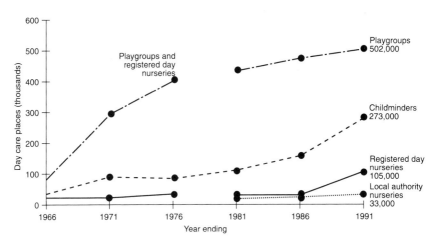

Figure 5.1   Number of preschool places in establishments registered with Social Services
Departments (i.e. forms of preschool provision that are not part of the education system),
United Kingdom 1966–92
(Adapted from CSO, 1987, Table 3.1; 1989b, Table 3.8; 1994, Table 3.2)
Note: Local authority nurseries include local authority playgroups up to 1976

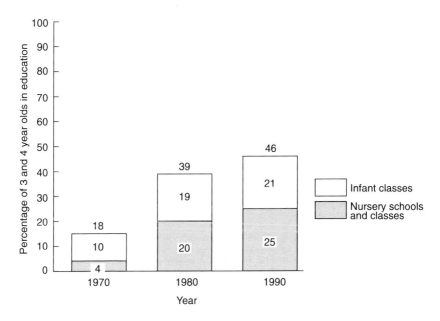

Figure 5.2   Percentage of 3- and 4-year-olds in full- or part-time maintained education,
England 1970–90
(Adapted from DES, 1981, Table A and DFE, 1993, Table 1)

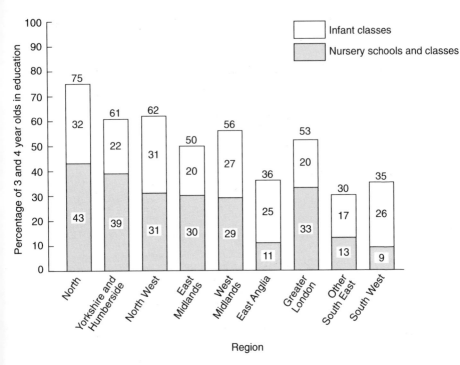

*Figure 5.3   Percentage of 3- and 4-year-olds in full- or part-time maintained education,
England 1992: regional variations
(Adapted from DFE, 1993, Table 2)*

secondary at the discretion of the LEA) and yet others for 10–14-year-olds
(deemed secondary). Middle schools are confined almost entirely to England;
Wales has just one, and Scotland, which never had more than two, now has
none.

F A C T   In the United Kingdom in 1991–2, there were nearly 24,000
maintained primary schools, including 547 middle schools deemed
primary. Virtually all were mixed-sex schools. Between them they
taught 4.7 million children and employed 223,000 teachers (82%
female). (GSS, 1994, Tables 11 and 15.)

Size of schools

Just over a quarter of all primary schools have between 100 and 200 pupils, and
over a third have more than 200. Very small schools (50 children or fewer)
accounted, in 1991–2, for around 8% of primary schools in the United

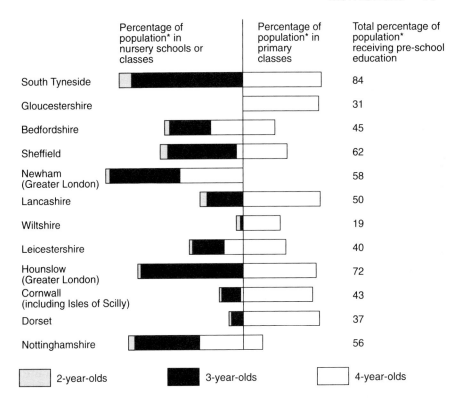

Figure 5.4   Percentage of 2-, 3- and 4-year-olds in education, England 1992: variations among selected LEAs (*Expressed as a percentage of the estimated total population of 3- and 4-year-olds)
(Adapted from DFE, 1993, Table 3)
Note: Any category with a percentage figure of less than 1 is omitted from the diagram

	0 year	1 year	2 years	3 years	4 years	5 years	6 years
Child 1	Childminder or day nursery			Nursery class		Primary class	
Child 2	Home			Nursery school		Primary class	
Child 3	Home			Nursery class		Primary class	
Child 4	Home				Playgroup	Primary class	
Child 5	Home						Primary class
Child 6	Combined nursery centre					Primary class	
Child 7	Home				Private nursery	Preparatory school class	

Figure 5.5   Some common patterns of early childhood experience

Kingdom, but the proportion varied greatly between countries and regions. For example, 14% of the primary schools in Wales and in Northern Ireland, and 19% in Scotland, had 50 pupils or fewer, compared with 6% in England as a whole, 3% in the South East region and none in Greater London (CSO, 1993, Table 5.3).

School closures and falling rolls

Between 1980 and 1992, more than 2,800 maintained primary schools closed in the United Kingdom (see Figure 5.6).

These closures have to be seen in the context of changes in the number of children at primary school; this is illustrated in Figure 5.7, using data for England.

Pupil/teacher ratios in primary schools fell during the 1970s and 1980s (especially the 1970s). This is illustrated in Figure 5.8.

The pupil/teacher ratio in maintained primary schools varies from country to country. Compared with the United Kingdom average of 21.8 to 1, it is rather higher in Northern Ireland (22.6 to 1), Wales (22.3 to 1) and England (22.0 to 1) and lower in Scotland (19.5 to 1) (GSS, 1994, Table 14: 1991–2 figures. See also Chapter 8 below, Part 2, pp. 144–5).

(C) SECONDARY

Secondary education is compulsory up to the age of 16, and pupils can stay on at school for up to three years longer.

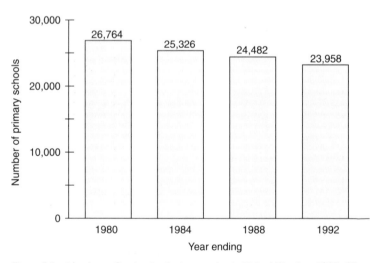

Figure 5.6   Numbers of maintained primary schools, United Kingdom 1980–92 (Adapted from GSS, 1983, 1985, 1989 and 1994, Table 2)

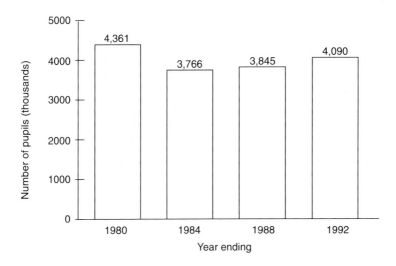

Figure 5.7   Primary school rolls, England 1980–92 (maintained schools, full- and part-
time pupils)
(Adapted from DES, 1989c, Table 1; GSS, 1994, Table 15)

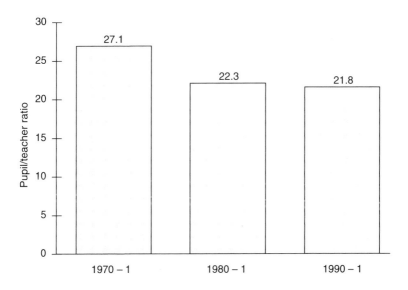

Figure 5.8   Pupil/teacher ratios in maintained primary schools in the UK, 1970–1 to
1990–1
(Adapted from GSS, 1994, Table 14)

F A C T   In the United Kingdom in 1991–2, there were nearly 4,700 maintained secondary schools (including 489 middle schools deemed secondary, virtually all in England). Between them they taught 3.5 million children and employed 233,000 teachers (52% male) (GSS, 1994, Tables 11 and 15; DFE, 1993, Table A1).

The following list of types of secondary schools includes some that no longer exist and others that now exist only in very small numbers, often in just a few LEAs.

Tripartite system

Grammar, secondary modern and technical schools in England and Wales (and, with different terminology, in Scotland and Northern Ireland – see below) form what is called the tripartite system, though in reality, technical schools have never existed in large numbers. The tripartite system now forms a very small and highly localised part of secondary schooling in Great Britain, where maintained secondary education is now almost entirely comprehensive (see Figure 5.9). The principal characteristics of tripartite schools are as follows:

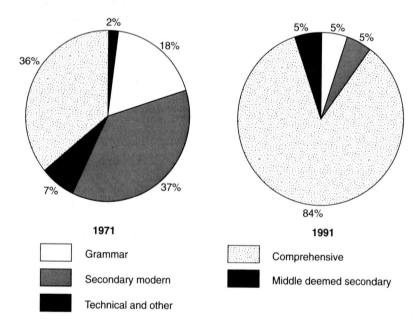

1971   1991

☐ Grammar   ▨ Comprehensive

▨ Secondary modern   ■ Middle deemed secondary

■ Technical and other

Figure 5.9   Percentages of pupils in different kinds of maintained secondary school, United Kingdom 1971 and 1991
(Adapted from GSS, 1989 and 1994, Table 18)

- *Grammar schools* provide a mainly academic education for pupils aged 11 to 19 who have been selected on the basis of ability.
- *Secondary modern schools* provide a general education for those who do not go to grammar schools, usually up to the minimum school-leaving age (though pupils can stay on longer).
- *Technical schools* provide a general education but with considerable emphasis on technical subjects. These never existed in large numbers and are now almost extinct: by 1992, only four remained in England and none in Scotland, Wales or Northern Ireland (GSS, 1994, Table 18).

In Scotland, the closest equivalent to English and Welsh grammar schools were called *senior secondary schools*, while the equivalents of secondary moderns were *junior secondary schools*. (However, the phrase 'grammar school' does sometimes appear in the names of particular schools in Scotland.)

In Northern Ireland, a selective system still predominates, though with a few comprehensive schools in certain areas. The closest equivalents to English and Welsh grammar schools are called *grammar secondary schools*; they can, however, accept some fee-paying pupils. (The schools called 'grammar preparatory schools' are fee-paying primary schools attached to voluntary grammar secondary schools (see Chapter 6); very few grammar preparatory schools remain.) Corresponding to secondary moderns are *secondary intermediate schools*. Until the mid-1970s, Northern Ireland also had *technical intermediate schools*, corresponding to the English technical schools, but none exist now. About 39% of secondary pupils in Northern Ireland attended grammar secondary schools in 1991–2, the remainder attending secondary intermediate schools. This represents a dramatic increase in grammar school attendance in recent years: in 1985–6, the figure was only 12%.

Direct-grant schools

Phased out by 1985, these used to bridge the gap between the maintained and independent sectors, being grammar schools which took fee-paying pupils but also provided free places for able children from poorer homes who were financed by a direct grant from the government. They were given the choice of becoming part of the maintained system or becoming independent; most chose the latter.

Grant-aided schools

In Scotland, these were schools that received part of their maintenance expenditure from the government and part from fees. They were phased out by 1985. In Northern Ireland, 'grant-aided' is the term equivalent to 'maintained' in Britain.

Comprehensive schools

Comprehensive schools take all pupils (except those attending special schools) regardless of ability. There is a great variety of schemes and great variation in the degree to which schools are fully comprehensive: if some schools in an area take the children who are thought to have greater academic ability, the remaining schools, even if called comprehensive, cannot be considered fully so. In 1992, there were 2,872 comprehensive schools in England.

Secondary schools with sixth form

These cater for the full age range from 11 (or following middle schools from 12, 13 or 14) to 18 or 19 years. In 1992 there were 1,962 comprehensive schools with sixth forms in England (including 1,585 comprehensive schools – 55% of all comprehensive schools).

Secondary schools without sixth form

These cater only for children up to the age of 16. Those pupils wishing to continue their education have either to transfer to a school which does have a sixth form, or to move outside the secondary school system into a sixth form, tertiary or further education college (see below).

Sixth form colleges

Sixth form colleges were moved in 1992 from the schools sector to the further education sector (see below).

Community schools

These are maintained schools which provide education for school pupils and mature students alongside social, recreational and cultural activities for the whole community.

City technology colleges

These new, relatively small colleges are set up by private sponsors, with government grants to provide a free education with a technological emphasis for 11–18-year-olds. The school day and terms are longer than the legal requirement for state schools. City technology colleges (CTCs) are independent of LEAs: the DFE pays running costs but promoters own or lease the premises and are responsible for their management, employing teachers, etc. By 1994, 15 CTCs had opened.

> **F A C T** Comprehensive schools are now (1991–2 figures) by far the most common form of secondary education for pupils in England (85%), Wales (99%) and Scotland (100%). But Northern Ireland retains a largely selective system, with 61% of its secondary pupils in secondary intermediate schools, and 39% in grammar secondary schools (GSS, 1994, Table 18).

Figure 5.9 shows, for the whole of the United Kingdom, how the pattern of maintained secondary school provision changed between 1971 and 1991, with a decrease in the number of grammar, secondary modern and technical schools (or their equivalents), and a corresponding increase in comprehensive schools.

Size of schools

Secondary schools are generally much larger than primary schools; in 1991–2 only 7% had fewer than 300 pupils on the roll and the most common size was between 400 and 1,000 pupils (65% of schools) (GSS, 1994, Table 15).

School closures and falling rolls

In the United Kingdom, between 1980 and 1992, 775 maintained secondary schools closed (see Figure 5.10).

These closures have to be seen in the context of changes in the number of children in secondary schools; this is illustrated in Figure 5.11, using data for England. The numbers declined throughout the 1980s, but in the 1990s, they have begun to increase again. Pupil/teacher ratios also fell during the 1970s and 1980s (see Figure 5.12 and Chapter 8, pp. 144–5). The pupil/teacher ratio in United Kingdom maintained secondary schools was 15.2 to 1 in 1991–2, and England, Wales and Northern Ireland were close to this figure. However, the ratio is distinctly lower in Scotland – 12.4 to 1 (GSS, 1994, Table 14).

(D) SPECIAL

Special schools provide education for children with special needs, on the grounds that they cannot be educated satisfactorily in an ordinary school. They are generally much smaller than mainstream schools: 83% of special schools in the United Kingdom have 100 pupils or fewer; 99% have 200 or fewer. Special schools often take the full age range, including nursery and post-16. They have a lower pupil/teacher ratio than any other type of school: 5.7 to 1 in the United Kingdom (1991–2 figures; GSS, 1994, Tables 14 and 15).

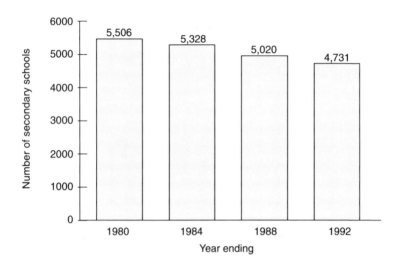

Figure 5.10   Numbers of maintained secondary schools, United Kingdom 1980–92
(Adapted from GSS, 1983, 1985, 1989 and 1994, Table 2)

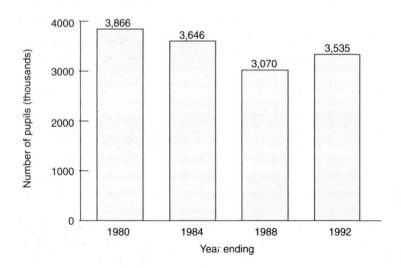

Figure 5.11   Maintained secondary school rolls, England 1980–92
(Adapted from DES, 1989, Table 1 and GSS, 1994, Table 15)

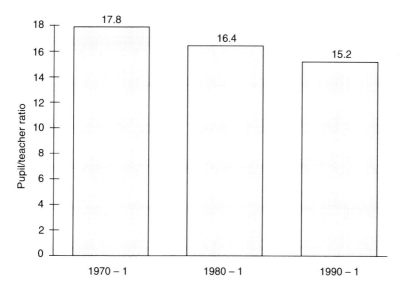

Figure 5.12   Pupil/teacher ratios in maintained secondary schools in the UK, 1970–1 to 1980–1
(Adapted from GSS, 1994, Table 14)

F A C T   In 1991–2 there were 1,792 special schools in the United Kingdom, including 43 hospital schools and 84 assisted independent schools, attended by 110,000 pupils. About 86% of them were day schools and the remainder boarding (GSS, 1994, Table 17).

Special classes and units may also be provided in mainstream schools (especially primary) for children with particular needs, e.g. the partially hearing or partially sighted, 'disruptive' children or slow learners. In England in 1986, the numbers of such units officially recognised by the DES were 1247 in primary schools and 660 in secondary schools. In addition, there are many other units not officially recognised – 'disruptive units', 'remedial classes', 'sanctuaries', etc.

The percentages of children with different types of handicap in special schools are shown in Figure 5.13 for England in 1982 – the last year for which such data were collected. Since the 1981 Education Act (see Chapter 4) came into force in 1983, children assessed as having special educational needs are given an individual 'statement' of these needs instead of being assigned to a category of handicap (see Chapter 3, 1978 Warnock). In 1992, 165,000

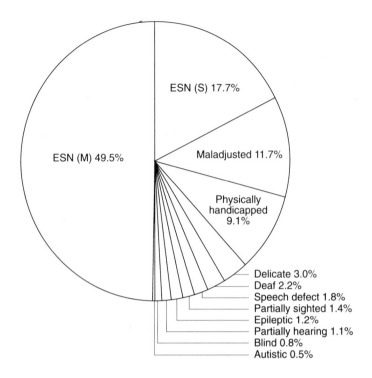

ESN (S) 17.7%

ESN (M) 49.5%

Maladjusted 11.7%

Physically
handicapped
9.1%

Delicate 3.0%
Deaf 2.2%
Speech defect 1.8%
Partially sighted 1.4%
Epileptic 1.2%
Partially hearing 1.1%
Blind 0.8%
Autistic 0.5%

Figure 5.13   Pupils, aged 5–15, attending special schools, England 1982, by pre-
Warnock categories of handicap
(Adapted from DES, 1986a)

children in England had statements of special educational needs – 1.8% of the
total school population. As Figure 5.14 shows, the great majority (70%) of
children with statements are educated in special schools, and a further 9% are
in officially recognised special classes and units in mainstream schools. About
21% are educated in ordinary classes in mainstream schools.

Since the 1981 Act, the percentage of the United Kingdom total school
population educated in special schools has fallen slightly, from just under 1.4%
in 1980–1 to just over 1.2% in 1991–2 (GSS, 1989, Table 14; GSS, 1994, Table
17).

(See Chapter 11 for more facts and figures on special education in relation
to sex and ethnic group.)

(E) INDEPENDENT

Independent schools are those outside the maintained education system. They
are not funded by the government or local authorities, and most charge fees

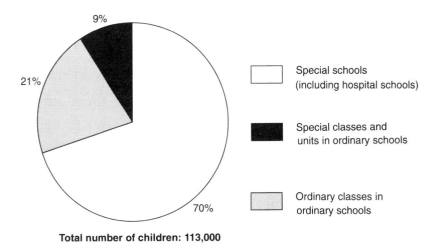

9%

21%

70%

Special schools
(including hospital schools)

Special classes and
units in ordinary schools

Ordinary classes in
ordinary schools

Total number of children: 113,000

Figure 5.14   Educational provision in maintained schools for children with statements of special educational need, England 1992
(Adapted from DFE, 1993, Tables A10 and A25)
Note: These figures are approximate, since they cover both full-time and part-time pupils, and some pupils attend more than one type of school.

(see Chapter 11); a few are wholly charitable institutions. All independent schools have to register with their LEAs (or with the local authority Social Services Department in the case of independent nursery schools) and they can be inspected by OFSTED.

Many independent schools provide a highly academic mainstream education for pupils selected on the basis of ability (usually through an entrance examination), but some are based on alternative philosophies of education, and others offer specialised provision: for example, for the musically gifted, for children with special needs, for children of foreign nationals, or for religious minorities. Independent schools generally have a relatively low pupil/teacher ratio – 10.6 to 1 in 1991–2, compared with 17.1 to 1 in all schools (combined figures for primary and secondary schools) (GSS, 1994, Table 14). About a quarter of pupils at independent schools are boarders, a much higher proportion than in maintained schools. Boarding is still common in the well-known public schools, but is declining very rapidly. Public schools normally take children from the age of 13 (usually the boys' boarding schools) or from the age of 11.

Independent schools are also referred to as public schools, private schools, preparatory schools and non-maintained schools. The terms are used loosely and sometimes interchangeably, but the most common meanings appear to be as follows.

Public schools

Especially in England, this term traditionally refers to independent fee-charging, but non-profit-making, secondary schools belonging to various highly prestigious associations. However, many of these now prefer the term 'independent schools', as in the title of the Independent Schools Information Service (ISIS). Associations about which ISIS collects and distributes information include the following. (The figures are for 1994.)

- *Headmasters' Conference (HMC)* – The most prestigious of associations of independent schools including around two hundred and forty schools, with some 159,000 pupils in total, 80% of whom are boys (many of the HMC schools admit girls only in the sixth form). Twenty-six per cent of HMC school pupils are full or weekly boarders. Within the HMC, there are smaller and more informal groups of schools, whose headmasters and senior masters meet several times a year to discuss matters of common interest. Two groups with particularly high prestige are the *Eton Group* (12 schools including, as well as Eton College, Dulwich College, Marlborough College, St Paul's and Westminster) and the *Rugby Group* (17 schools, including, as well as Rugby, Charterhouse, Harrow, Shrewsbury, Stowe and Winchester College). Between them, the schools in the Eton and Rugby Groups have about 20,000 pupils, fewer than 1% of the population in their age group (Walford, 1986, Table 1.1).
- *Society of Headmasters of Independent Schools (SHMIS)* and *Governing Bodies Association (GBA)* – The SHMIS and GBA schools are also predominantly for boys (71% of their 23,000 pupils). Thirty per cent are full or weekly boarders.
- *Girls' Schools Association (GSA)* and *Governing Bodies of Girls' Schools Association (GBGSA)* – The GSA and GBGSA schools are almost exclusively for girls (99% of their 114,000 pupils); 15% are full or weekly boarders.
- *Independent Schools Association Incorporated (ISAI)* – The ISAI schools have some 57,000 pupils, with roughly equal numbers of boys and girls; 7% of these are full or weekly boarders.

Overall, just under 50% of pupils in these schools are boys, just over 50% girls (ISIS, 1994).

In Scotland (as in most of the rest of the world), the term 'public schools' usually refers to maintained schools. The term is not used in Northern Ireland, although a few of the voluntary schools (see Chapter 6) belong to the Headmasters' Conference.

Non-maintained schools

This is a term used in the official government statistics for the United Kingdom for independent schools in Great Britain. It used to cover voluntary grammar schools in Northern Ireland too, but they are now classified in UK statistics as maintained schools.

Private schools

'Private schools' has a narrow sense, now slightly archaic, in which it refers to schools run for profit by teacher–entrepreneurs (a minority, especially at secondary level); in this sense, the term 'private schools' is *opposed* to 'public schools', which are not profit-making. However, the phrase 'private school' is nowadays more often applied (as in almost every other country) to independent schools generally; in this sense, it *includes* public schools.

Preparatory schools

These schools take boys from about eight and girls from about 11, until 13 and prepare them for competitive entry to the public schools. Many belong to the Incorporated Association of Preparatory Schools (IAPS), which has approximately 109,000 pupils, of whom 68% are boys. Twenty per cent of pupils in IAPS schools are full or weekly boarders (ISIS, 1994).

> **FACT** In 1991–2 there were 2489 non-maintained schools in the United Kingdom, excluding the non-maintained special schools, but including 13 City Technology Colleges. They provided education for some 594,500 children, 6.6% of the total school population (7.4% in England, 4.2% in Scotland, 2.5% in Wales, and 0.3% in Northern Ireland) (GSS, 1994, Table 15).

Children may move between the independent and maintained sectors at different stages of their school career; many different patterns of schooling are possible: some of these are illustrated in Figure 5.15.

(F) TERTIARY

The term 'tertiary education' is used for non-compulsory, post-school education, and covers both *further education* and *higher education*. Nowadays, 'further education' usually refers to courses of A-level standard or below, and 'higher education' to courses above A-level standard or its equivalent; this usage will be followed here. (In the past, courses above A-level standard but below degree level, and even degree courses at institutions other than

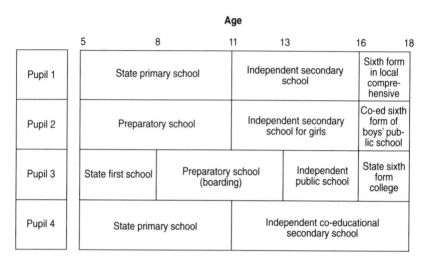

Figure 5.15   Some patterns of schooling

universities, were sometimes classified as 'advanced further education', or 'AFE,' other courses being 'non-advanced further education', 'NAFE'.)

Both the further and the higher education sectors have undergone substantial change in recent years, as a result of (in England and Wales) the 1988 Education Reform Act and the 1992 Further and Higher Education Act (which has a Scottish counterpart) (see Chapter 4). Further education in Northern Ireland is also currently under review.

FURTHER EDUCATION

Until the 1992 Acts, further education in Britain was financed and controlled by local education authorities (LEAs in England and Wales, EAs in Scotland). Thereafter, further education colleges became corporate bodies independent of local authorities, and financed by the central government. In England and Wales, this funding is indirect, provided on the advice of the Further Education Funding Council (FEFC) and the Further Education Funding Council for Wales. But in Scotland, further education is under the direct control of the Secretary of State, who allocates funds and may issue directives to colleges. (The 1992 Further and Higher Education (Scotland) Act authorises the Secretary of State to establish a Scottish Further Education Funding Council to assist him or her in disbursing funds, but none has as yet been established.) In Northern Ireland, following the recommendations of a Further Education Review Group, the existing 12 further education colleges are to be reduced by mergers to five.

> **F A C T**   In the United Kingdom in 1991–2, there were over 542,000 full-
> time students (including 'sandwich' students) and 3 million part-
> time students in further education. Almost three-quarters of the full-
> time students (73%) were aged 16–18. They represented 18% of
> the population aged 16–18. Two-thirds of the part-time students
> were over 25 (GSS, 1994, Table 22).

Sixth form colleges

These were transferred from the schools sector (and LEA control) to the
further education sector by the 1992 Further and Higher Education Act. They
are separate establishments for 16–19-year-olds, usually taking students from
several 'feeder' comprehensive schools without sixth forms in their area, and
catering for about 500 students. They may provide non-academic as well as
academic courses, but academic courses predominate. In 1973, there were 21
sixth form colleges in England; by 1992 there were 115, with almost 87,000
students in all. Their increase has been partly in response to declining numbers
of secondary school pupils, which makes it difficult for many smaller schools to
make up viable sixth form classes in less popular A-level subjects.

Tertiary colleges

Tertiary colleges combine the functions of a sixth form college and a further
education college. They are open to students of all abilities, and provide a wide
range of vocational and academic courses. Some cater for several thousand
students, full- and part-time. There were 51 tertiary colleges in England in
1994, and seven in Wales (Evans, M. et al. (ed.), 1994).

Colleges of further education

There are almost 600 colleges of further education in the United Kingdom.
They go by a variety of titles, including colleges of further education, colleges
of agriculture and horticulture, technical colleges, colleges of art and colleges
of commerce. They also offer a wide variety of types and levels of courses.

Independent further education colleges

A number of FE colleges outside the publicly maintained system offer full-time
and part-time courses in subjects such as art and architecture, drama, languages, and English for foreign students. Their qualifications are validated
either by the British Accreditation Council for Independent Further and

Higher Education (BACIFHE) or by one of the independent professional bodies such as the National Council for Drama Training or the Council for Dance Education, or are the college's own non-validated certificates or diplomas. Tutorial colleges, sometimes known as 'crammers', are privately run establishments offering intensive courses to prepare students for particular examinations, usually GCSE or A levels.

HIGHER EDUCATION

From the mid-1960s until the early 1990s, higher education was a 'binary system' with universities divided from polytechnics and other colleges of higher education. The universities were financed by central government, but this was done indirectly, on the advice of the University Grants Committee, leaving the universities a considerable degree of autonomy. (Exceptions were the Open University, which was funded directly by the Department of Education and Science, and the independent University of Buckingham, which did not receive government funding.) The polytechnics and other colleges were financed and controlled by local education authorities in England and Wales, and directly by the central government in Scotland. The universities awarded their own degrees; the polytechnics and other colleges had to have their degrees validated by the Council for National Academic Awards (CNAA), or by a university.

During the 1980s, the numbers of students in all types of higher education increased, but faster and more steadily in polytechnics and colleges of higher education than in universities. In 1979, the universities had 57% of all full-time students in higher education. By 1987, the two sectors had roughly equal numbers, and by 1991, the polytechnics and colleges, with 55% of all full-time students, had overtaken universities as the main providers of higher education (DES, 1989, Table 1; GSS, 1994, Table 22).

The binary division was blurred in England and Wales by the 1988 Education Reform Act, which removed polytechnics and the larger colleges of higher education from LEA control, making them 'free-standing statutory corporations'. But the funding of the two sectors was still kept separate, with resources allocated separately to a Universities Funding Council (UFC) and a Polytechnics and Colleges Funding Council (PCFC). The degrees of institutions other than universities still required outside validation. The one polytechnic in Northern Ireland had already merged with one of its two universities in 1985.

The binary division was formally dissolved by the 1992 Further and Higher Education Act and its Scottish counterpart. The UFC and PCFC were replaced by three unitary Higher Education Funding Councils (HEFC), one each for England, Wales and Scotland. All institutions of higher education in each country (including the Open University) now have to compete for the same pool of funds. The CNAA was abolished; subject to the approval of the Privy Council in each case, polytechnics and colleges of higher education became degree-awarding bodies in their own right. If they met certain criteria, they could also take the title of university; all 34 polytechnics in England and Wales (and two colleges of higher education) had done so by the end of 1993. Only one former polytechnic retained the word 'polytechnic' in its new title (Anglia Polytechnic University). Some smaller colleges of higher education still have to have their degrees externally validated. This is now usually done by a university, in many cases by the Open University, which has assumed some of the residual functions of the CNAA. In Northern Ireland, the two universities are to be funded by the Department of Education Northern Ireland with advice from the Northern Ireland Higher Education Funding Council (NIHEFC). It is planned that the NIHEFC will follow the methodologies of the other HEFCs, especially that for England.

As this book goes to press (mid-1994), however, the latest available government statistics on higher education still follow the binary division, with polytechnics lumped together with other colleges funded by the PCFC, and the pre-1992 universities appearing in separate tables and even separate publications. This is reflected in Figures 5.16 and 5.17 below.

Colleges and institutes of higher education

These resulted, in the 1970s, from the integration in England and Wales of teacher training outside universities with the rest of higher education. Many of the original colleges of education merged with other establishments such as technical and art colleges to form colleges and institutes of higher education (around 55 in England and five in Wales in 1994). (Scotland still had four colleges of education in 1994, and Northern Ireland two.) As well as teaching qualifications, colleges of higher education generally provide other degree and diploma courses, and so are similar to universities, although usually much smaller in size. Until 1992, their degrees had to be validated by the CNAA (or by a university). After 1992, many of the larger colleges were empowered to award their own degrees (and a much smaller number permitted to adopt the title of 'university'). The rest must have their degrees validated by a university – often the Open University.

Polytechnics

Polytechnics came into existence after 1966, and ceased to exist as a separate category after 1992. Almost all were in England, which ultimately had 33; Wales and Northern Ireland had one each, though the latter merged in 1985 with the New University of Ulster to form the University of Ulster. (For Scotland, see *Central Institutions*.) Often resulting from the merger of two or more existing colleges, polytechnics in England and Wales were under the control of local authorities until the 1988 Education Reform Act, which made them 'free-standing statutory corporations', funded by central government through the Polytechnics and Colleges Funding Council (PCFC), and under the direction of boards of governors. Half of the membership of these boards consisted of people experienced in industry, business, commerce and the professions; the other half was made up of representatives of staff, students and LEAs, plus co-opted members. Polytechnics offered degree courses, including higher degrees, plus other types of higher education, such as BTEC Higher National Certificates and Diplomas. Courses at polytechnics were often multi-disciplinary in content and modular in structure, with a technical or vocational emphasis. Polytechnics frequently had close links with business and industry, and their students, unlike those at the older universities, frequently had jobs and studied on a part-time or sandwich basis. Polytechnics also offered some further education courses, but the majority of these were taught at colleges of further education and other colleges of higher education. Until the Further and Higher Education Act of 1992, degree courses at polytechnics had to be validated by the CNAA, but thereafter the CNAA was dissolved and poly-technics were empowered to award their own degrees. This Act also replaced the PCFC (and the Universities Funding Council) with unitary Higher Educa-tion Funding Councils, and permitted polytechnics to adopt the title of 'university'. By 1993, all had done so.

> **F A C T**   In 1991–2 (i.e. just before the reorganisation of higher education), polytechnics and other PCFC- or LEA-funded colleges had 589,000 students on degree courses – 92% undergraduate, 8% postgradu-ate. Just under 60% were full-time (or sandwich) students. These figures represented a rise since 1988–9 of 43% for full-time and 15% for part-time students (DFE and OFSTED, 1994, Annex: Tables E and G).

For basic statistics of student numbers, see Figures 5.16 and 5.17 below.

Central Institutions

Until 1992, Scotland had 16 Central Institutions, which are similar in function to polytechnics in England and Wales, though they have always been controlled centrally by the Scottish Education Department rather than by local education authorities. Now there are only nine, the rest having become universities.

Universities

Until the 1992 Further and Higher Education Act and its Scottish counterpart, there were about 50 universities in the United Kingdom (the exact figure depending on whether a number of establishments are counted as colleges of the Universities of London, Wales and Manchester, or as universities in their own right). Now there are over 80, as all the polytechnics and several colleges of higher education have been granted university status. The number may continue to rise as more colleges may become universities. They are often classified, very roughly, along lines such as the following (see Bligh, 1990, though obviously he wrote before the 1992 Acts).

- *Ancient universities* – There are six of these, all more than 500 years old. Two are English (Oxford and Cambridge) and four Scottish (St Andrew's, Glasgow, Aberdeen and Edinburgh).
- *'Redbrick' or older civic universities* – These were founded in the later 19th century, usually in industrial cities (e.g. Leeds, Manchester).
- *Newer civic universities* – These were created after the Second World War by raising an existing college, often one that had prepared students for external degrees of the University of London, to university status (e.g. Newcastle, Leicester).
- *New universities* – Again after the Second World War, some entirely new institutions were created (e.g. Kent, Stirling).
- *The former Colleges of Advanced Technology (CATs)* – These were an entire category of institution, given university status after 1964 (e.g. Aston, Strathclyde).
- *The former Polytechnics (and some former Colleges of Higher Education)* – These became universities after 1992.

Traditionally, undergraduate courses at university have occupied three or four years of full-time study, but in recent years this has become much more varied and flexible. For example, the first degree courses at University of Buckingham last only two years, the Open University has part-time students who study by correspondence, and the former polytechnics have large numbers of part-time and 'sandwich' students.

The Department for Education has ultimate responsibility for universities in England; those in the other countries of the United Kingdom are the responsibility of the Scottish Office Education Department, the Welsh Office Education Department and the Department of Education Northern Ireland. But universities have a considerable and jealously guarded degree of independence. They appoint their own staff, decide on their own admissions policies and have traditionally had academic freedom in their teaching and research, though the last of these has arguably been eroded in recent years by the 'earmarking' of government funds for specific subjects, and the need to seek commercial sponsors for particular projects.

With one exception, all universities receive central government funding, which is allocated among them on the basis of advice by the appropriate Higher Education Funding Council (HEFC) rather than by the direct decision of the government. The exception is the University of Buckingham, which receives no government funds, though its students are eligible for mandatory grants.

In 1991–2, just before the reorganisation of higher education, universities in the United Kingdom (other than the Open University) had about 305,000 undergraduate and 91,000 postgraduate students. Just under 4% of the undergraduates, and just over half of the postgraduates were part-time students. University students represented about 8% of the population of 18–20-year-olds. The number of students at universities has increased rapidly and substantially in recent years – by 28% for full-time students, and 55% for part-time students on degree courses (again excluding the OU), in England between 1989 and 1992 (GSS, 1994, Table 22; DFE and OFSTED, 1994, Annex: Tables E and G).

The Open University (OU), established in 1969, teaches by correspondence and broadcasting. It is 'open' in the sense of not requiring any entrance qualifications for its undergraduate courses; admission is on a 'first come first served' basis. It has by far the largest number of students of any university in the United Kingdom. In 1993, it had about 87,000 undergraduate students, virtually all of them studying part-time, over 8,000 postgraduate students, and

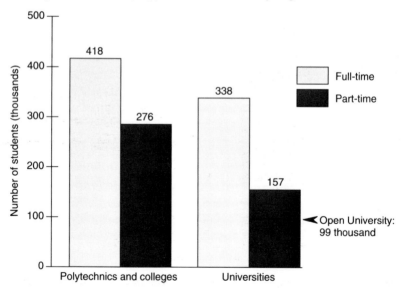

Figure 5.16   Numbers of full-time (including sandwich) and part-time students in higher education by type of institution, United Kingdom, 1991
(Adapted from GSS, 1994, Table 22)

some 32,000 registered students on non-degree courses. An additional 82,000 'study packs' were sold during the year to people who did not register as students. The OU accounted for two-thirds of all part-time undergraduate students in universities in the United Kingdom (OU Public Relations Department, 1993).

The largest conventional universities are the University of London (with 54,000 full-time students) and the University of Wales (with 28,000). But they are in effect federations of largely independent colleges – 22 for London, six for Wales. Apart from them, the largest universities are those of Oxford, Cambridge, Manchester and Leeds, with over 14,000 full-time students each.

Just under half of all university students (excluding OU students) live in colleges, halls of residence, or other accommodation provided by their university; another third live in lodgings or privately rented accommodation; and the rest live at home.

Figures 5.16 and 5.17 give some basic statistics about student numbers in higher education, comparing polytechnics and colleges with universities near the end of their separate lives. Figure 5.18 illustrates some of the routes that school leavers might follow through the main institutions offering further and higher education. (More detailed facts and figures on education and training after school can be found in Chapter 12.)

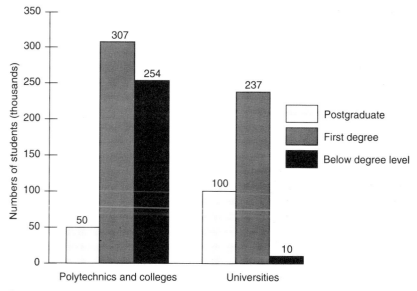

Figure 5.17   Numbers of higher education students taking full-time or part-time courses of different levels by type of institution, England 1991–2
(Adapted from DFE and OFSTED, 1994, Annex: Table G)
Note: The Open University is not included

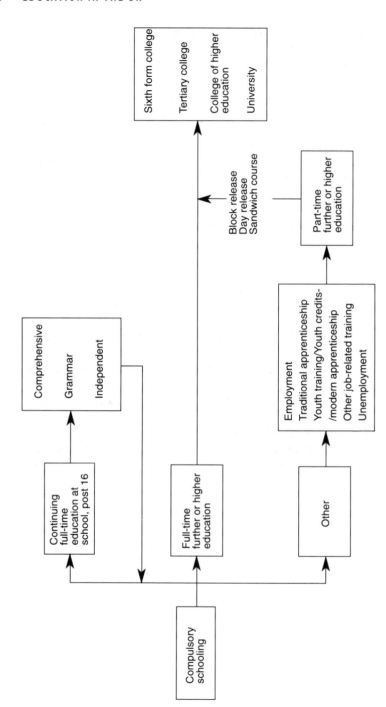

Figure 5.18   Further and higher education and training

SOURCES AND FURTHER READING

Bligh, D. (1990) *Higher Education*, London: Cassell.

COI (1994) *Britain 1994: an Official Handbook*, London: HMSO.

CSO (1987) *Social Trends*, No. 17, London: HMSO.

CSO (1989) *Social Trends*, No. 19, London: HMSO.

CSO (1993) *Regional Trends*, No. 28, London: HMSO.

CSO (1994) *Social Trends*, No. 24, London: HMSO.

DES (1981) *Statistical Bulletin 5/81: Pupils under five years in each local education authority in England – January 1980*, London: DES.

DES (1989) *Statistical Bulletin 8/89: Statistics of Schools in England – January 1988*, London: DES.

DFE (1993) *Statistical Bulletin 11/93: Pupils under five years of age in school in England – January 1992*, London: DFE.

DFE and OFSTED (1994) *Departmental Report/The Government's Expenditure Plans 1994–95 to 1996–97*, Cm 2507, London: HMSO.

Evans, M. et al. (ed.) (1994) *Education Year Book 1995*, Harlow: Longman.

GSS (1983) *Educational Statistics for the United Kingdom: 1983 Edition*, London: HMSO.

GSS (1985) *Educational Statistics for the United Kingdom: 1985 Edition*, London: HMSO.

GSS (1989) *Educational Statistics for the United Kingdom: 1989 Edition*, London: HMSO.

GSS (1994) *Educational Statistics for the United Kingdom: 1993 Edition*, London: HMSO.

ISIS (1994) *Annual Census 1994*, London: ISIS.

OU Public Relations Department (1993) *Basic Facts and Figures for 1993 (Fact Sheet No. X93)*, Milton Keynes: Open University.

Walford, G. (1986) *Life in Public Schools*, London: Methuen.

Education in the United Kingdom is administered as a partnership between local authorities and central government, though the balance of power and influence between the partners is at present changing, especially in England and Wales, with local authorities steadily losing powers. The exact division of responsibilities between central and local authorities varies from country to country, though in most respects England and Wales are more similar than the other countries. At central level, there are four government departments, one in each country, and at local level, each country is divided up into administrative areas for education. The local education authorities in England, Wales and Scotland are elected local councils, with many other responsibilities besides education, but those in Northern Ireland are not so closely linked to the rest of local government.

As we go to press in mid-1994, the government plans to reorganise the structure of local government in England, Wales and Scotland. How exactly this will be done has not yet been decided, but it seems likely to be a move away from having, for the same area, tiers of local authorities with different responsibilities (such as county councils and district councils) and towards unitary authorities, responsible for all functions. This could obviously have important consequences for the local government of education.

ENGLAND AND WALES

The central government department responsible for education in England is the *Department for Education* (DFE). Its responsibilities cover all schools (maintained and independent), and further and higher education in England, including universities, although in practice much of the latter is delegated to the *Further Education Funding Council* (FEFC) and the *Higher Education Funding Council* (HEFC). The DFE is also responsible for some aspects of the teaching profession in Wales.

The DFE has a staff of around 2500, 60% based in London, 40% in Darlington. At its head is a cabinet minister, the Secretary of State for Education. He or she is currently supported by a Minister of State and three Parliamentary Under-Secretaries of State. These are posts held by politicians. The civil servants who staff the DFE remain in post irrespective of changes of government. At their head is the permanent secretary, currently supported by three deputy secretaries (with responsibility, respectively, for schools, further and higher education, and the school curriculum and teachers).

Figures 6.1–6.3 show the divisions and the branches currently under the control of each of the three deputy secretaries. They illustrate how the DFE is concerned with all aspects of education, though at a broad, policy-making level;

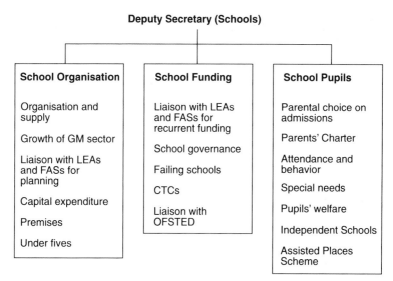

Deputy Secretary (Schools)

School Organisation	School Funding	School Pupils
Organisation and supply	Liaison with LEAs and FASs for recurrent funding	Parental choice on admissions
Growth of GM sector	School governance	Parents' Charter
Liaison with LEAs and FASs for planning	Failing schools	Attendance and behavior
Capital expenditure	CTCs	Special needs
Premises	Liaison with OFSTED	Pupils' welfare
Under fives		Independent Schools
		Assisted Places Scheme

Figure 6.1   Branches of the DFE: Schools
(Adapted from DFE and OFSTED, 1994, Figure 11)

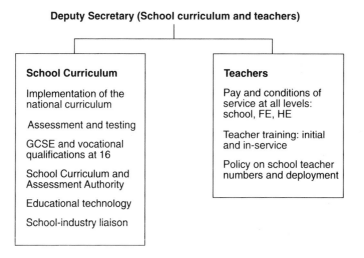

Deputy Secretary (School curriculum and teachers)

School Curriculum	Teachers
Implementation of the national curriculum	Pay and conditions of service at all levels: school, FE, HE
Assessment and testing	Teacher training: initial and in-service
GCSE and vocational qualifications at 16	Policy on school teacher numbers and deployment
School Curriculum and Assessment Authority	
Educational technology	
School-industry liaison	

Figure 6.2   Branches of the DFE: School curriculum and teachers
(Adapted from DFE and OFSTED, 1994, Figure 11)

the administration of most of the areas is at present the responsibility of the LEAs. In addition to the branches under the control of these three deputy secretaries, there are also a legal branch, a finance branch, an information branch and branches dealing with personnel and organisation, information technology, and analytical and statistical services within the DFE itself. The

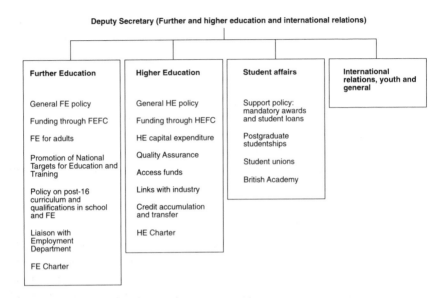

Figure 6.3   Branches of the DFE: Further and higher education and international relations
(Adapted from DFE and OFSTED, 1994, Figure 11)

Office for Standards in Education (OFSTED) is independent of the DFE (see below).

The *Welsh Office Education Department* is responsible for all aspects of education in Wales except the qualifications, probation, pay, superannuation and misconduct of teachers, which are the responsibility of the DFE.

The Welsh Office Education Department has four divisions, concerned with *schools curriculum, schools administration, further and higher education* and *culture and recreation.* The Office of Her Majesty's Chief Inspector of Schools in Wales is independent of the Education Department.

Educational structures and policies in Wales are much more similar to those in England than is true of Scotland or Northern Ireland. Much educational legislation applies to both England and Wales, and many official documents are issued in the joint names of the Secretaries of State for Education and for Wales.

England has 109 *local education authorities* (LEAs) — corresponding to 39 counties (plus the Scilly Isles), 36 metropolitan districts, 20 outer London boroughs and 12 inner London boroughs plus the City of London. Wales has eight LEAs, each corresponding to a county. The current boundaries of English and Welsh LEAs date from 1974, apart from those of inner London. The inner London boroughs (and the City of London) became local education authorities in April 1990, on the abolition of the Inner London Education Authority (ILEA) (see Figures 6.4–6.6).

The LEAs in England and Wales are part of the wider local councils and function through *education committees*. Elected councillors form the majority on these committees, which have ultimate authority and responsibility for education, although in practice the appointed education officers, who remain in post while councillors come and go, are often very influential. In most LEAs the education committee is composed of various subcommittees: usually one for finance, at least one for schools (in larger authorities there may well be separate ones for primary, secondary and special schools), at least one for further education (which may be subdivided into youth and community work, adult education and recreation), and one each for careers, libraries and museums, and sites and buildings.

Central versus local control

The 1944 Education Act set up a national educational system which was locally administered. Central government, in the form of the DFE and its predecessors, had overall responsibility and made policy decisions, but LEAs had control over most of the day-to-day running of the system. In the 1980s and 1990s, the balance of power shifted increasingly away from the LEAs and towards central government on the one hand, and individual schools and colleges on the other.

The most significant reduction of the LEAs' power began with the 1988 Education Reform Act. First, the Act and subsequent ministerial orders required LEAs to delegate important responsibilities to the governing bodies of almost all maintained schools (and colleges), in particular the responsibility for managing their budget and setting their own spending priorities, and for appointing and dismissing members of staff. An LEA is not allowed to use the allocation of funds to schools as a means of enforcing its policies. Funding levels must be determined by a standard formula, drawn up by the LEA but approved by the Secretary of State. It must place most weight on the numbers of pupils in the school, and must be applied even-handedly across all the authority's schools. This scheme has become known as the *Local Management of Schools* (LMS) (see Chapter 8). Secondly, the Act laid down procedures whereby individual schools could opt out of local authority control, acquiring *grant-maintained status*, and receiving their funding directly from the DES (see Chapter 4: 1988 Education Reform Act). By January 1994, 800 schools in England had successfully applied for grant-maintained status. Thirdly, it formalised the powers of the Secretary of State to enter into long-term agreements with private sponsors to fund City Technology Colleges (CTC) independent of LEAs (see Chapter 5). In the event, relatively few CTCs have been established – 15 by 1994.

The powers of LEAs are potentially diminished further by the 1993

Education Act, which established the Funding Agency for Schools (FAS) – for England – and the Funding Council for Wales (FCW). Members of these bodies are chosen by the respective Secretaries of State, who are empowered to issue directives to them. In the first instance, the FAS and the FCW are responsible for the funding of grant-maintained schools, but in addition they may assume some or all of the responsibilities currently held by LEAs for the planning of educational provision in their areas. When the percentage of the

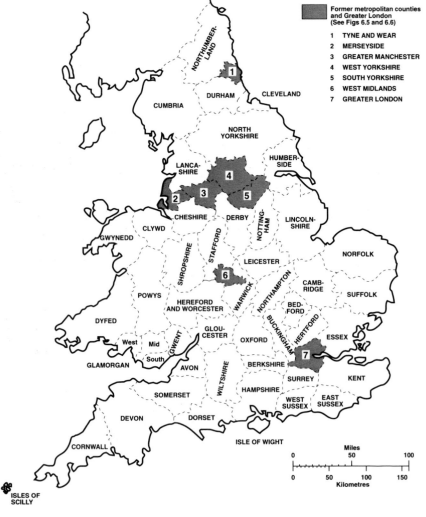

Figure 6.4   *LEAs of England and Wales: (i) Counties (and the Scilly Isles)*

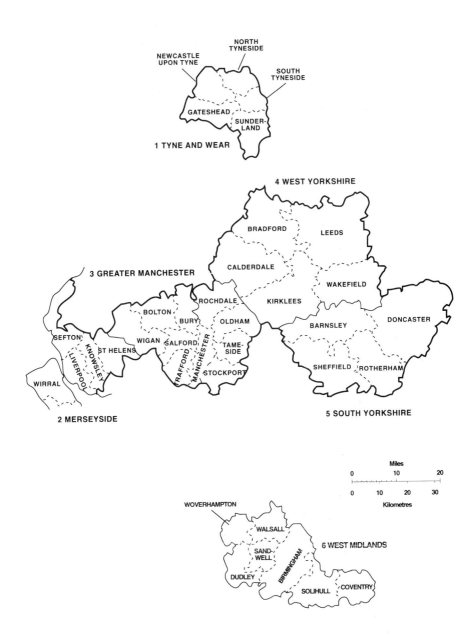

Figure 6.5   LEAs of England and Wales: (ii) Metropolitan districts

Figure 6.6   LEAs of England and Wales: (iii) London boroughs (and the City)

pupils in an LEA's area who attend grant-maintained schools reaches 10%, the Secretary of State is empowered to transfer part of these responsibilities; when it reaches 75%, he or she is empowered to transfer all the responsibilities. By mid-1994, partial responsibility for the planning of secondary schooling had been transferred to the FAS from 45 LEAs, and total responsibility from two (the London boroughs of Brent and Hillingdon). The extent to which control has moved out of the hands of the local authorities can be seen in Figure 6.7, where an asterisk (*) indicates a power traditionally held by the LEA which can now be taken over by schools which 'opt out'; a dagger (†)

DFE/WOED	LEA	Headteacher	Parents	Governors
Policy making	Provide 'adequate and efficient' education at primary and secondary level (nursery optional)	Care of pupils ('in loco parentis')	Send child to school (or 'educate otherwise')	Oversee implementation of national curriculum, conduct and discipline‡
Inspecting all schools and institutions	Establish, alter and close schools (after giving public notice)	Internal organisation of school	Express preference for a school‡	Financial management of school‡
Supply and training of teachers	Finance schools* and local education service	Rules, discipline, curriculum (subject to national curriculum and governors' general direction)	Be represented on governing body	Appointment and dismissal of teachers‡
Final court of appeal in disputes between parents and LEA	Enforce school attendance	Financial management of school (in association with governors)‡	Receive published information about school‡	Suspension/expulsion of pupils
Providing education support grants†	Student grants (England and Wales)		Be involved in assessment procedure for children with special educational needs‡	Sex education‡
Assisted places scheme†	Identify and provide for special educational needs		Withdraw child from religious instruction or sex education	Use 'best endeavours' to identify children with special educational needs‡
Financing further education (via FEFCs)	Health and safety		Decide whether a school should 'opt out' of LEA control‡	Publish information for parents about the school‡
Financing higher education (via HEFCs)	Careers service			
Collecting statistics	Ensure equal opportunities for both sexes and all races			
Educational building programme				

Figure 6.7 Powers and duties

indicates new powers which central government has taken on since 1979, often transferred from the LEA; and a double dagger (‡) in the parents, governors or headteachers column indicates new duties and rights they have received since 1979.

The control of schools

The 1944 Education Act created a unified framework which brought the church schools under state control (turning them into maintained schools), but left them with varying degrees of independence, usually over religious matters, according to how much financial support the church continued to provide. This system has remained relatively unchanged (apart from a recent increase of the proportion of parent and teacher representatives on the governing bodies of voluntary schools).

The LEAs created by the 1944 Act could set up new schools themselves; these are called *county schools*. Schools that had been established by a church body (or occasionally a trust) became *voluntary schools*, of which there are three types: 'aided', 'controlled' and 'special agreement', differing mainly in the extent to which the LEA finances and controls them.

- *Aided schools* (4,289 in number in 1992, roughly half Church of England and half Roman Catholic) provide their own premises and meet some of the maintenance costs in exchange for a degree of control.
- *Controlled schools* (3,033 in number, virtually all Church of England) provide their own premises, but the LEAs meet all the schools' costs. Before the 1988 Act, the governing bodies had control only over religious instruction.
- *Special agreement schools* are few in number (77, most of them Roman Catholic), and they arose from the government's offer in 1936 to pay 50–75% of the cost of building new secondary schools. By the outbreak of the Second World War, very few of the 500 or so 'special agreements' made with voluntary bodies had been implemented, and the 1944 Act allowed for their revival.

And, as mentioned above, the 1988 Education Reform Act established a further category, *grant-maintained schools*.

- *Grant-maintained schools* (just over 800 in England and Wales in mid-1994, but the number is increasing) are at present maintained schools whose governing bodies and parents have chosen to 'opt out' of LEA finance and control – though the 1993 Education Act has introduced further ways of establishing them. They own their premises and employ their staff, receiving grants from central government via the Funding Agency for Schools (in England) or the Funding Council for Wales. Services that cannot practicably be provided by a single school may be purchased from LEAs, or provided by a consortium of two or more grant-maintained schools. Grant-maintained schools remain subject to the national curriculum and its associated tests, and to inspection by OFSTED. They may not change their character (e.g. from comprehensive to selective) without permission from the Secretary of State, though in a number of cases such permission has been sought and given. Since the 1993 Act, independent schools may 'opt in' to grant-maintained status, or entirely new schools may be set up within the grant-maintained sector, on the initiative of local 'promoters' or of the appropriate Funding Agency or Council.

The main differences in funding and control between the different traditional types of school are summarised in Figure 6.8.

Voluntary schools in England account for about a third of primary schools and a fifth of secondary schools (see Figure 6.9). The majority of voluntary primary schools are Church of England, while just over half of voluntary secondary schools are Roman Catholic.

SCOTLAND

The central government department responsible for education in Scotland is the *Scottish Office Education Department* (SOED). It is responsible for all education in Scotland. Higher education is funded through the Scottish Higher Education Funding Council (SHEFC); further education is financed directly by the SOED. At local level, there are nine regional and three islands area education authorities (EAs). The current boundaries date from 1975 (see Figure 6.10).

Scotland has no statutory school curriculum, unlike the other countries of the United Kingdom. Central influence on what schools teach is more indirect (see Chapter 10).

The control of schools

Scotland does not have voluntary schools. Church schools which have chosen to transfer to the education authority, rather than be independent, become public schools (the term used in Scotland for maintained or state schools), although they can make separate arrangements for denominational instruction. Most are Roman Catholic, but there are also (in 1986) one Jewish, one Episcopalian and one Sikh school.

The Scottish counterpart to the grant-maintained school is the *self-governing school*. By 1994, there was just one (Dornoch Academy).

NORTHERN IRELAND

The central government department responsible for education in Northern Ireland, the *Department of Education Northern Ireland* (DENI), has overall

	County	Maintained schools			Independent schools
		Voluntary			
		Aided	Controlled	Special agreement	
Established by:	LEA	Voluntary organisations, usually religious bodies – C of E, Church in Wales, Roman Catholic Church, Jewish organisations		Voluntary organisations usually church bodies – but by special agreement the LEA pays 50–75% cost of building a new school	Private individuals Benefactors Trust and charities
Financed by:	LEA	Voluntary body responsible for external repairs and maintenance (assisted by 85% LEA grant) LEA pays running costs, internal repairs and teachers' salaries	LEA	Voluntary body responsible for external repairs and maintenance (assisted by 85% LEA grant)	Parental fees Assisted places scheme Benefactors/charities
Controlled by:	LEA and governing body Must offer non-denominational religious instruction to all pupils	Voluntary body appoints ⅔ majority of governors, and hence controls admissions and appointment of teachers Can offer denominational instruction to all pupils	LEA appoints majority of governors, but voluntary body nominates a third Can offer denominational instruction to families who request it	Voluntary body appoints majority of governors	Board of Governors (DES can enforce minimum standards for premises and staffing)

Figure 6.8 The administration and control of traditional schools (i.e. other than grant-maintained schools or CTGs) in England and Wales

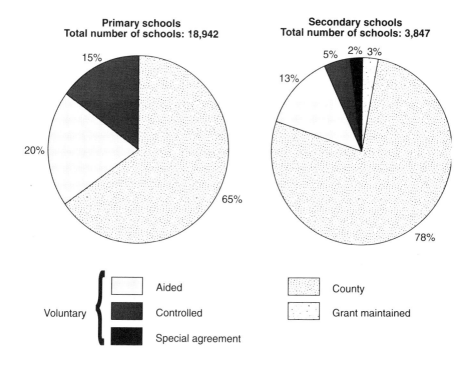

*Figure 6.9   Type of control of maintained schools, England 1992
(Adapted from DFE, 1993, Table A13)*

responsibility for schools, further education and universities. Local education authorities in Northern Ireland are called *Education and Library Boards*, and are responsible for the local provision and administration of schools and further education, as well as university awards. There are five of these; their current boundaries date from 1973 (see Figure 6.11). Unlike the local education authorities in Great Britain, Education and Library Boards in Northern Ireland are appointed centrally, by the DENI, though their membership includes nominated representatives of district councils, as well as teachers, local community representatives, trade union nominees, churches and maintained school trustees (see below).

The control of schools

Northern Ireland uses the terms 'controlled', 'voluntary' and 'maintained', but with meanings different from those that apply in England and Wales. There are three principal types of school management, described below; in all of them, the representation of parents and teachers has been strengthened, and that of the churches reduced, since 1984.

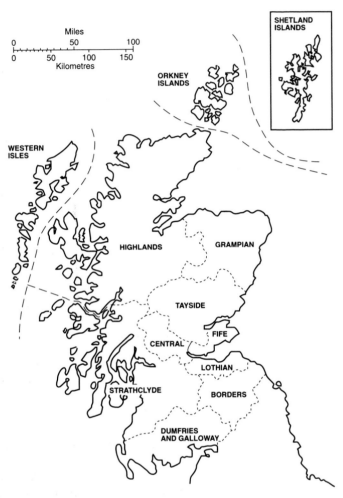

Figure 6.10   Education authorities in Scotland

- *Controlled schools* are managed by Education and Library Boards through boards of governors. The schools may be primary, secondary intermediate, grammar or special; membership of boards of governors differs for the different types of school, but they include representatives of parents, teachers, education and library boards, and sometimes churches (mainly the Protestant churches). The capital expenditure and running costs of control-led schools are met by the Education and Library Boards from funds provided by the DENI. (A *controlled integrated school* is a possible type of school under the 1978 Education (Northern Ireland) Act. The aim was to facilitate the development of schools which would be attended by pupils of different faiths. The proposal to change to a controlled integrated school

Figure 6.11 Education and Library Boards in Northern Ireland

has to be supported by three-quarters of the parents. No such schools as yet exist.)

- *Voluntary (maintained) schools* are managed by boards of governors, which consist of representatives of trustees (mainly Roman Catholic), parents, teachers and Education and Library Boards. Capital expenditure on these schools is partly met (up to 85%) by the DENI; running costs are met by the Education and Library Boards. There are several integrated primary voluntary (maintained) schools, and one integrated post-primary (Lagan College).
- *Voluntary (non-maintained) schools* are managed by boards of governors, whose constitutions vary from school to school, but which include representatives of parents and teachers, and sometimes of the DENI or an Education and Library Board. They are mainly grammar schools; there are separate Protestant and Roman Catholic schools. Capital expenditure on these schools is partly met (up to 85%) by the DENI; running costs are met from block grants direct from the DENI and from fees (although for many pupils these are paid or assisted by the Education and Library Boards).

SOURCES AND FURTHER READING

DFE (1993) *Statistics of Schools 1992*, London: DFE.

DFE and OFSTED (1994) *Department Report/The Government's Expenditure Plans 1994–95 to 1996–97*, Cm 2510, London: HMSO.

Department of Finance and Personnel (Northern Ireland Office)/HM Treasury (1994) *Northern Ireland Expenditure Plans and Priorities: The Government's Expenditure Plans 1994–95 to 1996–97*, Cm 2516, London: HMSO.

Departments of the Secretary of State for Scotland/Forestry Commission (1994) *Serving Scotland's Needs: the Government's Expenditure Plans 1994–95 to 1996–97*, Cm 2514, Edinburgh: HMSO.

Welsh Office and the Office of Her Majesty's Chief Inspector of Schools in Wales (1994) *The Government's Expenditure Plans 1994–95 to 1996–97: A Report by the Welsh Office and the Office of Her Majesty's Chief Inspector of Schools in Wales*, Cm 2515, London: HMSO.

(A) INTRODUCTION

The education service employs a wide variety of staff. Apart from those whose job is to teach (in schools, colleges and universities), there are the administrators, advisers and inspectors; the support staff who assist teachers (e.g. nursery assistants and laboratory assistants); the ancillary workers who maintain premises, provide the meals service and run the offices; and the professionals who offer specialist services, such as the educational psychologists.

> **F A C T** Out of a total workforce of 1.8 million (excluding police and other law and order services) in 1990, local authorities in England and Wales employed 906,000 (50%) in the education service; 517,000 of these (28% of all employees) were teachers and lecturers. These figures represent a reduction in staffing levels since 1980 of 5% for all employees, 9% for those in education (CIPFA, 1991, Table 5.4).

Figure 7.1 groups jobs in education into five main categories, although in practice the boundaries (e.g. between administrators and advisers) are not always well defined, and the term 'ancillary staff' is sometimes used to cover jobs categorised as 'educational support' too. All of the staff in Figure 7.1 are employed by the LEA, apart from those in further and higher education; and the HMIs, who are employed by the central government. However, the 1988 Local Government Act requires that a local authority's cleaning and maintenance work be put out to competitive tender: this is likely to result in fewer of these staff being employed directly by the LEA in future. And after the 1988 Education Reform Act, teachers, though still formally employed by LEAs, are appointed, and may be dismissed, by the governors of their schools.

(B) THE STAFF OF THE EDUCATION SERVICE

This section gives a brief description of the principal posts in the education service, at the level of central government, LEAs and schools. This is followed by some more detailed facts and figures about the teaching profession, and a description of some of the professionals involved in further and higher education.

Central government level

Inspectors

Inspection of schools in England is the responsibility of the Office for Standards in Education (OFSTED), a non-ministerial department (independent of the DFE) headed by Her Majesty's Chief Inspector of Schools. Before the 1992 Education (Schools) Act (and subsequent regulations issued by the Secretary of State), school inspections had been conducted directly by Her Majesty's Inspectors of Schools (HMIs), full-time professionals attached to, but independent of, the Department of Education and Science. Their principal role was to report to the Secretary of State on the education offered in schools and colleges; they also gave him or her professional advice, were involved in the in-service training of teachers, and helped to disseminate the government's thinking on curriculum and teaching. But now, the full-time professional inspectors are fewer (around 200 instead of just under 500) and play a more administrative and organisational part. OFSTED keeps a register of *Registered Inspectors*, not in the employ of OFSTED but 'fit and proper person[s] . . . able to conduct inspections competently and efficiently' (DFE, 1993, p. 4). Actual inspections of schools and colleges are now normally conducted by teams of independent *Inspectors* (not in the employ of OFSTED), headed by a Registered Inspector, and including at least one *Lay Inspector* who has not been involved professionally in education. All the members of the inspection team must normally have successfully completed a course of training organised or approved by OFSTED. A team offered a contract by OFSTED for the inspection of a school or college, after it has invited tenders from at least two Registered Inspectors. All maintained schools (including grant-maintained schools and CTCs) and some independent schools (notably those catering for children with special educational needs) are to have a four-yearly inspection, lasting not more than two weeks, and normally not more than one. The inspectors must report on the quality of education provided, the educational standards achieved, the efficiency of financial management and the 'spiritual, moral, social and cultural development' of the pupils (DFE, 1993, p. 5).

Similar arrangements now obtain in Wales, through the Office of Her Majesty's Chief Inspector of Schools in Wales (OHMCI), which is independent of the Welsh Office Education Department (See Welsh Office/Office of Her Majesty's Chief Inspector of Schools in Wales, 1994, Ch. 11).

In Scotland, however, Her Majesty's Inspectorate retains its traditional twin roles of directly inspecting schools and colleges (and now also publishing reports on individual institutions), and of giving professional advice to ministers and government departments and agencies on the formation of national policy. There are no proposals at present for any thoroughgoing reform of inspection in Scotland, but there are plans to involve lay people in inspections (Marker, 1994, Section 4).

LEA administrators	Teaching staff (schools)	Education support staff	Other education professionals	Ancillary staff	Further and higher education
Director of Education/Chief Education Officer (CEO)	Headteacher	Welfare assistant	Educational psychologist (EP)	Administration and clerical	Vice chancellor/Principal/Director/Chief Executive
Deputy CEO	Deputy head	Nursery assistant	Education welfare officer (EWO)	Kitchen and canteen	Professor
Assistant Education Officer (AEO)	Teacher	Teacher's aide	Adviser	Caretakers	Reader
Professional assistant	Nursery teacher	Student assistant	Youth and community worker	Porters	Principal lecturer
	Special school teacher	Laboratory technician	Careers officer	Gardeners	Senior lecturer
	Peripatetic teacher	Media resources officer	Schools-industry liaison officer	Cleaners	Lecturer
	Supply teacher	Librarian	Her Majesty's Inspector (HMI)	Security staff	Research fellow
	Home liaison teacher	Medical staff			Research officer
	Home tutor				Research associate
	Educational home visitor				Research assistant

Figure 7.1 Jobs in the education service
(Adapted from CIPFA, no single date)

Local education authority level

As local management of schools takes effect, many of the LEA posts described below are likely to change in character and lose some current functions.

Chief education officer (CEO)

Every LEA is required to have a chief education officer (known in some authorities as the director of education), who is the senior appointed official, with overall administrative responsibility for the running of the local education system. He or she is accountable to the education committee, on which elected councillors form the majority (see Chapter 6).

Deputy chief education officer

He or she coordinates the assistant education officers (see below), and deals with major initiatives such as secondary school reorganisation.

Assistant education officer

An assistant education officer is in charge of one of the half dozen or so branches into which the work of the education service is divided, such as secondary education or further education.

Professional assistant

This is a first-level administrative post within an education department, usually for an experienced teacher. He or she works under an assistant education officer. The post is sometimes also known as administrative assistant.

Adviser (sometimes called inspector)

Advisers are employed by the LEA to advise on the content and quality of courses, organise in-service training of teachers and, in some authorities, to inspect schools and colleges. They are usually responsible for a particular field, such as computing, preschool provision, adult education, political education or equal opportunities. There is no uniformity of numbers; some large authorities have 50 or more advisers while a few LEAs have none, relying on the centrally appointed HMIs for inspection and advice.

Educational psychologist

Every LEA has a team of educational psychologists headed by a principal educational psychologist. They generally have a psychology degree, a teaching qualification, some teaching experience and further specialist training. They work with children who have behavioural and/or learning problems in school, administering tests (traditional IQ testing used to be a central part of the job, but it is becoming less important) and designing remedial work in conjunction with teachers. Some educational psychologists visit the schools in their area on a regular basis so that teachers know when they will be coming in and can discuss children they may be worried about; others visit at the request of schools or when a child is formally referred to them. They are part of the LEA's

Schools Psychological Service or Child Guidance Service, and are often based in a Child Guidance Clinic. A large proportion of their time is taken up with identifying and assessing children's special educational needs, especially under the procedures introduced by the 1981 Education Act (see Chapter 3). Educational psychologists also work with children under school age who are likely to have special educational needs when they do start school, usually those children with a severe, or early-diagnosed, difficulty.

Education welfare officer (EWO) (also known as education social worker)

Education welfare officers liaise with Social Services Departments and are responsible for the general well-being of school children, not only ensuring that they attend school regularly but also dealing with grants, allowances and services which they may need to be able to attend (e.g. clothing, transport, free school meals). The job involves a substantial amount of fieldwork, such as visiting families where there is a record of absence, lateness or other difficulties at school, and the Educational Welfare Service (staffed by the EWOs) is usually based in the community rather than the Town Hall, in a school or small area office. EWOs are also involved with the families of children who have special educational needs, and in some LEAs they deliver to parents the 'Section 5 Letter' which initiates the formal assessment procedure for such children (see Chapter 13).

Careers officer

LEAs are obliged to set up a Careers Service, which is staffed by careers officers. As with education welfare officers, their job involves travelling in the community rather than being part of the central LEA administration, and so they also generally work in area teams based in a local school. Their job is part counselling, part provider of information. They liaise with secondary school careers teachers, and also with the employers in an area.

Youth and community worker/officer

Although youth work has many of the functions of social work, it is primarily an education service. Most full-time, qualified youth and community workers are employed by LEAs, although a few work for Social Services Departments. By far the greater part of youth work, however, is still done by volunteers. Qualified youth and community workers generally have a teaching qualification; some institutions offer a BEd degree or postgraduate courses in youth and community studies. They are generally based in youth clubs and centres, and work on a variety of projects including those for the unemployed.

Schools–industry liaison officer (SILO)

They are appointed by LEAs to coordinate the work of schools and industry within their areas.

School level

Headteacher
Virtually every school in the country has a headteacher who is responsible for the overall running of the school and for the rules, discipline and curriculum, under the guidance of the school's governors and subject to any requirements of the LEA and, since the 1988 Education Reform Act, to the national curriculum. While reducing headteachers' autonomy in curricular matters, the 1988 Act increases it in matters of financial management. Headteachers' salaries are linked to the number of pupils in their schools.

Deputy headteacher
The deputy head assists the head in the running of a school, often liaising between the head and the rest of the staff. Large secondary schools may have two or more deputy heads, with defined areas of responsibility (e.g. for the curriculum); primary schools normally have one. As with heads, their salaries are linked to the number of pupils in their schools.

Class teacher
Class teachers are the main category of professionals involved in the education of children, and more detailed information about them is given in the next section. Usually one teacher at a time works with a class of children, teaching a particular subject in the case of secondary schools, or teaching virtually all of the curriculum in the case of primary schools. Thus, children in a primary school will spend most of their time with the same teacher in any one year, while secondary school pupils will be taught by a variety of different teachers. A less common pattern is for teachers to combine classes and teach together ('team teaching'), usually for particular subjects or in open-plan primary schools.

Special school teacher
Teachers in special schools are paid an additional allowance, but the small size of the schools and the move towards integrating children with special needs into ordinary schools mean that they have fewer prospects for promotion than teachers in mainstream schools. They must be qualified teachers, and in Scotland must have previously taught in an ordinary school for at least a year (this is common practice but not compulsory in England and Wales). Teachers of the deaf, partially hearing and blind must in addition have a specialist qualification, and many other teachers in special schools (and increasingly in ordinary schools too) attend in-service training courses on children with special educational needs. With increasing integration, some special school teachers are spending part of their time in ordinary schools, supporting children with special educational needs in ordinary classes or special classes and units attached to the ordinary school.

Nursery school teacher
A nursery school teacher is a qualified teacher who usually specialises, during training, in the education of nursery and infant children. Nursery school teachers teach in either nursery schools or special nursery classes attached to a primary school, and are helped by nursery assistants and nursery students (doing the practical part of their training).

Nursery assistant
A nursery assistant is not qualified as a teacher, but holds a National Nursery Examination Board (NNEB) qualification (a theoretical and practical course studying the development and care of young children).

Teacher's aide
Also sometimes called an infant helper or primary helper, a teacher's aide is someone without formal teaching qualifications who works alongside the regular class teacher. The Plowden Report (see Chapter 3) recommended greater use of such posts, but they have never become common.

Welfare assistant
This is a person without teaching qualifications who is employed by the LEA to work alongside a class teacher, often with a particular child who has special educational needs. His or her job is to deal with the child's physical needs (e.g. arising from incontinence, lack of mobility or impaired speech) rather than to help teach the whole class.

Supply teacher
Each LEA has a supply of teachers who are sent in to schools to cover for absences of regular teaching staff. They may be attached to a particular school for a single day or even part of a day, or for a substantially longer period.

Peripatetic teacher
Some qualified teachers are not attached to a particular school but visit and work in several schools in an area, for instance teaching music or languages, or working with partially hearing children.

Home liaison teacher
In some LEAs there are qualified teachers whose job is to liaise between the school and the home, by visiting the child's family at home, seeing parents if they visit the school, and by organising activities, both during and after school hours, to encourage parental involvement with the school and with their children's education. They are most likely to be attached to primary schools in areas of social need, or to special schools.

Educational home visitor
Some LEAs employ teachers to visit families with preschool children before they start school, usually for about an hour a week, to play with the children

and involve the parents in finding out more about the children's development and needs. They perform a similar role to home liaison teachers in encouraging parental involvement in their children's education, but differ in working with children under five.

Home tutor
A home tutor is a teacher employed to teach children at home when they are unable to attend school for any length of time, for instance because of illness.

Laboratory technician/assistant
Laboratory technicians and assistants maintain laboratory and workshop equipment, usually in secondary schools or institutes of further or higher education. They provide technical assistance to teachers, especially in science subjects, and sometimes also deal with audio-visual equipment.

Audio-visual technician
Audio-visual technicians are responsible for the operation and maintenance of audio-visual equipment. Some posts exist attached to a particular secondary school, especially a very large comprehensive, but most A-V technicians are appointed to a local authority centre, or work in further or higher education.

Media resources officer
A few large authorities have created these posts, which involve not merely the operation and maintenance of audio-visual equipment and other educational technology, but also the preparation and production of audio-visual materials and the in-service training of teaching staff in the use of the equipment.

Ancillary staff
All educational establishments are dependent for their day-to-day running on the ancillary staff. They include the administrative and clerical staff, who often work part-time, especially in primary schools: the secretaries, clerical assistants, typists, and (especially in private boarding schools) bursars, who are responsible for the school's financial and domestic management. Another group are the kitchen and canteen staff, responsible for providing school dinners. Their numbers have decreased since 1980, when responsibility for the provision of school meals was delegated to LEAs, with a legal obligation to provide meals only to children in families receiving Supplementary Benefit or Family Income Supplement. The other main category of ancillary staff can be described as premises-related: they include caretakers, cleaners, porters, gardeners and security staff.

(C) THE TEACHING PROFESSION

Salaries and conditions

The 1991 School Teachers' Pay and Conditions Act established a review body, its members appointed by the government, to make annual recommendations to the Secretary of State for Education about teachers' salaries and conditions of employment in England and Wales. Final decisions are then made by the Secretary of State, after consultation with LEAs, teachers' representatives and other interested parties, and set out in a School Teachers' Pay and Conditions Document. These arrangements replace more complicated structures in which salaries and conditions were negotiated (see the first and second editions of *The Education Fact File*).

The current salary structure (from April 1994) consists of a single 'spine' for all qualified teachers (apart from heads and deputy heads), of 18 points from £11,571 to £31,323. Heads' and deputy heads' salaries range on a spine of 51 points from £23,055 to £52,052 (DFE, 1994).

The 1994 School Teachers' Pay and Conditions Document spells out explicitly and exhaustively the duties, and the working time, of teachers at all levels. The duties include the following. Teachers are required to plan and prepare lessons, assess and keep records of pupils' progress, and maintain discipline. They are to engage in appraisal of their own work, and attend in-service training. They must communicate with parents and others outside school, and attend meetings where necessary. They must provide cover for absent colleagues for up to three days, though this can be extended for a teacher whose assigned duties occupy less than three-quarters of his or her working week, or where the school authorities have 'exhausted all reasonable means' but failed to provide a supply teacher to replace the absent colleague. Finally, they must participate, when required, in the appraisal of other teachers' performance.

A teacher's working year is to consist of 1265 hours, spread reasonably over 195 working days. (This does not include travelling time to and from school.) In addition, teachers must work such extra hours as are needed to fulfil their professional duties, for example in preparing lessons and marking pupils' written work. Teachers are entitled to a reasonable midday break, and do not have to supervise pupils during this period as part of their normal duties (DFE, 1994, Part X).

In recent years, teachers' salaries have fallen behind those of other non-manual workers. Between 1975 and 1986, teachers' pay rose by 194%, on average, compared with an average rise of 259% for all non-manual earnings (New Society Database, 1986).

F A C T   Approximately 508,000 full-time teachers were employed in schools in the UK in 1990–1 (10% below the number employed in 1980–1, but 13% above the number in 1970–1). Of these, 91% taught in maintained schools (46% in secondary, 41% in primary and 4% in special schools) and the remaining 9% taught in the private sector (CSO, 1994, Table 3.25).

Women outnumber men in the teaching profession, making up over three-quarters of the teachers in primary schools, and just under half of the teachers in secondary schools. They are particularly highly represented as teachers of the youngest children. Figure 7.2 shows that as the age of the pupil increases, so the proportion of women teachers decreases.

Under the 1987 Teachers' Pay and Conditions Act (which was repealed in 1991) all teachers, apart from head and deputy head teachers, were paid on a single 'main scale', but with five levels of incentive allowance, from A (the lowest) to E. Although these categories no longer apply, the latest published statistics (for 1990) use them and they still illustrate the careers of male and female teachers in primary and secondary education, as Figures 7.3–7.5 show.

In both primary and secondary schools, women were more likely to be found at the bottom of the hierarchy of teaching posts. Figure 7.3 shows the women and the men on each level of incentive allowance as percentages of all teachers on that level. Figures 7.4 and 7.5 show the women and men on each level as percentages of all the women and of all the men in the teaching profession. (Primary and secondary schools are shown separately.)

The proportion of heads (and, therefore, the chance of becoming one) was higher in primary education, where there are many more, smaller schools. Differences between the sexes were very noticeable in both sectors. Particularly striking were the much higher percentage of men than of women who were heads, and the much higher percentage of women than of men who were on the lowest two scales, compared with the total numbers of men and women in all posts taken together. These discrepancies existed in both the primary and the secondary sectors, but were especially marked in the primary.

Ethnic minorities are under-represented in the teaching profession in comparison with their numbers in the population. In eight LEAs surveyed in 1987 by the Commission for Racial Equality, the overall percentage of teachers who were from ethnic minorities was 2% (Ranger, 1988); the percentage of the total population of these LEAs who are from ethnic minorities is about 8.5% (OPCS, 1982. However, the latter figure is based on answers to a question in the 1981 Census about the country of birth of one's head of household, and cannot be considered very accurate. See Chapter 2).

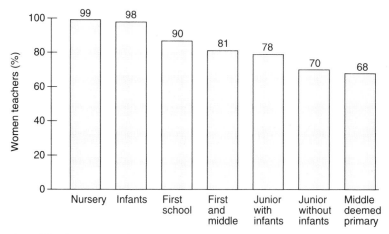

Figure 7.2   Percentages of women teachers in different types of primary school, England and Wales 1990
(Adapted from DES, no date, Table B12/90)

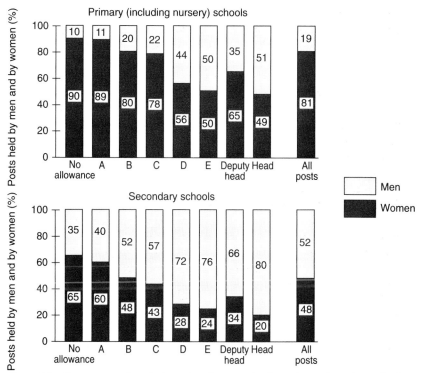

Figure 7.3   Percentages of each incentive allowance level on the main scale, and of deputy head and head teacher posts held by men and by women, England and Wales 1990
(Adapted from DES, no date, Table B12/90)

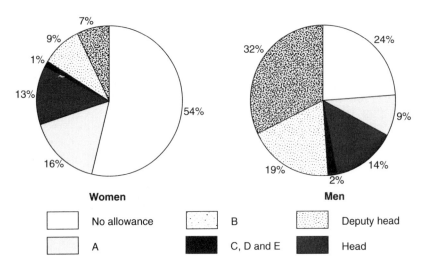

Figure 7.4   Percentages of men and of women teachers on each level of incentive allowance and in head and deputy head teachers' posts, in primary schools in England and Wales 1990
(Adapted from DES, no date, Table B12/90)

Teachers from ethnic minorities are more likely to be found in junior posts than are White teachers: in 1987 (before the abolition of salary scales), 78% of ethnic minority teachers were on scales 1 and 2 (the lowest), compared with 57% of White teachers. Ethnic minority teachers are twice as likely as White teachers to be teaching subjects in which there is a shortage of teachers (Ranger, 1988).

Training and qualifications

There are at present two main ways of becoming a qualified teacher in England and Wales: by taking an undergraduate course of initial teacher training – usually lasting four years and leading to a BEd degree; or, for graduates or the holders of equivalent qualifications in an appropriate subject, a postgraduate course of initial teacher training – usually lasting one year and leading to a Postgraduate Certificate in Education (PGCE). There are also some part-time PGCE courses, normally lasting two years, and two distance-learning PGCE programmes (run by The Open University and South Bank University).

In addition, LEAs and governing bodies can employ *licensed teachers*. These must be over 24 years old, and have successfully completed at least two years of full-time higher education (or its part-time equivalent), but need not have had any teacher training or teaching experience. The employer must provide 'tailor-made, on-the-job training' for such teachers, who can obtain qualified

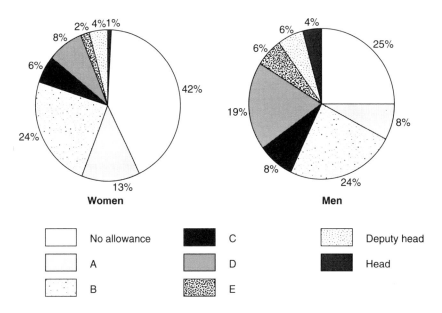

Figure 7.5   Percentages of men and women teachers on each level of incentive allowances, and in head and deputy head teachers' posts, in secondary schools, in England and Wales 1990
(Adapted from DES, no date, Table B12/90)

teacher status in two years or less. *Overseas trained teachers* can be employed, and gain qualified teacher status in England and Wales, in a similar way.

Currently there is also an *articled teacher* scheme, a two-year PGCE course which is predominantly school rather than university or college based. However, it is being phased out (with no new recruits after 1993) because the government proposes to make all teacher training more predominantly school based than at present (GSS, 1994, Appendix).

At present, all courses leading to qualified teacher status have to be approved by the Council for the Accreditation of Teacher Education (CATE), but the system is changing to one in which CATE approves *institutions* as providers of teacher training, not individual courses.

While this book is in press, the Education Act 1994 has been passed, making some alterations to these arrangements (see Chapter 4: 1994 Education Act).

Teacher training in Northern Ireland and Scotland follows a pattern similar to that in England and Wales. However, in Scotland there are separate courses for primary and secondary teachers, and the Teaching Qualification (Primary

Education) and the Teaching Qualification (Secondary Education) are distinct, making it more difficult for teachers in Scotland to move between the two sectors than in the rest of the United Kingdom (Marker, 1994, Section 15).

In 1991, a total of 64,100 students were enrolled on initial teacher training courses in the United Kingdom in universities or what was then in public sector higher education, i.e. polytechnics and colleges (see Figure 7.6). The proportion of the teaching force who have degrees has been steadily increasing (see Figure 7.7). It is higher among men than women, with the lowest proportion of graduates teaching in primary schools and the highest in non-maintained schools (see Figure 7.8).

An important aspect of the teacher's job is the size of the class he or she is expected to teach (on average, this is greater than the pupil/teacher ratio, as calculations of the latter include staff who do little or no classroom teaching). Primary classes are generally larger than classes in secondary schools. (For data on the pupil/teacher ratio, see Chapter 5; Figures 5.8 and 5.12.)

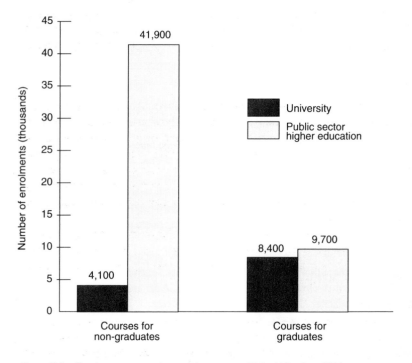

Figure 7.6   Enrolments on teacher training courses, United Kingdom 1991
(Adapted from GSS, 1994, Table 8)

(D) TEACHING STAFF IN FURTHER AND HIGHER EDUCATION

F A C T   In 1992–3, 61,300 academic staff were employed in further education colleges, and 59,400 in higher education, 56% in universities and 44% in polytechnics and colleges (many of which have subsequently become universities) (DFE/OFSTED, 1994, Tables D and E).

Men far outnumber women in further and higher education teaching, especially in senior posts. In 1992–3, there were over three men to every woman at lecturer level, almost nine men to every woman at senior lecturer level, and just over 19 men to every woman at the level of professor in British universities (see Figure 7.9). The discrepancy is particularly great in the sciences and mathematics, where male lecturers outnumber female by seven to one, and male professors outnumber female by 53 to one. However, the discrepancy between the sexes, though still huge, is currently decreasing. Women constituted 16% of all teaching staff in 1992–3, compared with 13% in 1988–9; and 5% of professors in 1992–3, compared with 3% in 1988–9.

Career structure

Most academic teaching posts in universities (but not the former polytechnics or colleges of higher education) have traditionally been offered on a 'tenured' basis, so that academic staff can lose their jobs only on grounds of professional misconduct (and not on such grounds as redundancy or financial exigency). However, under the 1988 Education Reform Act no new tenured appointments can be made. Academics already in post retain their tenure only so long as they do not move to another university or accept promotion within their present university.

The main traditional academic posts within universities are typically as described below, though there is a great deal of variation between universities, especially after the sudden expansion of the university sector following the 1992 Further and Higher Education Act.

Chancellor

The chancellor is the titular head of a university, with a purely ceremonial function, notably in conferring degrees. He or she is usually a well-known public figure, who need not have any connection with the academic world (such as a member of the Royal Family). In the ancient Scottish universities, the chancellor is elected by the graduates.

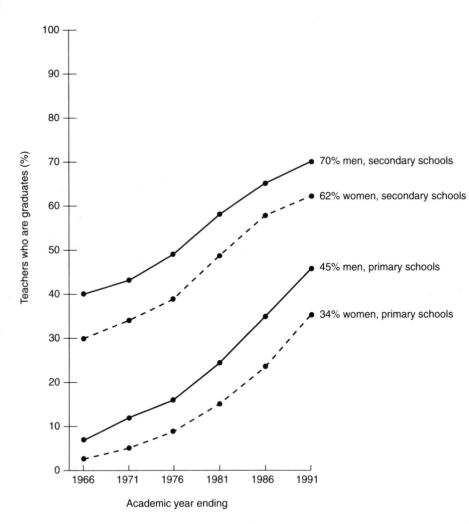

Figure 7.7 *Percentages of men and women teachers who are graduates, in public sector primary and secondary schools, United Kingdom 1966–91 (Adapted from GSS, 1994, Table 9)*

Pro chancellor

Nominally a deputy to the chancellor (for whom he or she sometimes stands in on ceremonial occasions, such as graduation ceremonies), the pro chancellor does have a substantial role, as chair of the council of a university, with overall responsibility for its financial and other non-academic affairs. It is usually a part-time appointment, often held by people distinguished in the world outside university, such as lawyers and business people.

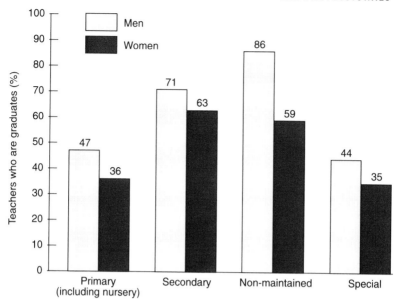

Figure 7.8   Percentages of men and women teachers who are graduates, in different types of school, United Kingdom 1991–2
(Adapted from GSS, 1994, Table 9)

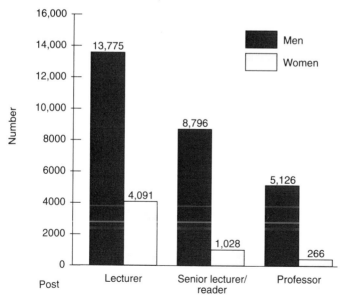

Figure 7.9   Numbers of men and women teaching staff in universities, Great Britain 1992–3
(Adapted from Universities' Statistical Record, 1993, Vol. 1, Table 28)
Note: The former polytechnics and colleges are not included

Vice chancellor (VC)

Again, the vice chancellor is nominally a deputy to the chancellor, but in reality is the chief academic and administrative officer of a university, in charge of its day-to-day running (though he or she also stands in for the chancellor on ceremonial occasions). He or she controls and coordinates the activities of committees and planning boards, oversees the working of academic departments and liaises with outside bodies. This is a full-time appointment, and in most universities a permanent one, though some (notably Oxford, Cambridge and London) elect their vice-chancellors for a period of several years at a time.

Principal

The chief academic and administrative officer of a Scottish university, he or she is usually styled 'principal and vice chancellor', the latter title used when standing in for the chancellor on ceremonial occasions. (The University of London has both a principal and a vice chancellor.)

Pro vice chancellor

Some universities now have deputy or pro vice chancellors, who chair major committees and stand in for the vice chancellors. These posts are often held for a limited term by senior academic members of the university.

Rector

A rector is the chair of the university court (the main finance committee) of one of the ancient Scottish universities. Elected by the students for a term of several years, rectors have been less exclusively drawn than most other senior officers of universities from 'establishment' circles: they have included a communist trade union leader and several television personalities, such as Malcolm Muggeridge, John Cleese and Muriel Gray. Most treat the position as purely ceremonial, but they can actively preside over their courts' proceedings if they choose, and in recent years a number have done so.

Master

A traditional title for the head of a college in Oxford and Cambridge Universities (and occasionally elsewhere).

Dean

A dean is the head of a faculty, such as a faculty of science, or a faculty of arts. A deanship may be a permanent appointment, or a temporary one held for a limited term by senior academic members of the faculty. The duties and powers of deans vary from university to university.

Professor

This is the highest purely academic appointment. Professors are responsible for conducting and promoting teaching and research in their subjects. A post as professor – known for historical reasons as a 'chair' – may be *established* or *personal*. An established chair is a permanent post in a university: when one occupant leaves it, another will normally be appointed in his or her place. A personal chair is conferred on a particular individual, usually for distinguished scholarship, research and published work, and continues only as long as his or her academic career. Traditionally, professors were the heads of academic departments. Often they still are, but in recent years it has become common for other senior academics to act as heads of departments, sometimes in rotation.

Reader

A reader engages in teaching and research. Like a personal chair, a readership is usually conferred on an individual for merit in scholarship, research and published work. In status, it lies between a professorship and a senior lectureship, but is equivalent to the latter in duties (and salary scale).

Senior lecturer

A senior lecturer engages in teaching and research. The criteria for promotion from lecturer are not clearly defined, but are generally concerned with qualities in teaching, research and, sometimes, administration. There is no sharp division of duties between senior lecturer and lecturer, but a senior lecturer is, in general, more likely than a lecturer to hold a post such as dean or head of department, or to chair university committees.

Lecturer

Lecturers engage in teaching and research. Despite their title, lecturers' teaching does not consist only, or even mainly, of giving lectures. They also hold tutorials and seminars, and comment on students' written work, as well as setting and marking examinations. (Lecturers at the Open University do not normally give lectures at all; they produce correspondence material for their students, as well as working with BBC colleagues on the production of radio and television programmes.) Most universities have no formal qualifications for the post of lecturer, but in practice, lecturers almost always have a good honours degree, and usually a higher degree and research experience.

In addition, there are sometimes temporary posts such as 'teaching fellow' or 'tutorial assistant', which are available for a limited period.

As well as the academic posts above, which carry responsibilities for both teaching and research, universities also have posts with research duties alone. Research posts often have short-term contracts and are rarely held on a tenured basis. They are increasingly being funded by external sources, such as industry. Definitions of different levels of appointment are varied and sometimes imprecise, but two broad levels can be distinguished:

Research fellow or research officer

People who hold these posts are deemed able to carry out research without supervision. They generally have a higher degree.

Research associate or research assistant
The work of research associates and assistants is carried out under supervision, sometimes as part of a research team. They are often allowed (and expected) to spend part of their time studying for a higher degree.

The former polytechnics had a similar, though not identical hierarchy of posts, though they were too recently established to have acquired the more colourful historic positions and titles of the universities. Now that they have acquired university status, however, many have adopted, or are adopting, some of the traditional university posts and job titles (such as vice chancellor and professor). At present, there is some confusion of nomenclature since some titles (for example, senior lecturer) have different meanings in the older universities and in the former polytechnics.

SOURCES AND FURTHER READING

CIPFA (no single date) *Financial Information Services*, Vol. 20, *Education*, London: CIPFA.
CIPFA (1991) *Local Government Trends 1990*, London: CIPFA.
CSO (1994) *Social Trends*, No. 24, London: HMSO.
DES (no date) *Statistics of Education: Teachers 1989 and 1990*, London: DES.
DFE (1993) *Circular 7/93: Inspecting Schools: a guide to the inspection provisions of the Education (Schools) Act 1992 in England*, London: DFE.
DFE (1994) *School Teachers' Pay and Conditions Document 1994*, London: HMSO.
DFE/OFSTED (1994) *Departmental Report/The Government's Expenditure Plans 1994–95 to 1996–97*, Cm 2510, London: HMSO.
Gordon, P. and Lawton, D. (1984) *A Guide to English Educational Terms*, London: Batsford.
GSS (1994) *Educational Statistics for the United Kingdom 1993*, London: HMSO.
Marker, W. B. (1994) *The Scottish Education System*, Edinburgh: Open University Scottish Region.
New Society Database (1986) Teachers' Pay, *New Society*, 31 October 1986.
OPCS (1982) *Census 1981: County Reports*, London: HMSO.
Ranger, C. (1988) *Ethnic Minority Teachers*, London: Commission for Racial Equality.
Rowntree, D. (1981) *A Dictionary of Education*, London: Harper and Row.
Universities' Statistical Record (1993) *University Statistics 1992–93: Vol. 1: Students and Staff*, Cheltenham: Universities' Statistical Record.
Welsh Office/Office of Her Majesty's Chief Inspector of Schools in Wales (1994) *The Government's Expenditure Plans 1994–95 to 1996–97: Departmental Report by the Welsh Office and the Office of Her Majesty's Chief Inspector of Schools in Wales*, Cm 2515, London: HMSO.

The funding of education in Great Britain (though not in Northern Ireland: see below) is shared between central and local government, in a fairly similar manner from country to country. Here, we first outline the English system, and then note some of the more significant differences in Scotland, Wales and Northern Ireland.

ENGLAND

PART I WHERE THE MONEY COMES FROM

The financing of education is shared between central and local government. Most of central government's contribution is indirect, consisting of grants to local authorities. Its direct expenditure is mainly for further and higher education. The local authorities' educational expenditure forms about 40% of their total expenditure; it is mainly on schools.

> **F A C T** In 1993–4, central government's direct expenditure on education was an estimated £6.5 billion, of which about 43% was for higher education, and 42% for further education. Local authorities' expenditure on education amounted to £16 billion, 76% of it on schools and approximately 9% on further education (DFE and OFSTED, 1994, Tables 1–3).

After the 1988 Education Reform Act and the 1992 and 1993 Education Acts, the local authorities' share of educational expenditure has diminished and will probably continue to diminish, though it is impossible to predict by how much. Under the terms of the Acts, further education and what used to be LEA-controlled higher education are now removed entirely from the control of LEAs, and are financed directly by central government – as are grant-maintained schools. As yet, these schools account for only a small amount of annual expenditure – an estimated £155 million in 1993–4 – but the govern-ment's expenditure plans provide for this sum to increase (to £593 million in 1996–7) as more schools choose to 'opt out' of LEA control and financing. If enough primary or secondary schools in the area served by an LEA become grant maintained, the Secretary of State may transfer some or all of the LEA's educational planning functions to the Funding Agency for Schools (see Chapter 4: 1993 Education Act; Chapter 6). In addition, the 1988 Act has reduced the LEAs' control even over those educational functions and services that they continue to finance (see Local Management of Schools below).

In principle, the creation of City Technology Colleges, entirely independent of LEAs, also diminishes the LEAs' control over education. In practice, however, only 15 CTCs have been created, accounting for an estimated £49 million of public funds in 1993–4. The official projections for future spending – £59 million in 1996–7 – suggest that the government does not anticipate a dramatic increase in the size of the CTC sector (DFE and OFSTED, 1994, Table 1).

Local government finance

Since 1993, the local authorities' money comes from three main sources. The first is the local community, through the Council Tax, the level of which is set by each local authority (though subject to 'capping' by central government). The second is central government, mainly in the form of a Revenue Support Grant (RSG). The third lies somewhere in between local and national revenue: the National Non-domestic Rate (or 'uniform business rate'), the level of which is set nationally and the proceeds of which are pooled nationally and distributed to local authorities in proportion to their populations. A small amount of money is also raised through fees and other charges, but this income is insignificant as a proportion of expenditure in the education service, unlike other services such as housing.

> **F A C T**   About half of local authority expenditure in England is financed by central government grants, an estimated 55% for 1994–5, of which 43% is Revenue Support Grant, and 12% grants for specific purposes. The rest is revenue raised by local authorities themselves – for 1994–5, an estimated 20% from Council Tax and 25% from business rates (Dept. of the Environment, 1994, Figure 107).

Each year, the government assesses the amount of expenditure it considers that each authority will require in order to provide a standard level of services. This takes into account the particular needs of the authority: some areas will have particularly high numbers of old people, for instance, or underprivileged groups, or bad housing, which require higher spending for the same level of services. Then, taking into account the resources of the authority, and the revenue available to it from the National Non-domestic Rate, the government decides how much Revenue Support Grant it will give, and how much revenue it considers should be raised by the authority itself through Council Tax.

However, a local authority decides its own level of Council Tax: it is not committed to following the government's recommendation. Of all the main sources of finance, only the level of Council Tax is within the control of the local authorities. Thus, any decision by an authority to spend more or less on services than the government's assumed level will be reflected directly in the level of tax it has to set. According to the government, this improves the accountability of local authorities to their electorate.

During the 1980s, the government introduced elaborate procedures to control the spending of local authorities, initially by financially penalising those authorities that exceeded the amount the government thought they should spend, and ultimately by imposing limits on the amount of revenue a re-calcitrant authority could raise ('rate capping') (see the first edition of *The Education Fact File*). This was necessary, the government argued, because the local authorities were not effectively accountable to anyone for their spending, as their rate-payers formed too small a proportion of their electorate. Under the current system, such controls should not be so necessary. Nevertheless, the Secretary of State for the Environment is empowered to 'cap' the tax levels set by local authorities whose levels of Council Tax he or she considers excessive. In 1993–4, the first year of operation of the current system, he used these powers to reduce the tax levied by three authorities.

Local management of schools

Under the terms of the 1988 Education Reform Act, the LEAs continue (subject to such constraints as Council Tax capping) to set the overall, authority-wide budget for schools under their control (known as the 'general schools budget'). But thereafter, the powers of LEAs are now greatly restricted.

First, they are required to distribute most (around three-quarters) of these funds (the 'aggregated schools budget') between schools strictly and even-handedly according to a formula, to be devised by each LEA but requiring approval by the DFE. An acceptable formula is expected to make each school's 'budget share' depend mainly on the numbers of pupils in the school, but also to take into account such factors as the ages of the children, the subjects they are studying, and the numbers with special needs; and also perhaps the levels of social advantage and disadvantage in the community the school serves. The intention is that an LEA will not be able to favour particular schools, or to use the granting and withholding of funds as a means of enforcing policies, or of promoting some educational practices and discouraging others (except to a marginal extent with some limited discretionary funds that can be kept outside the aggregated budget).

Secondly, the LEAs are required to delegate many of their responsibilities for the management and control of the schools' budget share, and for the appointment and dismissal of staff, to the governing bodies of the schools. The members of a governing body may in their turn delegate most of these responsibilities to the head teacher, or they may choose to discharge them themselves. In either case, decisions about spending priorities – e.g. on staffing as against computers, or educational visits as against redecoration – and about the hiring and firing of teachers, will now be made at the level of the school itself, not by the LEA.

This system, known as the Local Management of Schools (LMS), is intended to provide increased accountability, and therefore efficiency. A school's funding now depends above all on its pupil numbers, and open enrolment under the 1988 Act (see Chapter 4) allows parents much wider choice of school for their children to attend. Schools will therefore be liable to lose pupils and funds if they fail to satisfy parents. This, the government believes, will make schools more directly and effectively accountable to parents, and more responsive to their criticisms and wishes.

Capital expenditure

Spending by both central and local government is of two types: current and capital. Current expenditure covers day-to-day items such as salaries and services; capital expenditure covers items with a longer term use, such as buildings and machinery. About 96% of local authorities' educational expenditure for 1993–4 was current, and 4% capital (DFE and OFSTED, 1994, Table 3).

The amount that local authorities can raise and spend on capital items is subject to controls by central government. Here, too, a new system has recently been introduced, this time in the 1989 Local Government and Housing Act. Under this system, the government still controls the total capital expenditure of local authorities, but now allows the authorities almost complete freedom to decide their own priorities within that overall sum. Local authorities now have four main sources of funds for capital expenditure: *borrowing*, which is subject to approval by central government; *capital grants*, from central government, which will specify the purposes for which they are to be used, and the amount the local authority must itself contribute; *capital receipts*, from the sale of assets such as land and council houses, though the local authorities must first set aside 50% of these receipts (75% in the case of council house sales) towards repaying their debts; and *ordinary revenue* from the Council Tax, for which the government assumes the local authorities to be accountable to their voters (CIPFA, no single date, Chapter 3; HM Treasury, 1990, Chapter 21, paras. 4.8–4.10).

Direct government funding

In addition to its indirect funding of schools through local authorities, its direct funding of higher education and such programmes as the Assisted Places Scheme (see p. 186), the government provides some direct funding for education through various departments in addition to the Department for Education – including the Home Office and above all the Employment Department.

Under Section 11 of the 1966 Local Government Act, local authorities can apply to the Home Office for 75% of the costs of employing extra staff for educational (and other) purposes in areas with large numbers of Commonwealth immigrants for whom special provision is required because of differences in languages or customs. In 1993–4, an estimated £125 million was spent under this arrangement on education (CIPFA, 1993, Appendix B).

Much of the responsibility for education and training related to employment rests with the Training, Enterprise and Education Directorate (TEED) of the Employment Department. Its main current training programmes (see Chapter 12), and their estimated expenditure for 1993–4 are:

- *Employment Training* (ET) – £762 million;
- *Youth Training* (YT) – £520 million;
- *Youth Credits* (YC) – £122 million;
- the *Technical and Vocational Education Initiative* (TVEI) – £119 million;
- *Work-related Further Education* (WRFE) – £105 million.

The TEED's total spending on these and other, smaller programmes for 1993–4 was an estimated £1.8 billion (EDG, 1994, Table 4).

Funding of further education

From 1993, the funding of further education was transferred from LEAs to central government, through the Further Education Funding Council (see Chapter 4: 1992 Further and Higher Education Act, and Chapter 5). For 1993–4, the first full year of its operation, the expenditure of the FEFC is an estimated £2.7 billion, 94% of it being current expenditure (DFE and OFSTED, 1994, Table 1).

Funding of higher education

From 1993, the funding of higher education was unified. The Universities Funding Council and the Polytechnics and Colleges Funding Council were replaced by a unitary Higher Education Funding Council, funded by central government (see Chapter 4: 1992 Further and Higher Education Act, and Chapter 5). LEAs are immediately responsible for student grants, and thus for that proportion of the funding of higher education institutions that comes from tuition fees – an increasing proportion: see below – but the costs of mandatory grants to undergraduate students are reimbursed by central government. For 1993–4, the first year of its operation, the expenditure of the HEFC is an estimated £2.8 billion, 89% of it being current expenditure. Central government also paid £2.7 billion to LEAs to meet the cost of mandatory student awards, and £283 million in student loans. LEAs paid a further £222 million in discretionary awards (DFE and OFSTED, 1994, Tables 1 and 3).

Regardless of these administrative arrangements, institutions of higher education have received and continue to receive their money from two main sources: *direct funding* from central or local government, and *student fees*, which are themselves usually covered by mandatory or discretionary grants from LEAs.

In 1989–90, the UFC received £1.9 billion and the PCFC £1.1 billion in government funds. Local authorities paid a further £1.1 billion in mandatory and discretionary student awards (HM Treasury, 1990, Tables 11.1 and 11.2).

From 1990–1, however, the government altered the balance between these methods of finance, more than doubling the undergraduate tuition fees and correspondingly reducing the direct funding of higher education institutions. The fees are payable by local authorities, who are reimbursed for their extra expenditure. This change is intended to improve the performance of the institutions, by making their funding depend more on their ability to attract students in competition with one another. The change is reflected in the figures for 1992–3, the last year in which the UFC and the PCFC operated, though these figures are also affected by a substantial increase in student numbers (see Chapter 5). In 1992–3, the UFC received £1.8 billion and the PCFC £1.0 billion. Central government grants to LEAs to cover students' mandatory awards amounted to £2.5 billion (DFE and OFSTED, 1994, Table 1).

Also from 1990–1, the government introduced a new system of undergraduate student loans to supplement grants. The grants were initially frozen at their existing level, while the loans are to rise in line with inflation until they reach the level of the grant. Then the two will be kept equal, and allowed to rise together in line with inflation. A loan will be repayable when the student's earnings reach a level of 85% of the national average wage, and a period of 5 to 10 years allowed for the repayment (CIPFA, 1989, p. 17). In 1993–4, expenditure on mandatory grants in England and Wales was £1 billion and on student loans £166 million. By 1996–7, according to government plans, expenditure on grants will have fallen to £945 million, and that on loans will have risen to £898 million (DFE and OFSTED, 1994, Table 19).

In-service training of teachers

Since 1991–2, funds for the in-service training of teachers, and for education support and training more generally, have been covered by the Grants for Education Support and Training (GEST) programme. Since 1992–3, local authorities have been required to devolve the spending of an increasing proportion of GEST funds to schools; at present they must devolve about a third of the funds.

For 1994–5, the total expenditure on GEST is planned to be £271 million. Of this, 57% is for support and training in connection with the national curriculum and its assessment, 21% with school management and appraisal, 9% with special educational needs, 5% with truancy and disaffected pupils, and the rest (8%) for a number of smaller programmes (DFE and OFSTED, 1994, para. 89 and Table 10).

Unofficial parental contributions

In addition to their official funding, a number of schools receive cash payments and other gifts from parents of their pupils. These contributions are not shown in official statistics of educational expenditure, but in 1990 an attempt was made to quantify them by the *Mail on Sunday*, which commissioned a survey of a representative sample of primary schools by the National Foundation for Educational Research. Overall, the researchers estimated, parents contributed some £40 million per annum to primary schools in England and Wales. But this total sum was distributed very unevenly among the schools. At one extreme, 6% of primary schools received less than £1 per child, and a further 21% less than £5; at the other extreme, 3% of schools received over £50 per child and 0.2% over £100. (The highest figure found for an individual school was £248 per child.) In about 13% of schools, the money contributed by parents amounted to more than the schools' official funding from their LEAs.

Of this money, 18% was spent on computers – the largest single item of expenditure. A further 14% was spent on books, and other major items were educational visits, decoration and maintenance, science equipment and furniture (Lightfoot, 1990).

PART 2   WHERE THE MONEY GOES

Overall spending on education

Education is one of the largest consumers of public money: the total expenditure on education in 1992–3 by central and local government in England was an estimated £26.2 billion, some 13% of the total spending on all services. Only Social Security and Health had more spent on them. Figure 8.1 shows public expenditure for 1992–3 on the highest spending services.

Within the education service, estimated expenditure in 1993–4 planned by the DFE (most of it actually spent by LEAs) is divided as shown in Figure 8.2.

Of the £16.0 billion (59%) spent on schools, nearly all (£15.5 billion) is current expenditure by LEAs. This is divided as shown in Figure 8.3.

By contrast, since the 1988 and 1992 Acts, two-thirds of expenditure on further and higher education is current expenditure by central government, nearly all through the Further Education and Higher Education Funding Councils.

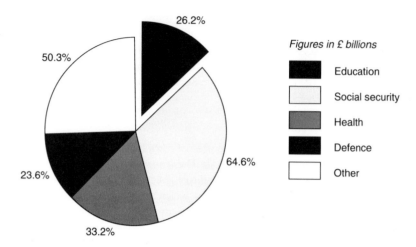

Figures in £ billions

■ Education
□ Social security
▨ Health
■ Defence
□ Other

Figure 8.1   Expenditure on major services (by government departmental responsibility: central and local government expenditure combined) England, 1992–3 (Adapted from HM Treasury, 1994, Tables 3.1 and 4.3)

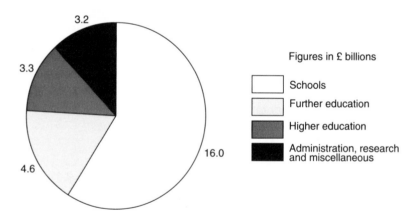

Figures in £ billions

□ Schools
□ Further education
▨ Higher education
■ Administration, research and miscellaneous

Figure 8.2   DFE and English LEA spending, 1993–4 (Adapted from DFE and OFSTED, 1994, Tables 1 and 3)

Taking all sectors together, LEA gross expenditure is divided among various categories as shown in Figure 8.4.

Trends over time in overall spending

Expenditure on education has increased fairly steadily over the last few years, even in 'real terms' after inflation is taken into account, as Figure 8.5 shows.

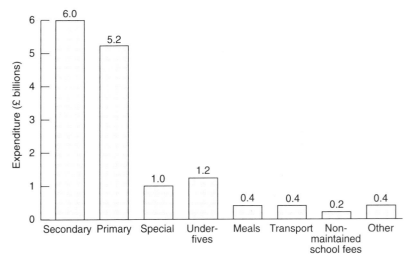

Figure 8.3   English LEA current expenditure on schools, 1993–4 (estimated)
(Adapted from DFE and OFSTED, 1994, Table 3)

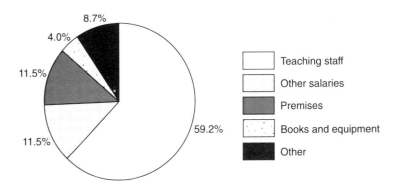

Figure 8.4   Percentage of LEA total gross expenditure in major categories, England and Wales, 1991–2
(Adapted from CIPFA, 1993, Figure 7)

However, as a percentage of total government expenditure, spending on education remained fairly constant over the 1980s and early 1990s, as Figure 8.6 shows. Furthermore, educational spending declined in the 1980s as a percentage of the gross domestic product (GDP) – from 5.5% of the United Kingdom GDP in 1980–1 to 3.6% in 1991–2 (CIPFA, 1993, Figure 6).

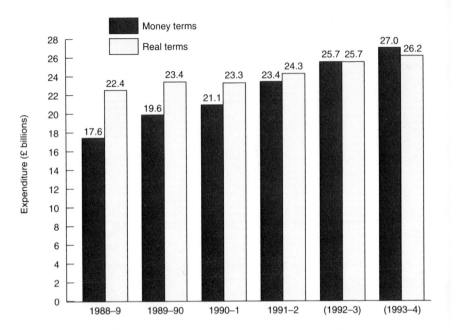

Figure 8.5   Total expenditure on education by central and local government and OFSTED,
England, 1988–9 to 1993–4, in money terms and real terms
(Adapted from DFE/OFSTED, 1994, Table 2)
Note: The 'real terms' figures are expressed in 1992–3 values using official estimates of
inflation; the 1992–3 figures are provisional, and those for 1993–4 are estimates

Expenditure per pupil or student

Educational expenditure is often expressed in terms of the amount spent per
pupil or student. This figure is known as the 'unit cost', and is arrived at simply
by dividing the total amount spent on a service (e.g. nursery schools) by the
number of children using it (expressed as 'full-time equivalents', so that two
part-time children could count as one full-time equivalent). Unit costs vary
considerably between different sectors of the education system, as is shown by
Figure 8.7. The Chartered Institute of Public Finance and Accountancy no
longer publishes such unit cost figures for special schools, on the grounds that
there is too much variation according to the precise nature of a child's disability
for such averages to have much meaning (see CIPFA, 1993, p. 9). When they
did publish these figures (e.g. CIPFA, 1990) the unit costs for special schools
were approximately twice as high as for secondary schools (over 16).
    Unit costs may be broken down further into the amounts spent on teachers,
books and equipment, ancillary staff, transport, and so on. Teachers' salaries

account for the largest proportion of education spending (just under 70%) in all types of school. A further 12% is spent on other staff, 13% on premises (including heating and lighting) and 4% on books and equipment (CIPFA, 1993, Table 7).

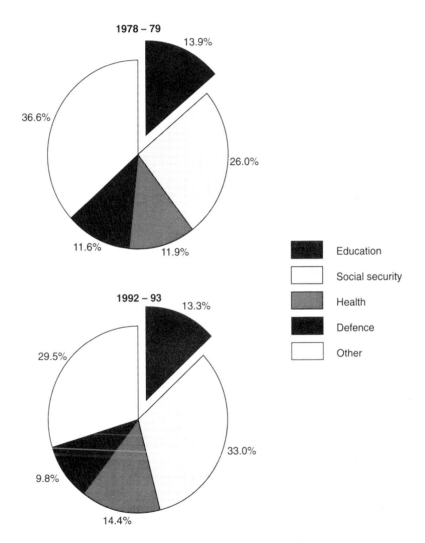

Figure 8.6   Percentage of public expenditure devoted to major functions, United Kingdom, 1978–9 and 1992–3
(Adapted from HM Treasury, 1994, Table 1.2)

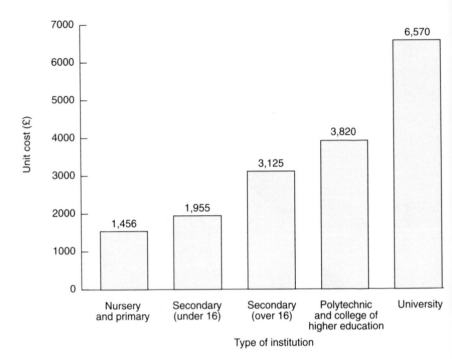

*Figure 8.7   Unit costs (per pupil or student per annum) of education, England, 1991–2
(Adapted from CIPFA, 1993, Table 7; DFE, 1993c, Table 3)*
Note: These figures include direct and indirect costs of providing tuition, but exclude costs
of transport, school meals and milk, central administration and financing of capital
expenditure. The university figure is for Great Britain; it and the polytechnic etc. figure
predate the unification of the funding of higher education. For universities, the costs cover
the research as well as the teaching duties of lecturers.

Regional variations in expenditure per pupil

There is considerable variation between regions in the amount spent per pupil,
as indicated in Figure 8.8. Unit costs in metropolitan authorities have been
consistently higher than in the shire counties. This is partly because of higher
rates and premises costs and the London weighting in salaries, and partly
because of the extra demands placed on the education service by inner-city
characteristics, such as high unemployment, widespread poverty and a greater
diversity of cultures and languages.

At the level of individual LEAs outside London, differences in spending
ranged from £1249 (Suffolk) to £1634 (Oxfordshire) per primary school child
in 1991–2, and from £1776 (Gloucestershire) to £2492 (Nottinghamshire) per
secondary school pupil (CIPFA, 1993, pp. 59 and 61).

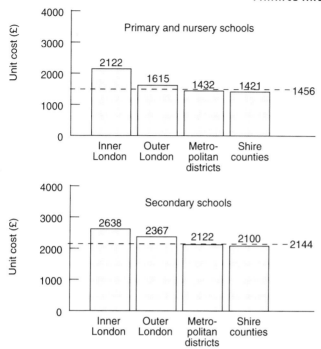

Figure 8.8   Unit costs (per pupil per annum) of education, for different types of school in different regions, England, 1991–2
(Adapted from CIPFA, 1993)

There are also regional variations in the proportions of the unit cost that is spent on different items. Figure 8.9 shows the range of spending on books and equipment.

Trends over time in unit costs

Unit costs for maintained schools have risen in real terms throughout the 1980s – by 50% between 1979–80 and 1991–2. This is only partly explained by a fall in pupil numbers over the same period of 15%. (If overall expenditure had remained the same in real terms, a fall in pupil numbers of 15% would have led to a rise in unit costs of 18% (DFE and OFSTED, 1994, Tables 4 and A).)

An increase in unit costs does not necessarily mean that a pupil gets proportionately more resources or better educational provision, as some costs are fixed (such as heating and cleaning) and they simply rise for each pupil as the school roll falls. However, spending per child on books and educational equipment did increase in real terms in the same period by 51%. In 1991–2 spending on books and educational equipment was £70 per child. The comparable figure for 1978–9, adjusted to 1991–2 values, would have been £46. Spending per child on books and equipment is much higher in secondary than in primary schools.

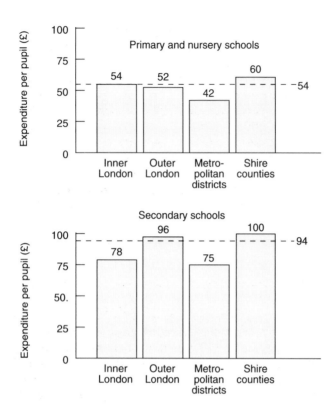

Figure 8.9   Expenditure per pupil on books and educational equipment in different regions, England, 1991–2
(Adapted from CIPFA, 1993, pp. 60 and 62)

By contrast, unit costs in higher education have fallen in real terms during the same period – by 45% in universities and 33% in polytechnics and colleges (HM Treasury, 1990, Table 11.16; DFE and OFSTED, 1994, Table 18).

Pupil/teacher ratio and class size

Another measure of the resources available in education is the pupil/teacher ratio (PTR), calculated by dividing the number of pupils by the number of qualified teachers or full-time teacher equivalents. It is lower in private than in maintained schools (i.e. there are fewer pupils per teacher), and it is lowest of all in special schools. As schools rolls have declined, the PTR has fallen.

Although the PTR is the measure on which decisions about resource allocation are often based, it is the size of the class as taught which has greater implications for children's learning experience. Class sizes are generally larger than PTRs, because not all teachers actually teach (heads, for instance, spend most of their time on administrative work), because marking and preparation duties restrict direct contact hours with pupils, and because sometimes classes are combined or split up for various periods.

Changes over time, and variations between different countries of the United Kingdom in PTRs are illustrated in Chapter 5 (see especially Figures 5.8 and 5.12). There is also variation between LEAs. For example, the PTR in English primary schools in 1993 varied from just over 17 to 1 in the London Borough of Westminster to 24 to 1 or more in Newham, Rochdale, Tameside and Staffordshire. And the PTR in English secondary schools in 1993 varied from 13 to 1 in the London Borough of Kensington and Chelsea to almost 18 to 1 in Northumberland. (The very lowest PTRs of any English LEA were in the Isles of Scilly and the City of London, but they each had only around 300 and 200 pupils respectively in total (DFE, 1994).)

School meals and milk

In 1980, responsibility for the provision of school meals passed from central government to the LEAs. They were initially required to provide free meals for children in families receiving Supplementary Benefit, and to provide a place for children to eat food they brought from home, but otherwise the level, type and price of provision, if any, was left to the discretion of the individual LEA. By 1986, however, all obligations on LEAs to provide meals were removed, and their powers to supply free meals reduced. (See Chapter 4: 1980 Education Act; 1986 Social Security Act.) Most authorities now operate a cafeteria system in secondary schools, although a fixed-price system is still more common in primary schools. The average cost of a primary school meal in 1988–9 ranged from 62p in metropolitan districts to 69p in shire counties; and that of a secondary school meal from 63p in metropolitan districts to 75p in shire counties (CIPFA, no single date, Table 20.10.1).

About half of the pupils in maintained schools take school meals, with the rest bringing their own food or making other arrangements (mostly going home for lunch). In 1986, some authorities provided no canteen facilities at all (e.g. Buckinghamshire), while in other authorities a substantial proportion of children took paid school meals (e.g. Derbyshire, with 56%). There is also considerable variation in the proportion of pupils receiving free school meals. The average in England and Wales in 1989–90 was 11%, but this figure masks variations, from 26% in the then ILEA to 6% in the Outer London boroughs. Some of the variation is due to differences in LEA policies and some to socioeconomic variation between the local populations. Figure 8.10 shows the national averages for various ways of taking meals at school.

Local education authorities' expenditure on meals and milk fell from 5.9% of recurrent expenditure in 1979–80 to 2.8% in 1989–90 (CIPFA, no single date, Table 20.10.2).

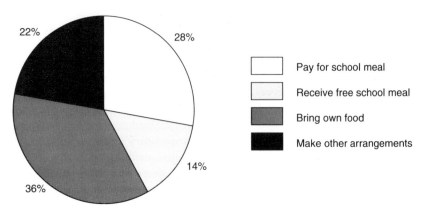

Figure 8.10   Types of meals at school, maintained schools, England, January 1992
(Adapted from DFE, 1993, Table A14/92)

SCOTLAND

Expenditure on education in Scotland is the responsibility, directly or indirectly (through influence on local authorities) of the Secretary of State for
Scotland. Together with such services as health, roads and transport, law and
order and housing, it falls within a category of spending programmes known as
the Scottish Block. The Block comprised over 97% of all expenditure within
the Secretary of State's responsibility in 1992–3. (The remaining 3%, though
formally within his responsibility too, was in practice for programmes determined by United Kingdom or European Community policies.) The total
Scottish Block is calculated each year by simply adopting the changes in
expenditure agreed for comparable programmes in England, adjusted for the
differences in population.

The Secretary of State then decides how to distribute this total among
individual services. In 1992–3, total expenditure in the Scottish Block was an
estimated £12.2 billion. Of this, £595 million was allocated to the central
government's (i.e. the Scottish Office's) own direct expenditure on education.
But this sum – under 6% of the Block – represents only a small part of spending
from the Block on education in Scotland. Much more money comes from it to
education in the shape of the funds allocated by the Secretary of State to local
authorities, mainly through the Revenue Support Grant and the distribution of
money raised from non-domestic rates: a total of £5.2 billion in 1992–3. The
local authorities decide how to distribute this money among the various
services they provide – together with the money they themselves raise from
Council Tax – but the Secretary of State each year indicates in advance what he
thinks their spending ought to be to provide a standard level of service. The
authorities need not follow his recommendations, but like his counterparts in

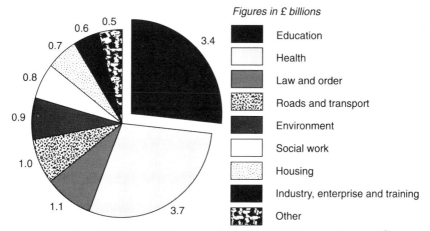

Figures in £ billions

- Education
- Health
- Law and order
- Roads and transport
- Environment
- Social work
- Housing
- Industry, enterprise and training
- Other

Figure 8.11   Scottish Office expenditure on major services (including central support of local authority expenditure), 1992–3
(Adapted from Scottish Office/Forestry Commission, 1994, Tables 1.3, 8.5 and 8.7)

England and Wales, he has powers to cap their Council Tax levels if he judges that they are overspending. For 1994–5, the total local authority spending necessary has been assessed at £5.9 billion, of which spending on education is £2.3 billion (39%).

The actual spending on education and other major services in 1992–3 by the Scottish Office (including support to local authorities) is shown in Figure 8.11. Only Health was a bigger spender than education; other services had much less money spent on them. (The spending in Scotland of the Department of Social Security and the Ministry of Defence is not included here.) Most of the educational expenditure (about 80%) was support for local authority current expenditure, and most of that (about two-thirds) was for wages and salaries. The remainder of the total educational expenditure in 1992–3 was direct spending by the Scottish Office, mostly on higher education: student awards and grants to higher education institutions (Scottish Office/Forestry Commission, 1994, Chapters 1, 6 and 8).

WALES

As in Scotland, the expenditure nominally under the control of the Secretary of State for Wales is partly determined by United Kingdom and European Union policies (just under 4%, mainly on agriculture, fisheries and food), but mostly (96%, known as the Welsh Office Block) more genuinely under his or her control. The total Welsh Office Block, and its distribution among the different services, are calculated each year by simply adopting the changes in expenditure agreed for comparable programmes in England, adjusted for the differences in population.

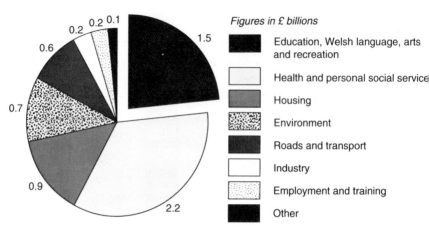

Figure 8.12   Expenditure on major services in Wales (Welsh Office and local authorities combined), 1992–3
(Adapted from Welsh Office etc., 1994, Figures 1.02 and 1.03)

In 1992–3, total expenditure in the Welsh Office Block was £5.8 billion, of which £142 million was allocated to the Welsh Office's direct spending on education. But this sum – under 3% of the Block – represents only a small part of spending from the Block on education in Wales. Much more money comes from it to education as funds allocated by the Secretary of State to local authorities, mainly through the Revenue Support Grant and the distribution of money raised from non-domestic rates: a total of £2.2 billion in 1992–3. The local authorities decide how to distribute this money among the various services they provide – together with the money they themselves raise from Council Tax – but the Secretary of State each year indicates what he thinks their spending should be to provide a standard level of service. The authorities need not follow his advice, but the levels of Revenue Support Grant are calculated on the assumption that they will, and like his counterparts in England and Scotland, he has powers to cap their Council Tax levels if he judges that they are overspending (Welsh Office etc., 1994, Ch. 1).

Expenditure on education and other major services in 1992–3 is shown in Figure 8.12 for the Welsh Office and local authorities combined. As in the rest of the United Kingdom, education is one of the highest spenders; only health spends more. (Of the category 'education, Welsh language, arts and recreation', education accounts for over 80% of the spending. Social security and defence are not part of the Welsh Office Block.)

Of the Welsh Office's direct expenditure on education, just under a third is on higher education, just over 10% on educational support and training (mostly in-service training of teachers) and just under 10% on schools (now including grant-maintained schools) (Welsh Office etc., 1994, Ch. 5).

NORTHERN IRELAND

As with public expenditure in Great Britain, the total Northern Ireland public expenditure and its division between services are announced in the government's annual expenditure plans. In 1992–3 expenditure on the major services

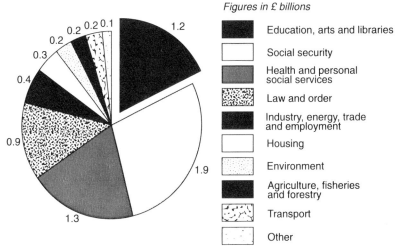

Figures in £ billions

- Education, arts and libraries
- Social security
- Health and personal social services
- Law and order
- Industry, energy, trade and employment
- Housing
- Environment
- Agriculture, fisheries and forestry
- Transport
- Other

Figure 8.13   Northern Ireland Office expenditure on major services, 1992–3 (Adapted from Northern Ireland Office Department of Finance and Personnel/HM Treasury, 1994, Table 1.1)

Note: Expenditure does not include that on the army in Northern Ireland

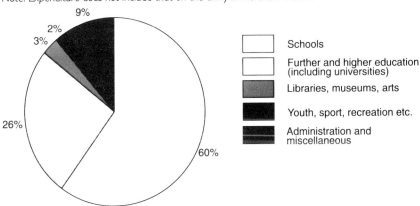

- Schools
- Further and higher education (including universities)
- Libraries, museums, arts
- Youth, sport, recreation etc.
- Administration and miscellaneous

Figure 8.14   Expenditure by DENI (including that by Education and Library Boards) on main groups of services, 1992–3 (Adapted from Northern Ireland Department of Finance and Personnel/HM Treasury, 1994, Table 8.1)

was as shown in Figure 8.13. As in the rest of the United Kingdom, education is one of the highest spenders; only health and social security spend more.

Unlike those in the rest of the United Kingdom, Northern Ireland's local educational authorities, the Education and Library Boards, receive all their funding from central government, here, the Department of Education Northern Ireland (DENI). The percentages of the total expenditure of the DENI and boards allocated to their five main groups of services are shown in Figure 8.14.

SOURCES AND FURTHER READING

CIPFA (no single date) *Financial Information Services*, Vol. 20, London: CIPFA.

CIPFA (1989) *Education Statistics: 1989–90 Estimates*, London: CIPFA.

CIPFA (1990) *Handbook of Education Unit Costs 1987/88*, London: CIPFA.

CIPFA (1993) *Education Statistics: 1991–92 Actuals, incorporating the Handbook of Education Unit Costs*, London: CIPFA.

DFE (1994) *Statistical Bulletin 3/94: Pupil-teacher ratios and information on the length of the taught week for each local education authority in England*, London: DFE.

DFE and OFSTED (1994) *Departmental Report/The Government's Expenditure Plans 1994–95 to 1996–97*, Cm 2510, London: HMSO.

Department of the Environment (1994) *Annual Report 1994/The Government's Expenditure Plans 1994–95 to 1996–97*, Cm 2507, London: HMSO.

Department of Finance and Personnel (Northern Ireland Office)/HM Treasury (1994) *Northern Ireland Expenditure Plans and Priorities: The Government's Expenditure Plans 1994–95 to 1996–97*, Cm 2516, London: HMSO.

EDG (1994) *Departmental Report: The Government's Expenditure Plans 1994–95 to 1996–97*, Cm 2505, London: HMSO.

HM Treasury (1990) *The Government's Expenditure Plans 1990–91 to 1992–93*, London: HMSO.

HM Treasury (1994) *Public Expenditure: Statistical Supplement to the Financial Statement and Budget Report 1994–95*, Cm 2519, London: HMSO.

Lightfoot, L. (1990) 'Scandal of our schools', *The Mail on Sunday*, 27 May 1990, pp. 1–2.

Scottish Office/Forestry Commission (1994) *Serving Scotland's Needs: the Government's Expenditure Plans 1994–95 to 1996–97*, Cm 2514, Edinburgh: HMSO.

Welsh Office and the Office of Her Majesty's Chief Inspector of Schools in Wales (1994) *The Government's Expenditure Plans 1994–95 to 1996–97: a report by the Welsh Office and the Office of Her Majesty's Chief Inspector of Schools in Wales*, Cm 2515, London: HMSO.

Qualifications are of many different kinds and levels. Some are predominantly academic, others vocational. Some are normally obtained through study at school, some through further or higher education, and some at the workplace. Courses leading to qualifications up to and including A level or its equivalent are now generally referred to as *further education* (FE); qualifications above A-level standard as *higher education* (HE).

Many have undergone considerable change in recent years. In schools, O level and CSE have been replaced by GCSE in England, Wales and Northern Ireland; and O grade has been replaced by Standard grade in Scotland. In vocational and 'pre-vocational' training, there have traditionally been very large numbers of different qualifications (and of awarding bodies), not always widely recognised or even understood; but more systematic frameworks for them have recently been introduced.

SCHOOL AND FURTHER EDUCATION: ACADEMIC

CSE (Certificate of Secondary Education)

Introduced in 1965, the CSE was replaced in 1988 by the GCSE. It was aimed at the top 60% of school pupils, and was usually taken by 15- and 16-year-olds.

GCE (General Certificate of Education) O level

Introduced in 1951, the GCE O level was also replaced in 1988 by the GCSE. It was aimed at the top 20% of school pupils, and again was usually taken by 15- and 16-year-olds.

SCE (Scottish Certificate of Education) O grade

This was the Scottish equivalent of the GCE O level and was introduced in 1962 for the top 30% of school pupils. From 1986 it was replaced by Standard grade.

GCSE (General Certificate of Secondary Education)

In 1986, GCSE courses were introduced to replace both CSE and GCE O levels, creating a single examination system in England, Wales and Northern Ireland for those aged 16 or over (though younger pupils can be entered).

GCSE is awarded on a 7-point scale, with much emphasis originally placed on assessment of course work as well as a final examination, though the relative importance of the examination has been subsequently increased.

SCE Standard grade

In 1984, the first SCE Standard grade courses started to replace O grades in Scotland, with the first examinations in 1986. They are taken by all pupils, but with three levels of study and award (Foundation, General and Credit). Pupils receive a certificate at the end of their fourth year giving a 'profile' of their attainments (see Chapter 3, 1977 Dunning). In 1992, the Howie Committee recommended that Standard grade courses should proceed more quickly, with pupils sitting exams at the end of their third year, and going on to more advanced studies in their fourth. This was rejected by the government, but it has decided to allow the most able pupils to sit Standard grade exams a year early.

GCE A level

Introduced in 1951 in England, Wales and Northern Ireland, A levels are aimed at the most academically able pupils. About 23% of 17-year-olds take two or more A levels, usually in full-time education in school, sixth-form college or FE college. They are widely used as entrance qualifications for higher education. In 1988, the Higginson Report recommended that A levels should cover a wider range of subjects, with candidates normally taking five A levels rather than two or three. However, the government immediately rejected this proposal.

SCE Higher grade

The SCE Higher is the Scottish alternative to the A level. Unlike A levels, Highers are taken one year after O grade rather than two, and over four or five subjects rather than two or three. They are normally taken between the ages of 16 and 18. In 1994, the government published proposals for the reform of the curriculum and assessment in the fifth and sixth years of Scottish secondary education (Scottish Office, 1994). These proposals were in response to the Report of the Howie Committee. The government accepted many of the committee's criticisms of current arrangements, but rejected its recommendations for radical reform, including the replacement of Highers with 'SCOTBAC' and 'SCOTCERT' (see Chapter 3: 1992 Howie). The government proposes to retain Highers, but with modifications: the courses will be modular in structure, and the recommended study time will be increased from 120 to 160 hours for each subject. In addition, Advanced Higher courses will be developed, requiring 320 hours of study time over two years. (These will replace the present CSYS.)

AS level (Advanced Supplementary)

This is an examination taken alongside A levels, involving about half the work of an A level, and aimed at broadening the curriculum. It has been available since September 1987, with the first examinations in summer 1989.

CSYS (Certificate of Sixth Year Studies)

The CSYS is a qualification available to Scottish pupils after a year of study following Highers. It is to be replaced by the Advanced Higher (see SCE Higher grade above).

SCHOOL AND FURTHER EDUCATION: PRE-VOCATIONAL AND VOCATIONAL

By the late 1980s, there were about 6000 different pre-vocational and vocational qualifications, awarded by about 600 different qualifying bodies (Rogers, 1988, p. 26). In the late 1980s, the government began to rationalise these, and by the early 1990s it had decided to unify them in frameworks provided by the National Council for Vocational Qualifications (NCVQ) in England, Wales and Northern Ireland, and the Scottish Vocational Education Council (SCOTVEC). The main bodies awarding qualifications are listed below, with brief descriptions of the traditional qualifications they have offered and in some cases still offer. These are followed by descriptions of the newer qualifications frameworks devised by the NCVQ and SCOTVEC, which are to replace many of them over the next few years.

Royal Society of Arts (RSA)

The RSA currently offers a range of qualifications for office and commercial work and languages. These can be taken on a full- or part-time basis, usually in FE colleges, but also in some schools. There are three stages of award: Elementary, Intermediate and Advanced.

London Chamber of Commerce and Industry (LCCI)

The LCCI currently offers a variety of qualifications in business, secretarial and language studies, again at three levels (Elementary, Intermediate and Higher).

City and Guilds of London Institute (CGLI)

The CGLI currently offers training and qualifications for most of the craft industries, offering over 200 subjects from hairdressing to engineering. Many job advertisements specify the precise City and Guilds Certificate required by number, e.g. CGLI 599 in construction services welding or CGLI 465 in tailoring. Three tiers of certificate are offered: Part 1, usually taken after one or two years part-time study; Part 2 or Final Certificate after another two years; and a Part 3 or Advanced Certificate is available in some subjects, usually including some training for management. The CGLI is an independent body and the courses are drawn up by specialist committees including representatives from government, industry and teaching.

Business and Technician Education Council (BTEC)

Formed in 1983 by an amalgamation of the Business Education Council and the Technician Education Council, the BTEC offers training for jobs in industry, commerce and administration. Each of the three levels of training (First, National and Higher National) can be taken as a Certificate (usually two years part-time alongside employment) or as a Diploma (normally two years full-time or three years sandwich). The National qualifications are a vocational equivalent to academic A levels, the Higher National to ordinary degrees. These qualifications replace the Ordinary and Higher National Certificates and Diplomas (ONC/OND, HNC/HND) that preceded them.

National Council for Vocational Qualifications (NCVQ)

The NCVQ is not an examining body in its own right but was established, in 1986, to monitor existing awarding bodies and their qualifications in England, Wales and Northern Ireland – approving those that meet certain standards, which it will set, and showing where they stand in relation to one another. Those it approves are designated National Vocational Qualifications (NVQ), or General National Vocational Qualifications (GNVQ). NVQs are intended mainly for people in work or in Youth Training. They are usually directed at specific occupations, and assessment normally takes place in workplace conditions. GNVQs are mainly for students aged 16–18 in full-time education, and, as their name suggests, directed at broad vocational areas rather than particular jobs, and uniform throughout the country.

NVQs may be taken at five levels:

1 Foundation
2 Basic craft
3 Technician/Advanced craft/Supervisor
4 Higher technician/Junior management
5 Professional/Middle management

GNVQs may be taken at three levels:

- Foundation (normally one year of full-time study)
- Intermediate (normally one year of full-time study after Foundation level)
- Advanced (normally two years of full-time study after Intermediate level)

GNVQs are awarded with pass, merit or distinction grades. They were introduced from September 1993, and are currently (mid-1994) available, at Intermediate and Advanced levels only, in Art and Design, Business, Health and Social Care, Leisure and Tourism, and Manufacturing. By the end of 1994, Foundation level courses will have been introduced, and the range of subjects extended to include Built Environment, Hospitality and Catering, and Science.

NVQ and GNVQ courses and qualifications may be combined with one another, and with GCE and GCSE courses and qualifications (DFE/Welsh Office, 1994; DFE/Welsh Office, no date).

Scottish Vocational Education Council (SCOTVEC)

Since 1984, the SCOTVEC has offered a National Certificate, modular in structure, with students receiving credits for units of up to 40 hours' study. It was designed to be equivalent in standard to existing qualifications, such as those of the RSA and CGLI, and to replace them in Scotland. National Certificate courses can be taken in FE colleges, central institutions or secondary schools, and students can transfer between these institutions, or between them and other forms of training. Now the SCOTVEC also accredits and awards Scottish Vocational Qualifications (SVQ) and General Scottish Vocational Qualifications (GSVQ) – equivalent to NVQ and GNVQ in the rest of the United Kingdom (see above: National Council for Vocational Qualifications).

COMPARING ACADEMIC AND VOCATIONAL QUALIFICATIONS

The government has taken the three GNVQ levels as the basis for specifying more general levels that apply across GNVQs, NVQs, GCSEs and GCE A and AS levels. These are:

Foundation Level

1 GNVQ at Foundation Level
or
1 NVQ at Level 1
or
4 GCSEs at grades D to G

Intermediate Level

1 GNVQ at Intermediate Level
or
1 NVQ at Level 2
or
5 GCSEs at grades A to C

Advanced Level

1 GNVQ at Advanced Level
or
1 NVQ at Level 3
or
2 GCE A levels *or* 4 AS levels *or* 1 A level plus 2 AS levels

Students or trainees are expected to attain Foundation level before proceeding to study at Intermediate level, and Intermediate level before studying at Advanced level. Advanced level qualifies for entry into Higher Education, or for advanced craft, technical, supervisory or administrative jobs (DFE/Welsh Office, 1994).

HIGHER EDUCATION

Diploma in Higher Education (DipHE)

The DipHE is a qualification, validated where necessary by a university, that is gained after two years of study in a college of higher education. A qualification in its own right, it is, however, often now extended by further study to a degree. It was first introduced in 1974.

Professional awards

These are specialised qualifications necessary for working in particular professions, such as architecture, law and accountancy; they are awarded by the professional body concerned. (Relevant BTEC diplomas and certificates sometimes count towards exemptions.)

Degree

Degrees are awarded by universities, colleges and institutes of higher education, and some FE colleges. Universities and some colleges have the right to award their own degrees; degrees from other colleges have to be validated (that is, approved and underwritten) by a university. Normally a degree (apart from those of the Open University) requires three or four years' full-time study, but it may be taken as a four-year sandwich course, or in five to six years' part-time study. At the Open University, degree studies are part-time, and mainly by correspondence.

Degrees may be 'first degrees' or 'higher degrees' (see below). Most first degrees carry the title 'bachelor': Bachelor of Arts (BA), Bachelor of Science (BSc), Bachelor of Education (BEd), Bachelor of Engineering (BEng) and so on. At the four ancient Scottish universities, however, first degrees in arts faculties are generally called Master of Arts (MA), although the newer Scottish universities follow the English system and award bachelor degrees. Labels such as 'arts' or 'science' do not necessarily indicate the content of a course; some institutions award a BA in almost every discipline, including science and engineering.

First degrees are normally awarded at honours and ordinary (or pass) levels, with honours degrees further divided into first class, second class (upper and lower) and third class.

PGCE (Postgraduate Certificate in Education)

This is a one-year teacher-training qualification for those who already have a first degree. It is offered by universities and colleges of higher education.

Higher degree

Higher degrees are normally available only to those who already hold a first degree (especially a 'good' degree, i.e. with first-class or upper-second-class honours). Higher degrees are of two basic kinds – taught degrees (for which one normally sits an examination) and research degrees (for which one normally submits a thesis) – and of three basic levels.

The lowest level – usually, but not always, called 'masters' degrees – may be by either teaching or research, and may require one or two years of full-time study (or the equivalent in part-time study). There is no uniformity of terminology between institutions: such degrees include MA, MSc, MEd, MBA, MPhil, MLitt, etc. However, the word 'master' does not always appear in the name of a postgraduate degree: BPhil, BLitt, LIB, BD and even sometimes BSc can be postgraduate degrees. Nor are all 'masters' degrees postgraduate: the four ancient Scottish universities call their first degree in arts an MA. Furthermore, a masters degree may not even be a qualification in the usual sense at all: Oxford and Cambridge University BA graduates can, after a specified number of years, obtain an MA without any further study or assessment.

The next level – usually called 'Doctor of Philosophy' (PhD or occasionally DPhil) regardless of the subject of study – normally requires the submission of a thesis based on original research, and is usually assumed to take three years of full-time study. Some institutions are now developing taught (rather than research-based) doctorates, with such titles as 'Doctor of Education' (EdD).

Finally, 'higher doctorates' (such as DSc, DLitt, DD) are awarded for distinguished contribution to an academic field, usually on the basis of books or other publications over a period of years.

Honorary degree

Awarded by universities according to any criteria they wish, honorary degrees are usually given as a mark of respect, congratulations or gratitude. They do not necessarily reflect or indicate any academic achievement. They normally take the form of higher degrees, occasionally masters degrees but more usually higher doctorates (Hon. DSc, Hon. LID, etc.); holders of honorary doctorates do not normally adopt the title 'Doctor'.

SOURCES AND FURTHER READING

COI (1994) *Britain 1994: an official handbook*, London: HMSO.

CRAC (1993) *Directory of Further Education 1993–94*, London: CRAC.

DFE/OFSTED (1994) *Departmental Report: The Government's Expenditure Plans 1994–95 to 1996–97*, Cm 2510, London: HMSO.

DFE/Welsh Office (1994) *The New Qualifications Framework*, London: DFE.

DFE/Welsh Office (no date) *General National Vocational Qualifications: the new vocational A Levels: a brief guide*, London: DFE.

Rogers, R. (1988) A is for acronym, *School Governor*, No. 2, March.

Scottish Office (1994) *Higher Still: opportunity for all*, Edinburgh: Scottish Office.

The 1988 Education Reform Act introduced a compulsory curriculum into maintained schools in England and Wales, together with arrangements for assessing how it is being learnt. These provisions were extended, with modifications, to Northern Ireland, by the 1989 Education Reform (Northern Ireland) Order. This curriculum is to occupy most, but not all, of pupils' time during the years of compulsory schooling. Scotland does not have a statutory curriculum; consistency between schools and regions of the country is achieved in other ways.

ENGLAND AND WALES

Before the 1988 Education Reform Act

For more than 40 years after the passage of the 1944 Education Act, central government had no formal role in determining the curriculum of schools. The 1944 Act specified only one compulsory subject – religious education – and even there individual pupils could opt out if their parents so wished. Other-wise, the curriculum was left formally to local education authorities, and in practice largely to headteachers – in association with governors after the 1986 Education Act (see Chapter 4).

In reality, of course, the structure and contents of school curricula during these years were subject to many constraints. These included such interrelated factors as GCE examination boards, university entrance requirements, HMI visits and reports, and the demands of parents. There was no single set pattern of subjects, but it would have been difficult for a school to neglect seriously those regarded as basic and normal. In 1984, four years before the introduction of the national curriculum, the percentages of time actually spent by the average pupil in England in the fourth and fifth year of secondary school (i.e. Years 10 and 11 in present-day terminology, and equivalent to Key Stage 4 as explained below) on what were to become the national curriculum subjects (or their nearest equivalents) were as shown in Figure 10.1.

The pattern of primary school curricula before 1988 is less well documented than that of secondary schools.

Introduction of the compulsory curriculum

The 1988 Education Reform Act, however, prescribed a compulsory *basic curriculum* for all maintained schools in England and Wales. This has two components. First, the Act introduced a *national curriculum*, determined centrally by the government. Secondly, the 1988 Act, like the 1944 Education

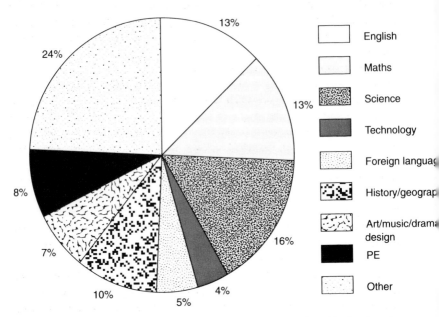

Figure 10.1   Percentage of time devoted to 'national curriculum subjects' by fourth and fifth year pupils, England, 1984
(Adapted from DES, 1987, Table 5)
Note: The national curriculum category of 'Technology' was not used in the DES 1984 survey; the figure for 'Craft-based CDT' has been used here in its place.

Act, made *religious education* compulsory, together with daily religious worship that would normally be 'broadly Christian' in character. Religious education is not part of the national curriculum, however: its syllabus is a matter for local agreement, not prescription by the central government, and parents may withdraw their children from it.

Since the 1993 Education Act, sex education (including education about HIV and AIDS) has a status similar to religious education, though in secondary schools only. It is compulsory for the schools to provide it, but it is outside the national curriculum and parents may withdraw their children from it. Sex education is required by the Act to have regard to moral considerations and the value of family life.

The 1988 Act does not itself lay down in detail what the national curriculum should be, or how it should be assessed. Instead, it provides a skeleton structure, and empowers the Secretaries of State for Education and for Wales to fill in the details in ministerial orders. To assist the Secretaries of State in these decisions, there are now two statutory bodies, the School Curriculum and Assessment Authority (for England, replacing two separate bodies originally established by the Act, the National Curriculum Council and the School Examinations and Assessment Council) and the Curriculum and Assessment Authority for Wales. Membership of these bodies is decided by the Secretaries of State. Before issuing an order under the Act, they must consult the appropriate body and, though not obliged to take its advice, must publish it and give reasons if it is rejected.

Although, as we go to press in mid-1994, almost six years have passed since the Act became law, the shape of the national curriculum and its testing arrangements have not been finally decided. The Act specified a number of subjects for the national curriculum (see below). After it was passed, the Secretaries of State began the process of implementing it by setting up subject working groups for these subjects, to make detailed recommendations as to their curriculum contents. These recommendations were cast within the framework proposed by a Task Group on Assessment and Testing (TGAT), under the chairmanship of Professor Paul Black, which had reported before the Act was passed (see below and Chapter 3: 1987 Black). They were the basis for a first generation of ministerial orders.

Several of the curriculum specifications proved controversial. In some cases, such as mathematics, there were fundamental disagreements within the working groups themselves; in others, such as English, there was basic agreement within the groups but conflict between them, their parent body, the now-defunct National Curriculum Council, and government ministers. Some working groups were asked to reconsider their recommendations; others found that the ministerial orders eventually produced differed in important respects from what they had proposed. Indeed, one subject (technology) was subject to such controversy and frequent change that its introduction as a compulsory subject has been postponed until 1996, and as we go to press the government is considering a similar postponement of a foreign language requirement.

Although many of the controversies in particular subjects were philosophical or ideological in character, the most widespread criticisms of the national curriculum as originally specified, and especially of the associated assessment arrangements, were that the curricula were too prescriptive, the assessment arrangements were too elaborate, and together they imposed too much work on both teachers and pupils.

Indeed, all the main teacher unions refused, on the grounds of excessive workload, to participate in the planned national assessment for 1993; the largest single union, the National Union of Teachers, did so again in 1994. In response to these concerns, the Secretary of State for Education asked the chairman of the new School Curriculum and Assessment Authority, Sir Ron Dearing, to review the national curriculum and assessment arrangements for England, and a parallel exercise was carried out by the Welsh authority. Dearing completed his final report at the end of 1993, recommending substantial reductions in both the curriculum and its assessment arrangements (see below and Chapter 3: 1993 Dearing). The Welsh inquiry, which had worked closely with Dearing, came to similar conclusions. These recommendations were accepted by the Secretaries of State, and made the basis of draft curriculum orders issued for consultation in May 1994.

Our description below is therefore in two parts. First, we outline the national curriculum as it stands now, according to the ministerial orders currently in force. Then we outline the principal changes proposed by the Dearing Report and the draft orders based on it; it should not be forgotten, though, that the latter are still provisional.

The subjects of the national curriculum

The national curriculum does not form the entire school curriculum, or even the whole of the compulsory basic curriculum. As we have seen, religious education and sex education, though compulsory for schools, are not part of the national curriculum.

The national curriculum itself is based on traditional school *subjects*. It consists of up to eleven *foundation* subjects, three or four of which are to form a *core*.

The core subjects are *English, mathematics* and *science* – for all ages and all parts of England and Wales. In addition, *Welsh* is a core subject in schools in Wales that use Welsh as their language of instruction.

The other foundation subjects are (for all ages) *art, geography, history, music, physical education* and *technology;* plus (for Key Stages 3 and 4: see below) a *modern foreign language*, as approved by the Secretary of State. Again, these apply to all parts of England and Wales. In addition, *Welsh* is a foundation subject in schools in Wales that do not use Welsh as their language of instruction.

The structure of the national curriculum

For the teaching and assessment of the national curriculum, the years of compulsory schooling are divided into four *key stages* (*KS*).

- Key Stage 1 – up to age 7 (Years 1 and 2)
- Key Stage 2 – up to age 11 (Years 3–6)
- Key Stage 3 – up to age 14 (Years 7–9)
- Key Stage 4 – up to age 16 (Years 10 and 11)

Each of the subjects of the national curriculum is specified by a number of *attainment targets* (*AT*), which were defined by the National Curriculum Council as 'objectives . . . setting out the knowledge, skills and understanding which pupils of different abilities and maturities are expected to develop'

(NCC, 1992, p. 20). The core subjects, for example, have attainment targets under the headings below. For science, these are the same throughout the age range, but for English and mathematics there are some differences between different key stages (DES/Welsh Office, 1991a; DES/Welsh Office, 1991b; DES/Welsh Office, 1991c).

English	Mathematics	Science
Speaking and listening	Using and applying	Scientific investigation
Reading	maths	Life and living processes
Writing	Number	Materials and their
Spelling	Algebra	properties
Handwriting	Shape and space	Physical processes
	Handling data	

Programmes of study (PoS) were defined by the NCC as 'the matters, skills and processes which must be taught to pupils during each key stage in order to meet the objectives set out in the [attainment targets]' (NCC, 1992, p. 21). As these definitions show, the distinction between attainment targets and programmes of study is not entirely clear, or free from overlap. Indeed in the actual curriculum orders, as the NCC itself acknowledged (NCC, 1992, p. 21), the terms 'attainment target' and 'programme of study', and the relationships between them, have been construed differently from subject to subject.

A *strand* is a sequence of ideas running through an attainment target/programme of study. Some strands run through all four key stages, whilst others are removed, added or modified from stage to stage. For example, the fourth attainment target in science – physical processes – has the following five strands at Key Stage 1.

- Electricity and magnetism
- Energy resource and energy transfer
- Forces and their effects
- Light and sound
- The Earth's place in the Universe

For each attainment target in most subjects, 10 successive *levels* of attainment are defined, setting out the way pupils should make progress from the beginning of their study of the subject (at age five for most subjects) to the end of compulsory schooling at age 16. Different pupils will attain various levels at different ages, but most pupils in each key stage are expected to be working within the following levels.

- Key Stage 1 – Levels 1–3
- Key Stage 2 – Levels 2–5/6
- Key Stage 3 – Levels 3–7/8
- Key Stage 4 – Levels 3/4–10

(These do not apply to a foreign language, or Welsh when it is taken as a second language, as all 10 levels have to be fitted into Key Stages 3 and 4.)

For most subjects, these levels are specified within each attainment target by *statements of attainment*, more precise objectives than the attainment targets themselves. Here, for example, are the statements of attainment for the electricity and magnetism strand of the fourth attainment target in science, physical processes, at the first two and last two levels.

Level 1:   Pupils should know that many household appliances use electricity, but that misuse is dangerous.

Level 2:   Pupils should know that magnets attract some materials, not others, and can repel each other.

●   ●   ●

Level 9:   Pupils should be able to use the quantitative relationships between charge, current, potential difference, resistance and electrical power.

Level 10: Pupils should understand the principles of electromagnetic induction.

But art, music and physical education do not have the 10-level scale, or such detailed statements of attainment. Instead, they have more general *end of key stage statements* (*EKSS*), specifying 'the knowledge, skills and understanding which pupils of different abilities and maturities can be expected to achieve by the end of the key stage in question' (NCC, 1992, p. 22).

The ministerial orders for English, mathematics, science, a modern foreign language, physical education and technology are common to England and Wales. But there have been some differences between the countries in the objectives and contents of the other subjects. In history and geography, greater emphasis is given in both England and Wales to the home country. The orders in the two countries have differences of emphasis for art and music, and Welsh is confined to the national curriculum in Wales (NCC, 1992, Part Two, Chapter 3; see also Moon, 1994).

The Dearing proposals and the 1994 draft orders

The Dearing Report recommended that the subject working groups review the current arrangements, with a view to reducing and simplifying the national curriculum and assessment arrangements. These reviews formed the basis for a new set of draft curriculum orders issued by the Secretary of State for Education in May 1994. (Those for English, mathematics, science, a modern foreign language, physical education and technology remain common to England and Wales.) It is planned that the final orders should be issued in January 1995, for implementation in schools from August 1995 for Key Stages 1–3, and from August 1996 and August 1997 for Key Stage 4. The Secretary of State has endorsed Dearing's hope that these final orders will be widely acceptable, and that no subsequent changes will need to be made to either the curriculum or the assessment arrangements for five years. The principal changes proposed in the Dearing Report and the draft orders are as follows.

1 Art, geography, history and music should be optional after Key Stage 3. (Originally it had been intended that all the foundation subjects, apart from the foreign language, should be compulsory for all ages.)

2 The compulsory national curriculum should occupy a smaller proportion of the total curriculum than originally intended, especially for older pupils. For example, Dearing's suggestions for the minimum amount of time at Key Stage 4 for each compulsory subject are shown in Figure 10.2. (These figures cannot be compared directly with the pre-1988 figures in Figure 10.1, as the latter gives an *average* of the varied individual curricula actually studied, whereas Figure 10.2 gives the suggested *minimum* for every child.)

3 The content of individual subjects, as specified in the attainment targets, should be reduced and simplified. For example, the proposed attainment targets in the new draft orders for the three core subjects are as follows (SCAA, 1994a; SCAA, 1994b; SCAA, 1994c).

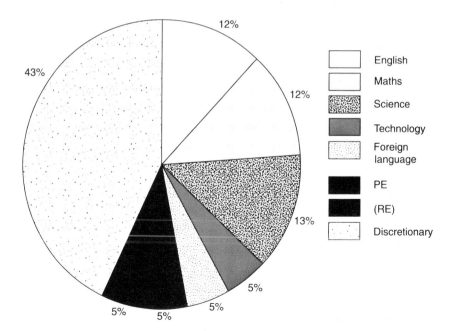

Figure 10.2   The Dearing Report's suggested minimum allocation of time to compulsory subjects at Key Stage 4
(Adapted from Dearing, 1993, Section 5)

English	Mathematics	Science
Speaking and listening	Using and applying	Experimental and
Reading	mathematics	investigative science
Writing	Number (KS 1 and 2)	Life and living
	Number and Algebra	processes
	(KS 3 and 4)	Materials and their
	Shape, space and	properties
	measures	Physical processes
	Handling data (KS 2–4)	

In English, this would reduce the attainment targets from five to three for all four key stages; in mathematics, it would reduce them from five to three for Key Stage 1.

4 Statements of attainment should be replaced by *level descriptions*. These would be fewer in number (some 200 level descriptions for the entire national curriculum, compared with almost 1000 current statements of attainment), they would be more general, and their relationship to programmes of study would be more clearly defined. The level descriptions would indicate 'the types and range of performance which pupils working at a particular level should characteristically demonstrate' (SCAA, 1994, Introduction), rather than specify exactly what they should be able to do. The planning, teaching and day-to-day assessment of pupils' work should now be guided by the programmes of study.

In science, for example, there would no longer be detailed statements of attainment at each level for every strand (as in the electricity and magnetism examples above). Instead, an entire attainment target would have just one level description to characterise each level. By way of comparison with the examples above, here are the proposed level descriptions for the attainment target 'physical processes' at Levels 1, 2, 9 and 10 (SCAA, 1994c, pp. 48–9).

Level 1:   Pupils observe and describe simple events such as the movement of familiar things, pushes and pulls or changes. They recognise that phenomena, such as light, come from a variety of sources.

Level 2:   Pupils recognise and describe in everyday terms similarities and differences between pairs of related objects or events; for example, between two light sources or between the movements of two toys.

• • •

Level 9:   Pupils use their knowledge of models to explain more complex phenomena; for example, they use the wave model to explain reflection and diffraction. In quantitative work, pupils use abstract ideas such as the connection between potential difference and energy transfer in electrical components. They use their scientific knowledge and understanding, and quantitative and qualitative data, for example in considering the appropriateness of different sources of electricity generation.

Level 10: Pupils should distinguish clearly between related phenomena, such as electromagnetic forces and electromagnetic induction, and between related applications, such as motors and generators. Their quantitative work includes problems in which the solution is found by making the connection between two relationships. They work with non-linear relationships, such as that between the velocity of a car and its braking distance. Pupils link their knowledge and understanding of physical processes in discussing complex systems, such as the structure of the Earth and the origin of the Universe.

5 The 10-level scale of attainment should now apply only to Key Stages 1–3. At Key Stage 4 (ending at age 16), assessment should instead be by GCSE and possibly GNVQ (see Chapter 9). In the light of this recommendation, the Secretary of State has suggested reducing the scale to eight levels, removing the current Levels 9 and 10 (though he has expressed concern that this might remove an incentive for the ablest pupils at Key Stage 3 and their teachers).

Assessment of the national curriculum

Assessment has been a fundamental part of the national curriculum from its inception. Indeed, the first national curriculum working group to be established, even before the 1988 Education Reform Act was passed, was a Task Group on Assessment and Testing (TGAT). The TGAT, under the chairmanship of Professor Paul Black, reported in 1987. Its recommendations were initially accepted virtually in full by the then Secretary of State for Education and Science, Mr Kenneth Baker, and, as mentioned above, became the framework for the working groups devising the curricula of the individual subjects in the national curriculum, and for the first generation of ministerial orders (see Chapter 3: 1987 Black).

The system of assessment that evolved from the TGAT recommendations was sophisticated and complicated, combining national standard tests with carefully 'moderated' assessment of pupils by their teachers, in terms of numerous statements of attainment at each of 10 levels, agregated at the end of each of four key stages. It was widely criticised for being too elaborate, for taking up too much time and making too many demands of both teachers and pupils. More fundamentally, according to Dearing, the system of standard tests developed 'distorts the nature of the different subjects, . . . serves to fragment teaching and learning in that teachers are planning work from statements of attainment, and . . . has at times reduced the assessment process to a meaningless ticking of myriad boxes' (Dearing, 1993, p. 61).

Dearing's recommendation, therefore, was to retain the basic principles of assessment as set out in the TGAT Report, but to simplify their implementation considerably, by reducing the number of attainment targets, reducing both the number and specificity of the statements of attainment or even gathering them together into 'level descriptors', and confining the 10-level scale of attainment to the first three key stages. This, according to Dearing, would not only significantly reduce teachers' workload, by greatly reducing the sheer number of assessments they have to make and record, but make the assessment process more realistic and credible. As we have seen, the draft ministerial orders went even further, proposing to reduce the number of attainment targets, to eliminate statements of attainment altogether, replacing them with level descriptions that were duly fewer in number and less specific, and also to reduce the 10 levels of attainment to eight.

NORTHERN IRELAND

The 1988 Education Reform Act does not apply to Northern Ireland, but parallel reforms were introduced there by the 1989 Education Reform (Northern Ireland) Order. These include the introduction of a Northern Ireland curriculum and a pattern of assessment much as in England and Wales, for all children of compulsory school age in grant-aided schools (see Chapter 6), though the first key stage ends there at the age of eight, not seven.

In Northern Ireland, Irish is a foundation subject in schools that use it as their language of instruction. Apart from that, the subjects in the Northern Ireland curriculum are the same as in the national curriculum in England, though there are some differences in structure and content within these subjects (see Moon, 1994).

Unlike England and Wales, Northern Ireland still has a predominantly selective (rather than comprehensive) system of secondary education, which gives added significance to attainment tests at age 11. The government favours using these tests as a replacement for the traditional tests at that age for admission to grammar secondary schools, which emphasise verbal reasoning rather than attainment.

SCOTLAND

The 1988 Education Reform Act does not apply to Scotland, which has no statutory curriculum. However, there is considerable similarity across the country in what pupils study, especially from the age of 14, for two main reasons. First, Scotland, unlike England, has only one examination board, and so pupils throughout the country who are taking its examinations follow the same syllabuses. Secondly, although the central government cannot issue directions about the curriculum, as in the rest of the United Kingdom, the Secretary of State for Scotland can and does offer national advice (to advise him or her, there is a Scottish Consultative Council on the Curriculum) (Marker, 1994).

An important influence on that advice is the Munn Report, which recommended a common curriculum for the third and fourth years of Scottish secondary schools (equivalent to Key Stage 4 in the rest of the United Kingdom). This was a complicated structure of a two-tier core plus an elective area (see Chapter 3: 1977 Munn). The percentages of pupils' time recommended by Munn for the various subjects are shown in Figure 10.3.

The recommendations of the Howie Committee, for curriculum and assessment in the fifth and sixth years of Scottish secondary schools, have not been accepted by the government (see Chapter 3: 1992 Howie).

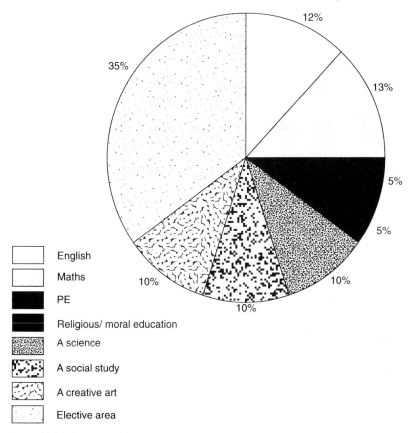

Figure 10.3   The Munn Report's suggested allocation of time to subject areas in the third and fourth years of Scottish secondary education
(Adapted from SED, 1977)

SOURCES AND FURTHER READING

Dearing, R. (1993) *The National Curriculum and its Assessment: Final Report,* London: SCAA.

DES (1987) *Statistical Bulletin 10/87: The Secondary Schooling Staffing Survey – Data on the Curriculum in Maintained Secondary Schools in England,* London: DES.

DES/Welsh Office (1991a) *English in the National Curriculum,* London: HMSO.

DES/Welsh Office (1991b) *Mathematics in the National Curriculum,* London: HMSO.

DES/Welsh Office (1991c) *Science in the National Curriculum,* London: HMSO.

Marker, W. B. (1994) *The Scottish Education System,* Edinburgh: The Open University Scottish Region.

Moon, B. (1994) *A Guide to the National Curriculum,* 2nd ed., Oxford: Oxford University Press.

NCC (1992) *Starting Out with the National Curriculum: an Introduction to the National Curriculum and Religious Education,* York: NCC.

SCAA (1994a) *English in the National Curriculum,* London: SCAA/COI.

SCAA (1994b) *Mathematics in the National Curriculum,* London: SCAA/COI.

SCAA (1994c) *Science in the National Curriculum,* London: SCAA/COI.

SED (1977) *The Structure of the Curriculum in the Third and Fourth Years of the Scottish Secondary School,* Edinburgh: HMSO ('The Munn Report').

As measured by examination performance, educational achievement in secondary schools in the United Kingdom has increased during the last two decades, as Figure 11.1 shows. A much smaller percentage of pupils now leaves school without any qualifications.

There is some variation in educational achievement from country to country within the United Kingdom. A higher percentage of school leavers achieves one or more A level passes in Northern Ireland (30%) than in England (28%) and Wales (27%); but at the same time, a much higher percentage of pupils leaves school with *no* GCSE qualifications in Northern Ireland (13%) and Wales (12%) than in England (5%). In Scotland, 10% of leavers have no qualifications. (The percentage of Scottish leavers with Highers, 43%, is not directly comparable with the A-level figures elsewhere.) (GSS, 1994, Table 30.)

During the 1980s, there has been an increase in the percentage of young people aged 16–18 staying on in full-time education, as Figure 11.2 shows (see also Chapter 5, Figure 5.19 and Chapter 12, Figure 12.5).

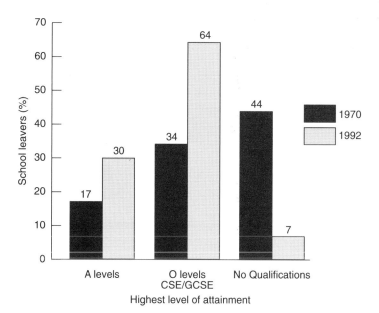

Figure 11.1   *Highest level of attainment of school leavers in the United Kingdom, 1970 and 1992*
(Adapted from GSS, 1994, Table 30)
Note: For Scotland, Highers are counted in place of A levels, and O grades or Standard grades in place of O levels or GCSE.

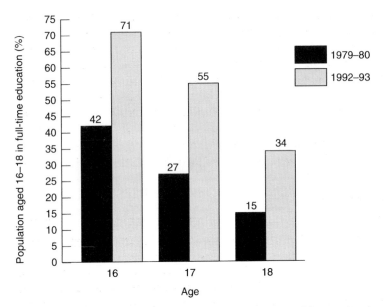

Figure 11.2   Percentage of population aged 16–18 staying on in full-time education, England, 1979–80 and 1992–3
(Adapted from DFE, 1993c, Tables 6 and 9)

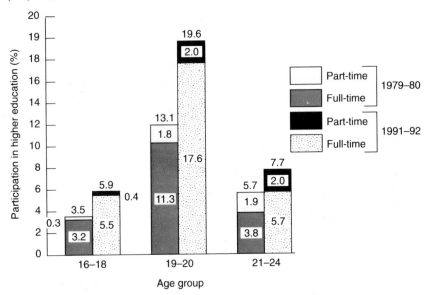

Figure 11.3   Percentage of population in higher education, United Kingdom, 1979–80 and 1991–2
(Adapted from GSS, 1982, Table 29, and 1994, Table 22)

Educational achievement as measured by participation in higher education has also increased during the past decade, as Figure 11.3 shows.

Different types of school achieve different levels of success in GCE and GCSE examinations. This is illustrated in Figure 11.4 for A levels in England in 1992. A substantially lower percentage of pupils in comprehensive schools achieve A level passes than in independent schools – though the highest levels of all are achieved in the small number of grammar schools remaining within the maintained sector. (These differences do not necessarily reflect any differences in the quality of teaching in the different types of school, as grammar schools and most independent schools select their pupils by tests of ability and attainment.)

INEQUALITY

Education in the United Kingdom is characterised by numerous inequalities in achievement and provision, not only between individuals but also between social groups and categories. The rest of this chapter provides data about three different dimensions of inequality: sex, ethnic group and social class; it also gives some information about educational achievement in independent schools.

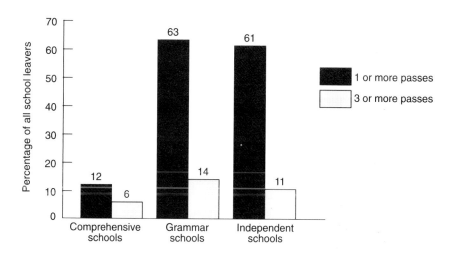

Figure 11.4   Percentage of school leavers gaining one or more, and three or more A levels, England, 1992
(Adapted from DFE, 1993b, Table 4)
Note: Sixth form colleges are included under 'comprehensive schools'

SEX

Differences between the sexes in educational participation and achievement are much better documented than any other dimensions of inequality. This is because sex is one of the principal categories used in the collection and publication of official statistics on education. The measures of educational achievement discussed above all show differences between the sexes. Figure 11.5 shows how girls do better, overall, than boys in school examinations at all levels.

However, sex differences in achievement are not uniformly in favour of girls across all subjects: while girls regularly achieve higher numbers of passes in some subjects, boys consistently achieve higher numbers in others. Figures 11.6 and 11.7 illustrate this for England, showing the number of 'passes' by boys and by girls in some of the most popular subjects, at GCE A level, and GCSE (and their Scottish counterparts).

By the sixth form, a pattern is well established of arts subjects (especially languages) being 'girls' subjects', and maths and sciences (other than biology) being 'boys' subjects'. Figures 11.8 and 11.9 show how these patterns have been reflected during the past decade, in England, in A level passes held by school leavers.

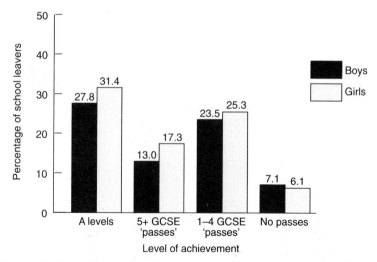

Figure 11.5   School leavers with different levels of achievement as percentage of appropriate age group of each sex, United Kingdom, 1991–2
(Adapted from GSS, 1994, Table 32)
Note: SCE H or Standard grades are taken as equivalent to GCE A level and GCSE respectively; 'passes' are GCSE (SCE Standard grade) A–C; 'no passes' are lower grades or no graded results

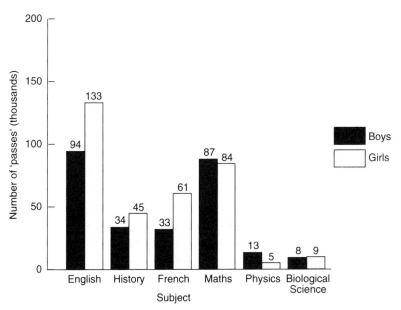

Figure 11.6   GCSE grades A–C, England, 1992
(Adapted from DFE, 1993b, Table 8)

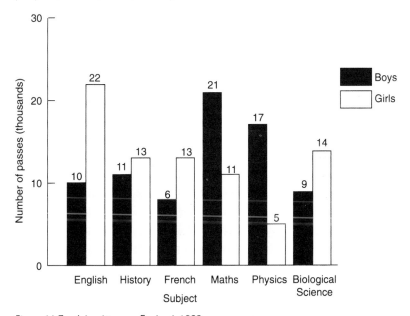

Figure 11.7   A level passes, England, 1992
(Adapted from DFE, 1993b, Table 14)
Note: AS levels are included, with each AS level pass counted as half an A level pass

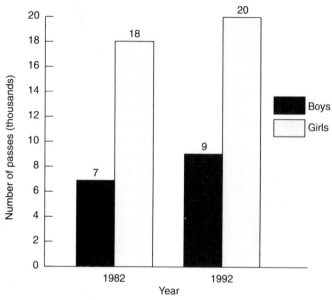

Figure 11.8 A level passes in French and other modern languages held by school leavers, England, 1982–92
(Adapted from DES, 1982, Table C13; DFE, 1993b, Table 14)

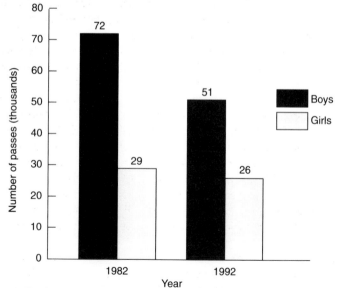

Figure 11.9 A level passes in maths, physics and chemistry held by school leavers, England, 1982–92
(Adapted from DES, 1982, Table C13; DFE, 1993b, Table 14)

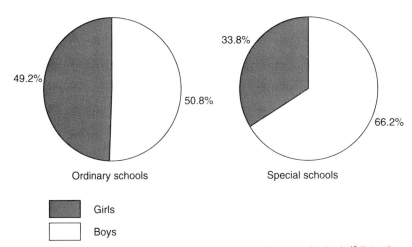

Figure 11.10   Percentages of boys and girls in ordinary and in special schools (full-time)
England, 1992
(Adapted from DFE, 1993a, Tables A1 and A10)

Boys are over-represented and girls under-represented in special schools, as compared with their numbers in the population as a whole; this is illustrated in Figure 11.10 using the data for England.

Figures published in the mid-1980s by the now-abolished Inner London Education Authority (which published more detailed information on special education than central government or other LEAs) showed boys to be in the majority, not just overall, but in schools and units catering for every type of special need. They were particularly over-represented in schools for children with emotional and behavioural difficulties (87%) and in units for the language impaired (79%) (ILEA Research and Statistics, 1984, Table 2).

Participation in higher education also shows overall differences between the sexes, though here it is men who predominate. In 1991–2, there were 695,000 men and 602,000 women in higher education in the United Kingdom (full- and part-time, universities, polytechnics and colleges). However, the gap between the sexes is narrowing: men now make up 54% of students in higher education, compared with 63% in 1980–1 and 69% in 1970–1 (GSS, 1994, Table 27).

The discrepancy between men and women is greater at higher degree level than at first degree level. This is illustrated by Figure 11.11, which shows the numbers of degrees of various types obtained by full-time university students in 1991.

As with schools, though, these global figures conceal great variation from subject to subject. Figure 11.12 shows the numbers of full-time first-degree courses, in different subject areas, taken by men and by women in the United Kingdom in the academic year 1991–2. (These figures do not include Open University courses.)

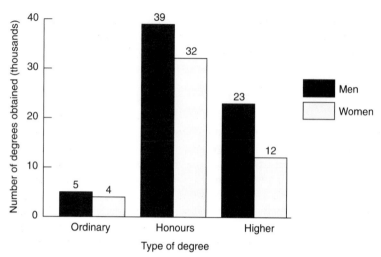

Figure 11.11   Numbers of men and women obtaining different types of degree, full-time
university students, United Kingdom, 1991
(Adapted from CSO, 1994a, Table 5.16)

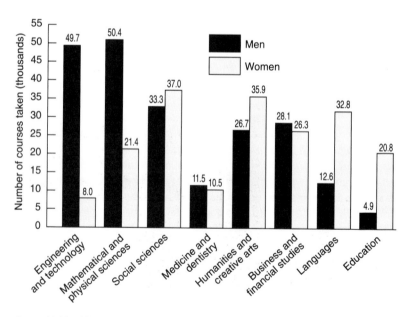

Figure 11.12   Numbers of men and women taking selected full-time first-degree
university courses (other than Open University), United Kingdom, 1991–2
(Adapted from GSS, 1994, Table 24)

Differences between the sexes in education patterns are also discussed below in the section on independent schools. For differences in patterns of employment in educational institutions, see Chapter 7.

ETHNIC GROUPS

Information about educational differences and similarities between ethnic groups is more scarce, less recent and less reliable than that available for the sexes. Ethnic divisions are not categories used in the national collection and publication of official statistics on education; data have to be taken from sample surveys. The most comprehensive surveys are still those conducted for the Rampton/Swann Committee (see Chapter 3: 1981 Rampton; 1985 Swann), as long ago as 1979 and 1982, in five LEAs with high proportions of ethnic minority pupils. All five LEAs were inner city areas, where the average educational attainment for every ethnic group is lower than the national average.

Children and young people from different ethnic groups show differences in educational attainment: White and Asian children and young people achieve higher results, on average, than Afro-Caribbean, as Figure 11.13 illustrates.

However, this picture needs to be qualified in a number of ways.

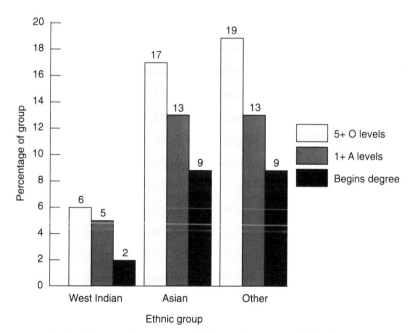

Figure 11.13   Educational attainment of different ethnic groups, 1981–2
(Adapted from DES, 1985, Chapter 3)

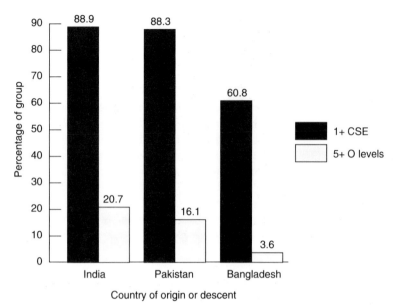

Figure 11.14   Examination results of fifth-year Asian pupils in the ILEA, by country of origin or descent, 1986
(Adapted from ILEA Research and Statistics, 1987, Table 6)
Note: '1 + CSE' means at least one CSE grade 5 or higher; '5+ O levels' means at least five O levels grade C or higher.

First, different ethnic groups are often of very different social class composition (see Chapter 2, Figure 2.14). Since educational attainment is strongly linked to social class (see below), some of the ostensible differences in achievement between ethnic groups may be reflections of these class differences.

Second, none of these ethnic categories are monolithic. The 'Asian' group, for example, is itself made up of groups of different levels of achievement. This is illustrated by data from the now-abolished ILEA in Figure 11.14, which compares the examination results of fifth-year pupils of Indian, Pakistani and Bangladeshi origin or descent.

Third, data collected by the former ILEA (which published more detailed statistics than central government or other LEAs on differences between ethnic groups) have shown Asian pupils as having distinctly higher average educational attainment than either White or Afro-Caribbean pupils (see, e.g., ILEA Research and Statistics, 1987).

Fourth, the Rampton/Swann statistics themselves provide evidence that the educational achievements of Afro-Caribbean children and young people are increasing from year to year at a higher rate than those of other groups.

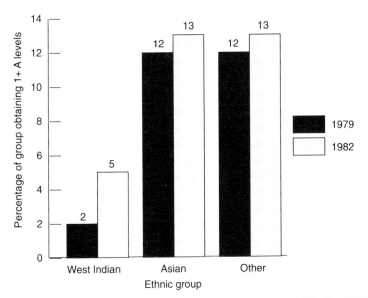

*Figure 11.15   Educational attainment of different ethnic groups, 1978–9 and 1981–2
(Adapted from DES, 1981, Chapter 1, Table D; DES, 1985, Chapter 3, Annex B)
Note: There is a minor discrepancy between the 1978–9 figures for Asians as given in the
Rampton Report (13%) and in the Swann Report (12%). Here we have followed Swann*

Figure 11.15 compares A level results in 1979 (when data were gathered for
the Rampton Report) with those in 1982 (when comparable data were
collected for the Swann Report).

Finally, the data are now very old: even those for the Swann Report are 12
years old as we go to press.

Some more recent – though sketchy – evidence suggests a more complicated picture. In 1993, differences were found between ethnic groups (and
between men and women) in the percentages of people of working age who
have *no* qualifications. The highest percentage is among people of Pakistani and
Bangladeshi origin: 60% of women and over 50% of men have no qualifications. For people of Indian origin, the figures are just under 40% for women
and under 30% for men. Of White people, just under 30% of women and just
over 20% of men have no qualifications. And among Black people (mainly
people of Caribbean or African origin), just under 30% of people have no
qualifications; this is the only ethnic category where there are (slightly) more
men than women without qualifications (CSO, 1994b, Table 3.23).

Figures published in the mid-1980s by the ILEA showed some differences
between ethnic groups in the proportions of children attending special
schools. English/Scottish/Welsh/Irish children and Afro-Caribbean children
were over-represented in special schools as compared with their numbers in
ordinary schools. Asian and 'other' children were under-represented. The

discrepancies were not dramatic, however. At primary level, for example, English/Scottish/Welsh/Irish children constituted 56% of the population of ordinary schools and 61% of special schools; for Afro-Caribbean children, the figures were 16% and 17% respectively, and for Asian children, 11% and 8%. (The percentages at secondary level were similar.)

The ILEA figures also showed some differences between ethnic groups in the *types* of special school or unit that children were likely to attend, but there was no obvious pattern to this variation. The largest single difference was that, of Asian children in special schools or units, only 1% were in schools catering for children with emotional or behavioural difficulties, compared with 22% of the Afro-Caribbean children and 16% of the English/Scottish/Welsh/Irish children in special schools or units (ILEA Research and Statistics, 1984, Table 2).

For differences between ethnic groups in patterns of employment in schools, see Chapter 7.

SOCIAL CLASS

Although social class is one of the census categories (see Chapter 2), it is not widely used in the publication of official statistics on education. Nor have there been many recent sample-survey investigations of the relationship between social class and educational attainment. One reason for this relative neglect may be that so many earlier surveys gave such clear and unequivocal results: at virtually every stage of education, by virtually every criterion of achievement, middle-class children had higher levels of achievement than working-class children. This was documented particularly thoroughly in surveys conducted for a succession of official reports in the 1950s and 1960s (see Chapter 3, especially 1954 Gurney-Dixon, 1959 Crowther, 1963 Newsom, 1963–4 Robbins and 1967 Plowden), whose criteria of educational achievement ranged from 11 plus passes to class of university degree.

In the 1950s and 1960s, most of those surveyed were, or had been, at school under the tripartite system. There has been little research in most of the United Kingdom into the relative effects of social class on achievement under the tripartite and comprehensive systems. In Scotland, however, while differences between the social classes in educational attainment remain, they are smaller in the comprehensive system than they were in the tripartite. The trend towards equality of attainment is especially marked in schools that have been comprehensive for a long time. It has been a result of the raising of working-class attainment, not the lowering of middle-class attainment (McPherson and Willms, 1987).

Such recent survey evidence as exists for Great Britain as a whole shows that, whatever the effects of comprehensivisation, the link between social class and educational achievement remains strong. For example, Figure 11.16

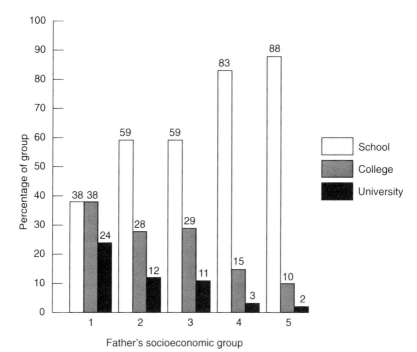

Figure 11.16   Last educational establishment attended full-time, by father's socioeconomic group, Great Britain, 1991–2
(Adapted from OPCS, 1993, Table 10.4a)
Key to socioeconomic groups: 1 Professional; 2 Employers and managers; 3 Intermediate and junior non-manual; 4 Skilled manual and self-employed non-professional; 5 Semi-skilled and unskilled manual
Note: Categories 3 and 5 each combine two OPCS categories; 'college' includes polytechnics and colleges of further and higher education, before the 1992 reorganisation of higher education.

shows, for adults in Great Britain aged 25–49 in 1991–2, the relationship between their fathers' socioeconomic groups (as defined by the OPCS) and the last educational establishment they attended full-time. Roughly speaking, the lower the socioeconomic group of someone's father, the more likely it is that his or her full-time education ended in school, rather than college or university.

However, the number of people with fathers in the professional group is relatively small, so that they are still a minority of those who have been in higher education. Figure 11.17 illustrates this (from the same sample) for universities.

The likelihood that a person enters higher education continues to be strongly related to his or her family's social class. In Great Britain in 1991, 67% of people who had attended universities or polytechnics full-time had fathers in non-manual occupations, and 33% had fathers in manual occupations. By comparison, 36% of men in the population as a whole were in non-manual occupations and 64% in manual occupations (OPCS, 1994, Table 10.4b).

People's own occupational levels are also strongly related to their levels of educational attainment. This is illustrated in Figure 11.18, which shows the percentages of people in each socioeconomic group with various levels of educational qualification.

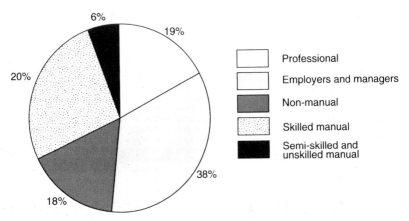

Figure 11.17   Socioeconomic groups of fathers of people whose last full-time education was at university
(Adapted from OPCS, 1993, Table 10.4b)

INDEPENDENT SCHOOLS

Pupils in independent schools (see Chapter 5) form a small percentage of all school pupils – just over 7% in the United Kingdom in 1991–2. However, independent schools retain a much higher proportion of their pupils after the legal minimum school-leaving age than do maintained schools, so that in 1991–2, 18% of all boys and 15% of all girls aged 16 or over were in independent schools. This shows a percentage decline since 1951 (when the corresponding figure for boys was 29%, or 38% including direct grant schools); during this period, there was a substantial increase in *absolute* numbers over the minimum leaving age in independent schools, but this was overshadowed by a much larger increase, proportionately as well as absolutely, in maintained schools. (Figures for 1951 have been taken, and rounded, from Halsey, Heath and Ridge, 1984, Table 1; 1991–2 figures from CSO, 1994b, Table 3.7; GSS, 1994, Table 15).

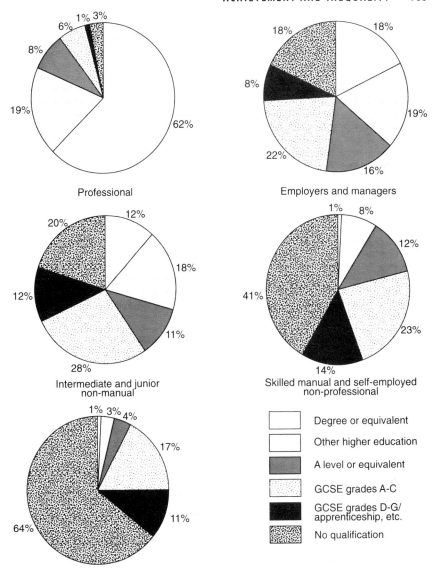

Professional

Employers and managers

Intermediate and junior
non-manual

Skilled manual and self-employed
non-professional

☐ Degree or equivalent

☐ Other higher education

▨ A level or equivalent

▨ GCSE grades A-C

■ GCSE grades D-G/
apprenticeship, etc.

▨ No qualification

Semi-skilled and unskilled manual

*Figure 11.18   Highest qualification shown as percentage of each socioeconomic group,
Great Britain, 1992–3*
(Adapted from OPCS, 1994, Table 8.3a)
*Note: The figures for 'intermediate and junior non-manual' and for 'semi-skilled and
unskilled manual' each combine two OPCS categories; people with qualifications other
than those above (e.g. from abroad) are omitted; the sample is confined to economically
active people aged 25–69, not in full-time education*

The percentage of pupils in independent schools is significantly higher in England (8%) than in Scotland (3%), Wales (3%), or Northern Ireland (1%).

Fees for independent schools are high. For example, the average annual fees in Headmasters' Conference Schools in 1994 were £10,700 for boarders, and £4,450 for day pupils. In schools belonging to the Girls' Schools Association, the average annual fees were £9,800 for boarders, and £4,100 for day pupils (ISIS, 1994).

Approximately 32,000 pupils, 5% of pupils in independent schools in the UK, hold places under the Assisted Places Scheme, which provides assistance with tuition fees and certain other expenses. A further 81,500 in schools belonging to ISIS (18%) receive help with fees from the schools themselves, 9,500 (2%) from local authorities and 3000 (1%) from other sources (ISIS, 1994, Table 7).

Independent schools have drawn their pupils very unequally from the different social classes. The most detailed evidence of this — now very old — comes from the Oxford Social Mobility Study's sample of men in England and Wales who had completed their education by 1972 (women were not included in the study). This is illustrated in Figure 11.19 which shows the percentages of men with fathers in each of the three main social classes identified in the study

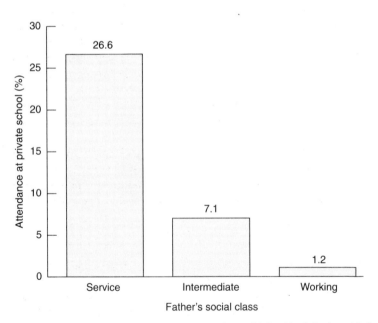

Figure 11.19   Percentages of men of each social class (defined by father's social class) who had attended private (including direct-grant) schools, England and Wales 1972 (Adapted from Halsey, Heath and Ridge, 1980, Table 4.8)

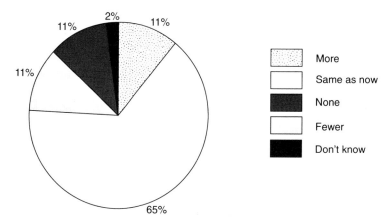

Figure 11.20   Attitudes to private schools, Great Britain, 1987
(Adapted from Flather, 1988, p. 22)

who had attended private schools. (The *service* classs covers professional and managerial occupations; the *intermediate*, routine non-manual jobs and small proprietors; and the *working*, manual workers and their supervisors.)

Pupils in independent schools achieve higher levels of success in public examinations than those at maintained schools (see Figure 11.4 above).

At the other extreme, the percentage of pupils leaving school with no qualifications is lower for independent schools (1.8%) than for maintained schools (7.5%) (England, 1990–1 figures; DFE 1992, Table C3).

Attitudes to private schools are summarised in Figure 11.20, which shows the percentages of people in Great Britain (in 1987) who thought there should be more, fewer, none, or about the same number as then.

There is little variation with age or sex in these attitudes, but some variation between social classes. Respondents in non-manual occupations are more likely to think that there should be more private schools, or the same number as now, than respondents in manual occupations (77% compared with 62%).

SOURCES AND FURTHER READING

CSO (1994a) *Annual Abstract of Statistics*, No. 130, 1994 edn, London: HMSO.
CSO (1994b) *Social Trends*, No. 24, 1994 edn, London: HMSO.
DES (1981) *West Indian Children in our Schools: Interim Report of the Committee of Inquiry into the Education of Children from Ethnic Minority Groups*, Cmnd. 8273, London: HMSO ('The Rampton Report').
DES (1982) *Statistics of Education 1982: School Leavers CSE and GCE*, London: HMSO.

DES (1985) *Education for All: Report of the Committee of Inquiry into the Education of Children from Ethnic Minority Groups*, Cmnd. 9453, London: HMSO ('The Swann Report').

DFE (1992) *Statistics of Education: School Examinations: GCSE and GCE, 1991*, London: HMSO.

DFE (1993a) *Statistics for Education: Schools, 1992*, London: HMSO.

DFE (1993b) *Statistics of Education: Public Examinations: GCSE and GCE, 1992*, London: HMSO.

DFE (1993c) *Statistical Bulletin 16/93: Participation in Education by 16–18-Year-Olds in England, 1979/80 to 1992/93*, London: DFE.

Flather, P. (1988) Education matters, in Jowell, R., Witherspoon, S. and Brooks, L. (eds) *British Social Attitudes: The 1986 Report*, Aldershot: Gower.

GSS (1982) *Educational Statistics for the United Kingdom 1982*, London: HMSO.

GSS (1994) *Educational Statistics for the United Kingdom 1993*, London: HMSO.

Halsey, A. H., Heath, A. F. and Ridge, J. M. (1980) *Origins and Destinations: Family, Class and Education in Modern Britain*, Oxford: Clarendon Press.

Halsey, A. H., Heath, A. F. and Ridge, J. M. (1984) 'The political arithmetic of public schools', *in* Walford, G. (ed.) *British Public Schools: Policy and Practice*, pp. 9–44, London: Falmer Press.

ILEA Research and Statistics (1984) *Characteristics of Pupils in Special Schools*, RS 962/84, London: ILEA.

ILEA Research and Statistics (1987) *Ethnic Background and Examination Results*, RS 1120/87, London: ILEA.

ISIS (1990) *Annual Census 1990*, London: ISIS.

McPherson, A. F. and Willms, J. D. (1987) Equalisation and improvement: some effects of comprehensive reorganisation in Scotland, *Sociology*, Vol. 21, No. 4.

OPCS (1993) *General Household Survey 1991*, No. 22, London: HMSO.

OPCS (1994) *General Household Survey 1992*, No. 23, London: HMSO.

Vocational and pre-vocational training programmes, aimed primarily at school leavers and long-term unemployed adults, are similar in the different countries of the United Kingdom, but they are organised and administered separately. In this chapter, we first describe the English arrangements in some detail, then note the principal similarities and differences in Wales, Northern Ireland and Scotland.

ENGLAND

The percentage of young people staying on in full-time education after the legal minimum leaving age has increased substantially in recent years, as has the likelihood that their post-compulsory education will be in a college of further (or higher) education rather than a school. This is shown, for 16-, 17- and 18-year-olds, in Figure 12.1.

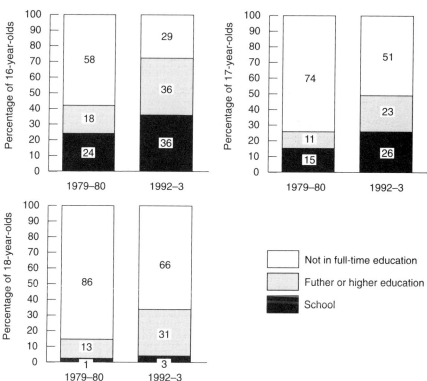

Figure 12.1   Percentages of 16-, 17- and 18-year-olds in full-time education, England, 1979–80 and 1992–3
(Adapted from DFE, 1993, Tables 3, 6 and 9)

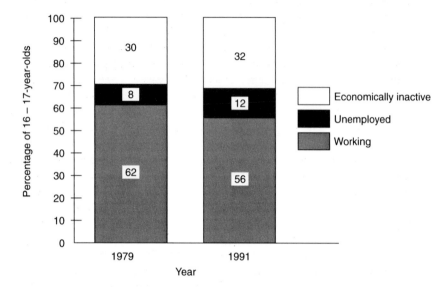

Figure 12.2   Percentages of 16–17-year-olds working, unemployed, and economically inactive, Great Britain, 1979 and 1991
(Adapted from OPCS, 1994, Table 7.3)
Note: Those in full-time education are included among the 'economically inactive', but since 1989 those on government training schemes are classified as 'working'.

Over the same period, there has been a significant, though far from steady, fall in employment and rise in unemployment among young people. This is illustrated for 16–17-year-olds in Figure 12.2.

In addition to employment and conventional education in schools or colleges, young people, especially school leavers aged 16 and 17, have a number of training schemes available to them under the auspices of the Employment Department. Some of these schemes operate within, or partly within schools and colleges, others outside. (The Department also offers some training schemes for older people, especially the long-term unemployed.)

EMPLOYMENT DEPARTMENT TRAINING SCHEMES

Much of the government-funded vocational and pre-vocational training in England is the responsibility of the Training, Enterprise and Education Directorate (TEED) of the Employment Department. TEED has a main office (in Sheffield) and had 10 regional offices, employing about 1500 staff in total – though from April 1994, the regional offices of the Employment Department were integrated with those of the Departments of the Environment, of Trade and Industry, and of Transport. The estimated total expenditure for 1993–4 by TEED on training and enterprise (i.e. supporting new businesses) was £1.8 billion – compared with £9.8 billion in the same year by the Department for Education (EDG, 1994a, Table 4; DFE and OFSTED, 1994, Table 1).

Unlike its predecessors, the Manpower Services Commission (MSC) and the Training Agency, TEED does not itself organise training programmes and courses, but instead delegates the tasks to Training and Enterprise Councils (TECs) throughout the country. TECs are independent, non-profit-making companies, with boards of directors led by business people from the private sector. There are currently (mid-1994) 75 TECs in England. The Employment Department enters into contracts with each of these for managing the provision in its locality of training for young people and unemployed adults, and fostering links more generally between business and education. The TECs in their turn enter into contracts with local providers of training, such as colleges and employers. TECs are encouraged to negotiate with those providers lower payments than they themselves have negotiated with the Department. Savings thus made, known as 'efficiency savings', may be used to fund other activities by the TECs. Both the Department in its payments to TECs, and the TECs in their payments to training providers, are currently experimenting with various forms of 'payment by results'. (TECs also have major responsibilities for supporting new businesses; and they enter into contracts with other government departments as well as the Employment Department.)

The four main current educational and training schemes under the auspices of TEED are described below. There are numerous other, smaller schemes, but these four between them account for over 90% of the expenditure of TEED on training and enterprise.

Training for Work (TfW)

The Training for Work programme began in April 1993, with the aim of helping long-term unemployed people – especially those who have been unemployed for over 12 months – to improve their skills and find jobs. It is designed to be flexible, allowing the TECs who run it to offer the types of training and combinations of training and work experience that they judge appropriate for individual needs and local labour market conditions. An estimated 240,000 people will have enrolled on TfW programmes in 1993–4, with an average of 121,000 people taking part at any one time.

TfW replaces various earlier training programmes for unemployed adults, most recently Employment Training. Of those leaving Employment Training in 1992–3, 35% were in employment six months later, and 6% in full-time education or further training; 52% were unemployed. 54% had studied for a qualification, and 39% had gained one, or credit towards one (EDG, 1993, Table 9.3).

Youth Training (YT), Youth Credits and Modern Apprenticeships

Youth Training was introduced in 1990–1 to fulfil the government's guarantee of a suitable training place to all 16- and 17-year-olds not in employment or full-time education. It is flexible, allowing the TECs who run it to offer the types of training and combinations of training and work experience that they judge appropriate for individual needs and local labour market conditions. However, programmes have typically lasted two years for 16-year-olds and one year for 17-year-olds, combining 'on the job' and 'off the job' training with work experience. The programmes must be directed towards the acquisition of NVQ or equivalent qualifications (see Chapter 9).

Of those leaving Youth Training in 1992–3, 50% were in employment six months later, and 17% in full-time education or further training; 28% were unemployed. 62% had studied for a qualification, and 48% had gained one, or credit towards one (EDG, 1993, Table 9.4).

Youth Training replaced the Youth Training Scheme (YTS), and is itself being increasingly replaced in its existing form by Youth Credits. Under the latter scheme, young people, instead of being offered places on pre-arranged training programmes, are to be issued with 'Youth Credits' which they are supposed to use to arrange their own training. A third of TECs were offering or developing Youth Credits by early 1994. It is planned that they should be available throughout the country by 1995–6. An estimated 133,000 people enrolled on YT programmes in 1993–4, representing three-quarters of entrants to the labour market. Of these, a fifth arranged their own training through the Youth Credits scheme.

From 1995, the government proposes to introduce a Modern Apprentice-ship Scheme of work-based training for technician, supervisory and equivalent skills. (A number of TECs are piloting these apprenticeships in 14 occupational sectors from September 1994.) The scheme is intended to build on the best of traditional apprenticeships in sectors which have used them, and to introduce apprenticeship to other sectors. The apprentice, his or her employer and the responsible TEC are required to sign an 'apprenticeship pledge', describing the training to be provided, and committing all parties to seeing it through. The standards to be achieved are specified in terms of the NVQ framework (see Chapter 9). Eventually, the government intends that some 40,000 young people each year should attain NVQ Level 3 and above through Modern Apprenticeships.

By 1996–7, according to government plans, Modern Apprenticeships arranged through the Youth Credits scheme will account for 90% of expenditure on the employment training of young people, and conventional Youth Training for only 10%.

Technical and Vocational Education Initiative (TVEI)

TVEI is a scheme whereby LEAs and some grant-maintained schools and colleges receive grants for approved programmes of technical and vocational education for 14–18-year-olds in schools or colleges, irrespective of ability. TVEI was introduced in 1983 as a series of pilot projects in a small number of LEAs, and was extended in 1987 to cover the whole country. It is now being phased out (87% of LEAs participated in 1993–4, compared with 98% in 1992–3), and its funding will finally cease in 1997. An estimated 1.3 million students – 78% of all 14–18-year-olds – participated in TVEI in 1993–4.

Work Related Further Education (WRFE)

Since April 1993, when colleges of further education became independent of LEAs, payments under the Work Related Further Education scheme have been made directly to colleges by TECs for particular courses and programmes contracted between them. These payments amount to 5% of the total funding of further education colleges by central government. However, WRFE monies are now to be transferred from TECs to the Further Education Funding Council established by the 1992 Further and Higher Education Act.

The percentage of TEED's budget spent on each of the four programmes described above is shown in Figure 12.3.

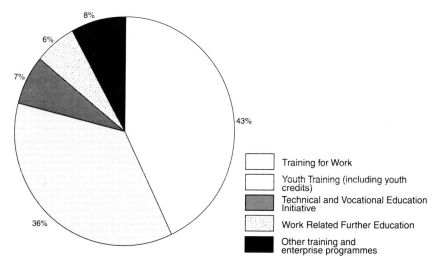

Figure 12.3   Percentages of the estimated 1993–4 expenditure of TEED devoted to major training programmes
(Adapted from EDG, 1994a, Table 4)

WALES

Training in Wales is the responsibility of the Welsh Office. Although the Welsh arrangements are separate from those in England, they are very similar. Thus Wales also has Training for Work and Youth Training schemes, a Technical and Vocational Education Initiative and Work Related Further Education; a system of Youth Credits is being developed. Trainees are encouraged to use their training to acquire NVQs. These programmes are managed and delivered through seven Training and Enterprise Councils (Welsh Office etc., 1994, Chapter 4).

An estimated £150 million was spent by the Welsh Office on training and employment in 1993–4, 36% of it on adult training, and 31% on youth training (Welsh Office etc., 1994, Figure 4.01).

SCOTLAND

Training in Scotland is the responsibility of the Scottish Office Industry Department, much of it organised and financed through the Scottish Enterprise and the Highlands and Islands Enterprise programmes. Like England and Wales, Scotland operates Youth Training and Training for Work schemes, and a Technical and Vocational Education Initiative. Much of the training is delivered through 22 Local Enterprise Companies (LECs), the Scottish counterpart to Training and Enterprise Councils, though with slightly different responsibilities. (LECs, for example, have some responsibilities for environmental protection, but have never been responsible for Work Related Further Education.) Since 1991, Youth Credits have been introduced as a pilot scheme in one region (Grampian) in place of Youth Training as it currently exists, and the government has found the results encouraging.

In 1993–4, an estimated 31,000 school leavers began Youth Training, and an estimated 34% of those leaving gained recognised qualifications. The 1994–5 budget for Youth Training is £94 million. (In these figures, Scottish Enterprise and Highlands and Islands Enterprise programmes are taken together.)

In 1993–4, an estimated 23,000 adults began Training for Work, and an estimated 25% of those leaving gained recognised qualifications. The 1994–5 budget for Training for Work is £91 million. (In these figures, Scottish Enterprise and Highlands and Islands Enterprise programmes are again taken together.)

As in England, the Technical and Vocational Education Initiative is to be phased out by 1997. In 1993–4, an estimated 265,000 students took part – 88% of the age group – with a total expenditure of £14 million (Departments of the Secretary of State for Scotland etc., 1994, Chapter 3).

NORTHERN IRELAND

Training in Northern Ireland is the responsibility of the Training and Employment Agency of the Northern Ireland Office Department of Economic Development. The Agency has a staff of 1,350, and had a 1993–4 budget of £195 million. The main training and employment schemes under its auspices are described below (Northern Ireland Office Department of Finance and Personnel/HM Treasury, 1994, Chapter 6).

Youth Training Programme (YTP)

The Youth Training Programme offers full-time training to all school leavers under 18, through a network of training providers. These are paid a fixed sum per trainee, and required to meet specified standards. The average number of YTP trainees at any one time in 1993–4 was an estimated 12,000; 20% of those leaving YTP during 1994 were expected to attain NVQ at level 2 or above. The estimated expenditure on the YTP for 1993–4 was £48 million.

Job Training Programme (JTP)

The Job Training Programme aims to assist long-term unemployed people to find work through training, either by updating their existing skills or by acquiring new skills. The training is delivered through a network of training providers, mainly employers in the private sector. The average number of JTP trainees at any one time in 1993–4 was an estimated 4,900; 17% of those leaving JTP during 1994 were expected to attain NVQ at level 2 or above. The estimated expenditure on the JTP for 1993–4 was £21 million.

Action for Community Employment (ACE)

The Action for Community Employment programme provides temporary employment – up to one year – for long-term unemployed adults, on projects deemed to be of benefit to the community; most of the projects are run by voluntary organisations. Recently an element of structured training has been introduced into the programme. The average number of jobs created through ACE at any one time in 1993–4 was an estimated 9,200. The estimated expenditure on the ACE for 1993–4 was £51 million.

SOURCES AND FURTHER READING

Departments of the Secretary of State for Scotland and the Forestry Commission (1994) *Serving Scotland's Needs: The Government's Expenditure Plans 1994–1995 to 1996–1997*, Cm 2514, Edinburgh: HMSO.

DFE (1993) *Statistical Bulletin 16/93: Participation in Education by 16–18-year-olds in England: 1979/93*, London: DFE.

DFE and OFSTED (1994) *Departmental Report: The Government's Expenditure Plans 1994–95 to 1996–97*, Cm 2510, London: HMSO.

EDG (1993) *Employment Gazette*, Vol. 101, No. 12, London: EDG.

EDG (1994a) *Departmental Report: The Government's Expenditure Plans 1994–95 to 1996–97*, Cm 2505, London: HMSO.

EDG (1994b) *Employment Gazette*, Vol. 102, No. 5, London: EDG.

Northern Ireland Office Department of Finance and Personnel/HM Treasury (1994) *Northern Ireland Expenditure Plans and Priorities: The Government's Expenditure Plans 1994–95 to 1996–97*, Cm 2516, London: HMSO.

OPCS (1994) *General Household Survey 1992*, London: HMSO.

Welsh Office and Office of Her Majesty's Chief Inspector of Schools in Wales (1994) *The Government's Expenditure Plans 1994–95 to 1996–97: Departmental Report by the Welsh Office and the Office of Her Majesty's Chief Inspector of Schools in Wales*, CM 2515, London: HMSO.

Aided School
type of voluntary school where the voluntary body retains control over the employment of teachers, religious instruction and admissions policy, in exchange for meeting part of the external maintenance costs

Ancillary Staff
non-teaching staff in schools (e.g. laboratory assistants, caretakers, secretaries) and unqualified classroom assistants

Assessment of Performance Unit
section of the DES which monitored the performance of children at different stages of their education (now dissolved)

Assisted Places Scheme
a scheme introduced in the 1980 Education Act whereby central government pays part of the tuition costs (on a means-tested basis) for children who have been in state schools to attend selected independent day schools

Banding
modified form of streaming, where pupils are divided into broad bands of ability (e.g. average, below average, above average) and each band follows a similar curriculum

Capping
mechanism by which central government sets limits to the amount of money a local authority is allowed to raise through the Council Tax

Catchment Area
the area from which a school takes its pupils

City Technology College
school with a technological bias, set up by private sponsors with government grants

Community Home
replaced approved schools under the 1969 Children and Young Persons Act. Administered by Social Services Departments

Comprehensive School   secondary school which does not select children for admission on the grounds of ability

Consortium   group of schools which join together for a particular purpose, for example to purchase equipment or to teach certain subjects (especially at fifth- and sixth-form level, where falling rolls would otherwise result in sixth-form groups being too small)

Continuous Assessment   judging students on the basis of work done during a course rather than, or in addition to, a formal examination at the end

Controlled School   in Great Britain, a type of voluntary school where all costs are met by the LEA but the voluntary body retains some rights over religious instruction. In Northern Ireland, a school financed and managed by an Education and Library Board

'Crammer'   private institution providing intensive coaching for examinations

Curriculum   course of study followed by a pupil or student

Developmental Curriculum   a type of curriculum deemed suitable for children with severe learning difficulties. It has closely defined educational and social objectives, and aims to encourage a degree of personal autonomy (see also Mainstream plus Support Curriculum; Modified Curriculum)

Dyslexia   disability in using and interpreting written language and symbols, irrespective of general intelligence and spoken language skills. (Its existence is widely, but not universally, accepted by educational psychologists and LEAs.)

Education Authority the Scottish term for a local education authority. As in England and Wales, EAs form part of the local government structure

Education and Library Board in Northern Ireland, one of the five regional educational authorities, centrally appointed by the Department of Education for Northern Ireland, though partly consisting of local council representatives. It is funded by the DENI. It has complete responsibility for controlled schools and for some services to all schools in its geographical area

Education Otherwise an organisation offering support and help to parents wishing to educate their children out of school (the name is based on a phrase in the 1944 Education Act)

Education Support Grant sum of money earmarked in the Government's Revenue Support Grant for specific projects which the Secretary of State has decided are important, e.g. science teaching in primary schools. LEAs then bid for this money

Educational Priority Area term suggested in the Plowden Report to describe areas of particular social deprivation that should receive extra educational funding

First School primary school taking children from age five up to the age of transfer to middle school at eight or nine

Governor elected, co-opted, appointed or foundation member of the governing body which every school is now required to have

Grammar School in the tripartite system in England and Wales, a secondary school taking only children of high academic ability, usually measured by a test taken at age 11 (the tripartite system is now largely replaced, in Great Britain, by comprehensive schools)

Initial Teaching Alphabet
a 44-letter phonetic alphabet with only one sound per letter, developed to help children learn to read. Popular in the 1960s but now little used

Inner London Education Authority
until April 1990, the largest LEA in the UK, responsible for schools and colleges in the inner London boroughs. With the abolition of the Greater London Council, the ILEA became the only LEA whose members were directly elected, rather than part of the local government system. It was itself abolished by the 1988 Education Reform Act

Integration
the education of children with special educational needs alongside their peers in ordinary, rather than special, schools. The term is also used in Northern Ireland to refer to education without denominational segregation

Intermediate Treatment
a form of provision dating from the Children and Young Persons Act (1969) for children deemed to be at risk and in trouble, which often includes persistent truants and pupils whom schools are unable to contain. Run by social services, but LEAs may provide teachers

Junior Secondary School
the Scottish equivalent of the secondary modern school in England and Wales

Local Education Authority
in England and Wales, part of the local government structure, responsible for the day-to-day running of the state education service in a particular geographical area (for Northern Ireland, see Education and Library Board)

Mainstream

an ordinary, rather than a special, school, class, etc. (in America, the term 'mainstreaming' is the equivalent of 'integration')

Mainstream plus Support Curriculum

a type of curriculum deemed suitable for children with particular kinds of special need. As the name suggests, this is comparable to ordinary curricula in aims, content and standards, but with support appropriate for pupils' distinctive needs – whether in organisation, equipment or style of teaching (see also Modified Curriculum; Developmental Curriculum)

Maintained School

in Great Britain, a school maintained by the state (see also Voluntary Schools). In Northern Ireland, a school provided by the Roman Catholic Church, though with a large measure of state support and controlled by the Maintained Schools Commission (similar to an aided school in Great Britain)

Middle School

comprehensive school catering for children aged from eight to nine to 12 or 13. Legally designated as either primary or secondary depending on whether most children are under or over age 11. Confined almost entirely to England

Modified Curriculum

a type of curriculum deemed suitable for children with moderate learning difficulties. Similar to ordinary school curricula, but with objectives suited to the children's special needs (see also Mainstream plus Support Curriculum; Developmental Curriculum)

National Curriculum

a set of 'essential subjects' which the government decides all children must study, with their performance assessed against set criteria at various ages. At present, applies to England and Wales and, with modifications, to Northern Ireland (see Northern Ireland Curriculum)

Northern Ireland Curriculum   the Northern Ireland equivalent of the English and Welsh National Curriculum

Open Tech   not an institution, but a range of distance learning materials on technical and business subjects, developed by various institutions with funding from the MSC. Ceased operating in 1987

Peripatetic Teacher   visiting teacher, i.e. one who is not attached to any one school but travels to several (e.g. to teach music or to give specialist help for deaf children)

Pooling   mechanism for sharing expenses between LEAs on services which may be used by all authorities but are concentrated in a few, e.g. the advanced further education pool for colleges of higher education

Portage   scheme first developed in Portage, USA, to help parents teach their handicapped child at home before he or she starts school, by working on an agreed programme with a trained home visitor

Preparatory School   private, fee-charging school for children between the ages of eight and 11 (girls) or 13 (boys), preparing them for entrance examinations for the independent secondary and public schools

Public School   usually used, especially in England, to refer to one of the prestigious independent schools for boys. In Scotland, however, 'public school' refers to a maintained school

Pupil Profile	form of evaluation designed to give more detailed information about a pupil than an examination result. It may include academic grades, but also such things as internal school assessments, material selected by the pupil and teachers' comments
Reception Class	the first class of an infant or first school, taking children at (or before) the age of five
Revenue Support Grant	money allocated to local authorities by the government to supplement the local Council Tax. Each authority decides what proportion to spend on education
Rising Fives	children who are not yet five years old, admitted to schools in the term before their fifth birthday, or in some areas at the beginning of the school year in which they will become five
Sandwich Course	course with periods of study at a university or college, alternating with periods of training and experience in industry, commerce or the professions.
Secondary Intermediate School	the Northern Ireland equivalent of the secondary modern school in England and Wales
Secondary Modern School	in the tripartite system in England and Wales, a secondary school which caters for those children, identified as of average and below average academic ability, who do not go to grammar schools. (The tripartite system is now largely replaced, in Great Britain, by comprehensive schools.)
Section 5 Letter	the letter sent by the LEA to parents to inform them that the authority intends to begin the full assessment procedure to determine a child's special educational needs – a procedure begun when it has been decided that the child's needs cannot

be met within the ordinary resources of the school. ('Section 5' refers to the relevant part of the 1981 Education Act and means that the procedure was initiated by the LEA; parents themselves can also initiate the procedure, under Section 9 of the Act.)

Senior Secondary School
the Scottish equivalent of the grammar school in England and Wales

Setting
grouping pupils according to ability in a particular subject. A student may thus be in one set for English, another for mathematics, etc.

Sixth Form College
separate school for 16–19-year-olds, taking pupils from several schools in an area

Special Agreement School
type of secondary school with rights and responsibilities similar to those of an aided school. Set up by a special agreement for joint provision made between a voluntary body and an LEA before the 1944 Education Act

Special Educational Needs
term introduced by the Warnock Report to replace the old categories of handicap

Special School
separate school for children with mental, physical or emotional difficulties

Statement
formal document drawn up by an LEA (in consultation with parents) describing the special educational needs of a child who needs more help than can be provided within the ordinary resources of a school. The assessment procedure leading to a statement was first laid down in the 1981 Education Act

Streaming
allocating pupils, on the basis of perceived ability, to 'streams', i.e. classes in which pupils stay for all subjects, usually following different curricula

Supply Teacher

teacher appointed by an LEA to fill in for absent school staff, for periods ranging from half a day to several weeks

Teacher Placement Service

government-funded scheme operating in England, Wales and Scotland to support short-term teacher placements in industry, business, and the public sector

Technical and Vocational Education Initiative

scheme funded by the Department of Employment for schools and colleges to develop their own work-related courses for pupils between the ages of 14 and 18. Now being phased out

Tertiary College

college for young people over the age of 16 that combines the functions of a sixth form and FE college by offering a full range of academic and vocational courses

Training and Employment Agency

the Northern Ireland equivalent of the Training, Enterprise and Education Division in Britain

Training, Enterprise and Education Division (formerly, Training Agency)

replacement for the Manpower Services Commission. Now an integral part of the Department of Employment

Twenty-one-hour Rule

rule enabling claimants of Unemployment or Supplementary Benefit to take part-time further education courses, provided that these do not exceed 21 hours a week, and that the claimant remains 'available for work'

Upper School

comprehensive school taking children after they have left a middle school at 12 or 13. (Some secondary schools also use the term to describe the senior half of the school, as opposed to the 'lower school' comprising the first, second and third years.)

Urban Programme	administered by the Department of the Environment. Some grants are given for educational purposes, e.g. setting up nurseries in deprived areas
Vocational Education	employment-related rather than academic education
Voluntary School	school provided by a voluntary body (usually the church) but maintained by the LEA in England and Wales, and partly aided by the DENI in Northern Ireland (see Aided, Controlled and Special Agreement Schools)
Youth Training	training programme in England and Wales for school leavers, combining education and work experience. Run by Training and Enterprise Councils (TECs) on behalf of the Department of Employment. In Scotland, run by Local Enterprise Councils (LECs) on behalf of the Scottish Office. In Northern Ireland, the equivalent scheme is called the Youth Training Programme, and is run jointly by the Departments of Economic Development and Education. Since September 1988, 16- and 17-year-olds who choose not to take a YT/YTP course have not been eligible for welfare benefit payments
Youth Training Programme	the Northern Ireland equivalent of Youth Training

The use of acronyms and abbreviations is extremely widespread in writings about education; this chapter contains only a highly selective list of some of the most common and most important.

ACE	Advisory Centre for Education *or* Action for Community Employment (Northern Ireland)
AEB	Associated Examining Board
AMA	Association of Metropolitan Authorities
AMMA	Assistant Masters and Mistresses Association
APS	Assisted Places Scheme
APU	Assessment of Performance Unit
AS	Advanced Supplementary (examination)
AT	Attainment Target
ATC	Adult Training Centre
AUT	Association of University Teachers
BA	Bachelor of Arts
BACIE	British Association for Commercial and Industrial Education
BACIFHE	British Accreditation Council for Independent Further and Higher Education
BD	Bachelor of Divinity
BEd	Bachelor of Education
BERA	British Educational Research Association
BLitt	Bachelor of Letters
BPhil	Bachelor of Philosophy
BPS	British Psychological Society
BSc	Bachelor of Science
BSL	British Sign Language
BTEC	Business and Technician Education Council
CACE	Central Advisory Council for Education
CAL	Computer Assisted Learning
CASE	Campaign for the Advancement of State Education
CAT	Credit Accumulation and Transfer
CATE	Council for the Accreditation of Teacher Education
CDT	Craft, Design and Technology
CE2L	Centre for Teaching English as a Second Language
CEE	Certificate of Extended Education
CEO	Chief Education Officer
CGLI	City and Guilds of London Institute
CHES	Child Health Education Study
CIPFA	Chartered Institute of Public Finance and Accountancy

CNAA	Council for National Academic Awards (dissolved in 1992)
COPE	Committee on Primary Education (Scotland)
COSE	Committee on Secondary Education (Scotland)
CPVE	Certificate of Pre-vocational Education
CQSW	Certificate of Qualification in Social Work
CRAC	Careers Research and Advisory Centre
CRE	Commission for Racial Equality
CSE	Certificate of Secondary Education
CSO	Central Statistical Office
CSYS	Certificate of Sixth Year Studies (Scotland)
CTC	City Technology College
CVCP	Committee of Vice Chancellors and Principals of the Universities of the United Kingdom
DD	Doctor of Divinity
DENI	Department of Education Northern Ireland
DES	Department of Education and Science (now renamed: see DFE)
DFE	Department for Education
DipHE	Diploma in Higher Education
DLitt	Doctor of Letters
DPhil	Doctor of Philosophy
DSc	Doctor of Science
DSS	Department of Social Security
EA	Education Authority (Scotland)
EATE	Economic Awareness in Teacher Education
EBD	Emotional and Behavioural Difficulties
ECATT	Economic Awareness and the Training of Teachers
ED	Employment Department
EDG	Employment Department Group
EFL	English as a Foreign Language
EIS	Educational Institute of Scotland
EOC	Equal Opportunities Commission
EPA	Educational Priority Area
ERA	Educational Reform Act (of 1988)
ERIC	Educational Resources Information Centre
ESG	Education Support Grant
ESL	English as a Second Language
ESN	Educationally Subnormal. **ESN (M)** = moderate. **ESN (S)** = severe. (No longer used)
ET	Employment Training (replaced: see TFW)
EWO	Education Welfare Officer
FAS	Funding Agency for Schools
FCW	Funding Council for Wales

FE	Further Education
FEFC	Further Education Funding Council
FEFCW	Further Education Funding Council for Wales
FTE	Full-time Equivalent
GAMMA	Girls and Mathematics Association
GBA	Governing Bodies Association (of boys' public schools)
GBGSA	Governing Bodies of Girls' Schools Association
GCE	General Certificate of Education
GCSE	General Certificate of Secondary Education
GEST	Grants for Education Support and Training
GIST	Girls into Science and Technology
GMS	Grant-Maintained School
GNVQ	General National Vocational Qualification
GPDST	Girls' Public Day School Trust
GRE	Grant-related Entitlement
GSA	Girls' Schools Association
GSVQ	General Scottish Vocational Qualification
HE	Higher Education
HEFC	Higher Education Funding Council
HEFCS	Higher Education Funding Council for Scotland
HEFCW	Higher Education Funding Council for Wales
HMC	Headmasters' Conference
HMCI	Her Majesty's Chief Inspector of Schools
HMI	Her Majesty's Inspector (or Inspectorate)
HMSO	Her Majesty's Stationery Office
HNC	Higher National Certificate
HND	Higher National Diploma
IAPS	Incorporated Association of Preparatory Schools
IB	International Baccalaureate
ILEA	Inner London Education Authority (now abolished)
INSET	In-service Education of Teachers
IQ	Intelligence Quotient
ISAI	Independent Schools Association Incorporated
ISIS	Independent Schools Information Service
IT	Information Technology
	or
	Intermediate Treatment
ITA	Initial Teaching Alphabet
ITB	Industrial Training Board
ITT	Initial Teacher Training
JBPVE	Joint Board for Pre-vocational Education
JTP	Job Training Programme (Northern Ireland)
JTS	Job Training Scheme (replaced: see **TfW**)

KS	Key Stage
LAPP	Lower Attaining Pupils Programme
LCCI	London Chamber of Commerce and Industry
LEA	Local Education Authority
LEATGS	Local Education Authorities Training Grants Scheme
LEC	Local Enterprise Company (Scotland)
LFM	Local Financial Management (renamed: **LMS**)
LLB	Bachelor of Laws
LLD	Doctor of Laws
LMS	Local Management of Schools
MA	Master of Arts
MBA	Master of Business Administration
MEd	Master of Education
MESP	Mini Enterprise in Schools Project
MLD	Moderate Learning Difficulties
MLitt	Master of Letters
MPhil	Master of Philosophy
MSc	Master of Science
MSC	Manpower Services Commission (replaced: see **TEED**)
NAGM	National Association of Governors and Managers
NAHT	National Association of Head Teachers
NAME	National Antiracist Movement in Education (formerly National Association for Multiracial Education)
NAS/UWT	National Association of Schoolmasters/Union of Women Teachers
NATE	National Association for the Teaching of English
NATFHE	National Association of Teachers in Further and Higher Education
NCB	National Children's Bureau
NCC	National Curriculum Council (now dissolved)
NCDS	National Child Development Study
NCDT	National Council for Drama Training
NCES	National Council for Educational Standards
NCVQ	National Council for Vocational Qualifications
NEC	National Extension College
NFER	National Foundation for Educational Research
NICED	Northern Ireland Council for Educational Development
NICER	Northern Ireland Council for Educational Research
NNEB	National Nursery Examination Board
NRA	National Record of Achievement
NUS	National Union of Students
NUSS	National Union of School Students
NUT	National Union of Teachers

NVQ	National Vocational Qualification
OECD	Organisation for Economic Cooperation and Development
OFSTED	Office for Standards in Education
OHMCI	Office of her Majesty's Chief Inspector of Schools in Wales
ONC	Ordinary National Certificate
OND	Ordinary National Diploma
OU	Open University
PAT	Professional Association of Teachers
PCFC	Polytechnics and Colleges Funding Council (now dissolved)
PGCE	Postgraduate Certificate in Education
PhD	Doctor of Philosophy
PICKUP	Professional Industrial and Commercial Updating
PoS	Programme of Study
PPA	Preschool Playgroups Association
PTA	Parent–Teacher Association
PTR	Pupil/Teacher Ratio
QTS	Qualified Teacher Status
REB	Regional Examining Body
ROSLA	Raising of the School Leaving Age
RSA	Royal Society of Arts
RSG	Rate Support Grant
SAT	Standard Assessment Task
SATRO	Science and Technology Regional Organisation
SCAA	School Curriculum and Assessment Authority
SCCC	Scottish Consultative Council on the Curriculum
SCDC	Schools Curriculum Development Committee
SCE	Scottish Certificate of Education
SCIP	School Curriculum Industry Project
SCOTVEC	Scottish Vocational Education Council
SEB	Scottish Examination Board
SEC	Secondary Examinations Council
SED	Scottish Education Department (renamed: see **SOED**)
SEN	Special Educational Needs
SEO	Society of Education Officers
SHA	Secondary Heads Association
SHMIS	Society of Headmasters of Independent Schools
SILO	Schools Industry Liaison Officer
SLD	Severe Learning Difficulties
SMP	School Mathematics Project
SOED	Scottish Office Education Department
SSTA	Scottish Secondary Teachers Association
STOPP	Society of Teachers Opposed to Physical Punishment
SVQ	Scottish Vocational Qualification

TEC	Training and Enterprise Council
TEED	Training, Enterprise and Education Directorate
TEFL	Teaching English as a Foreign Language
TES	*Times Education Supplement*
TESL	Teaching English as a Second Language
TESOL	Teaching of English to Speakers of Other Languages
TfW	Training for Work
TGAT	Task Group on Assessment and Testing
THES	*Times Higher Education Supplement*
TOPS	Training Opportunities Programme (replaced: see **TfW**)
TPO	Teacher Placement Organiser
TPS	Teacher Placement Service
TTA	Teacher Training Agency
TVEI	Technical and Vocational Education Initiative
UBI	Understanding British Industry
UCAS	Universities and Colleges Admissions Services
UFC	Universities Funding Council (to replace **UGC**, now itself dissolved)
UGC	University Grants Committee (replaced by **UFC**)
UNESCO	United Nations Educational, Scientific and Cultural Organisation
VC	Vice Chancellor
WEA	Workers' Educational Association
WISE	Women into Science and Engineering
WOW	Wider Opportunities for Women
WRFE	Work Related Further Education
YC	Youth Credits
YOP	Youth Opportunities Programme (replaced: see **YT**)
YT	Youth Training
YTP	Youth Training Programme (Northern Ireland)
YTS	Youth Training Scheme (replaced: see **YT**)

INDEX